CASEBOOK SERIES

GENERAL EDITOR: A. E. Dyson

PUBLISHED

Jane Austen: *Emma* DAVID LODGE
William Blake: *Songs of Innocence and Experience* MARGARET BOTTRALL
Charlotte Brontë: *'Jane Eyre' and 'Villette'* MIRIAM ALLOTT
Emily Brontë: *Wuthering Heights* MIRIAM ALLOTT
Browning: *'Men and Women' and Other Poems* J. R. WATSON
Byron: *'Childe Harold's Pilgrimage' and 'Don Juan'* JOHN JUMP
Chaucer: *The Canterbury Tales* J. J. ANDERSON
Coleridge: *'The Ancient Mariner' and Other Poems* ALUN R. JONES AND
    WILLIAM TYDEMAN
Conrad: *The Secret Agent* IAN WATT
Dickens: *Bleak House* A. E. DYSON
Donne: *Songs and Sonets* JULIAN LOVELOCK
George Eliot: *Middlemarch* PATRICK SWINDEN
T. S. Eliot: *Four Quartets* BERNARD BERGONZI
T. S. Eliot: *The Waste Land* C. B. COX AND ARNOLD P. HINCHLIFFE
Henry Fielding: *Tom Jones* NEIL COMPTON
E. M. Forster: *A Passage to India* MALCOLM BRADBURY
Hardy: *The Tragic Novels* R. P. DRAPER
Gerard Manley Hopkins: *Poems* MARGARET BOTTRALL
Jonson: *Volpone* JONAS A. BARISH
James Joyce: *'Dubliners' and 'A Portrait of the Artist as a Young Man'*
    MORRIS BEJA
John Keats: *Odes* G. S. FRASER
D. H. Lawrence: *Sons and Lovers* GĀMINI SALGĀDO
D. H. Lawrence: *'The Rainbow' and 'Women in Love'* COLIN CLARKE
Marlowe: *Doctor Faustus* JOHN JUMP
The Metaphysical Poets GERALD HAMMOND
Milton: *'Comus' and 'Samson Agonistes'* JULIAN LOVELOCK
Milton: *Paradise Lost* A. E. DYSON AND JULIAN LOVELOCK
John Osborne: *Look Back in Anger* JOHN RUSSELL TAYLOR
Pope: *The Rape of the Lock* JOHN DIXON HUNT
Shakespeare: *Antony and Cleopatra* JOHN RUSSELL BROWN
Shakespeare: *Hamlet* JOHN JUMP
Shakespeare: *Henry IV Parts I and II* G. K. HUNTER
Shakespeare: *Henry V* MICHAEL QUINN
Shakespeare: *Julius Caesar* PETER URE
Shakespeare: *King Lear* FRANK KERMODE
Shakespeare: *Macbeth* JOHN WAIN
Shakespeare: *Measure for Measure* C. K. STEAD
Shakespeare: *The Merchant of Venice* JOHN WILDERS
Shakespeare: *Othello* JOHN WAIN
Shakespeare: *Richard II* NICHOLAS BROOKE
Shakespeare: *The Tempest* D. J. PALMER
Shakespeare: *Twelfth Night* D. J. PALMER
Shakespeare: *The Winter's Tale* KENNETH MUIR

Swift: *Gulliver's Travels* RICHARD GRAVIL
Tennyson: *In Memoriam* JOHN DIXON HUNT
Virginia Woolf: *To the Lighthouse* MORRIS BEJA
Webster: *'The White Devil' and 'The Duchess of Malfi'*
   R. V. HOLDSWORTH
Wordsworth: *Lyrical Ballads* ALUN R. JONES AND WILLIAM
   TYDEMAN
Wordsworth: *The Prelude* W. J. HARVEY AND RICHARD GRAVIL
Yeats: *Last Poems* JON STALLWORTHY

TITLES IN PREPARATION INCLUDE

Jane Austen: *'Sense and Sensibility', 'Pride and Prejudice', and 'Mansfield Park'*
   BRIAN SOUTHAM
Bunyan: *Pilgrim's Progress* ROGER SHARROCK
Peacock: *Satirical Novels* LORNA SAGE
Shakespeare: *Troilus and Cressida* PRISCILLA MARTIN
Shelley: *Shorter Poems and Lyrics* PATRICK SWINDEN

Gerard Manley Hopkins

Poems

A CASEBOOK

EDITED BY

MARGARET BOTTRALL

M

Selection and editorial matter © Margaret Bottrall 1975

First published 1975 by
THE MACMILLAN PRESS LTD
London and Basingstoke
Associated companies in New York Dublin
Melbourne Johannesburg and Madras

SBN 333 14968 8 (hard cover)
      333 14969 6 (paper cover)

Printed in Great Britain by
THE ANCHOR PRESS LTD
Tiptree, Essex

24/7/90

CONTENTS

Acknowledgements   7

General Editor's Preface   9

Introduction   11

Part One: *Contemporary and Early Criticism*

1. Extracts from the Notebooks and from Letters by
   Hopkins   27

2. Extracts from Letters to Hopkins and from Contemporary
   Correspondence about him: RICHARD WATSON
   DIXON, p. 32 – COVENTRY PATMORE, p. 35 – SIR
   ROBERT STEWART, p. 38 – C. N. LUXMOORE, p. 38 –
   ANONYMOUS CONTEMPORARIES, p. 39 – JOSEPH
   KEATING, S.J., p. 40

3. Early Criticism: ROBERT BRIDGES, p. 41 –
   J. MIDDLETON MURRY, p. 48 – FREDERICK PAGE, S.J.,
   p. 55 – 'PLURES', p. 60 – EDWARD SAPIR, p. 65 –
   I. A. RICHARDS, p. 69

Part Two: *Critical Appraisals, 1930–44*

CHARLES WILLIAMS: From 'An Introduction to the
Poetry of Hopkins' (1930)   81

WILLIAM EMPSON: Ambiguities in Hopkins (1930)   87

HARMAN GRISEWOOD: The Impact of G. M. Hopkins
(1931)   92

6

HERBERT READ: Creativity and Spiritual Tension
(1933)   101

T. S. ELIOT: A Note on Hopkins (1934)   107

HUMPHRY HOUSE: A Note on Hopkins's Religious
Life (1935)   109

CHRISTOPHER DEVLIN, S.J.: Hopkins and Duns
Scotus (1935)   113

BERNARD KELLY: 'The Wreck of the *Deutschland*'
(1935)   117

VINCENT TURNER, S.J.: 'Many a Poem that both
Breeds and Wakes' (1944)   126

HUMPHRY HOUSE: In Praise of Hopkins (1944)   140

Part Three: *Modern Studies*

GEOFFREY GRIGSON: A Passionate Science (1953)   143

DENNIS WARD: 'The Windhover' (1955)   168

ELISABETH SCHNEIDER: 'The Windhover' (1960)   183

ELIZABETH JENNINGS: The Unity of Incarnation
(1960)   186

DONALD McCHESNEY: The Meaning of 'Inscape' (1968)   202

PATRICIA A. WOLFE: Hopkins's Spiritual Conflict in
the 'Terrible' Sonnets (1968)   218

JOHN SUTHERLAND: 'Tom's Garland': Hopkins's
Political Poem (1972)   235

Bibliography   247

Notes on Contributors   250

Index   532

ACKNOWLEDGEMENTS

The author and publishers wish to thank the following, who have kindly given permission for the use of copyright material: Chatto & Windus Ltd and New Directions Publishing Corporation for extracts from *Seven Types of Ambiguity* by William Empson, all rights reserved, reprinted by permission of New Directions Publishing Corporation; Lady Madeleine Devlin for extracts from *Spiritual and Devotional Writings* and *Sermons and Devotional Writings of Gerard Manley Hopkins*, ed. Christopher Devlin, and for 'Hopkins and Duns Scotus' by Christopher Devlin from *New Verse*, no. 14 (April 1935); Faber & Faber Ltd and Harcourt Brace Jovanovich Inc. for an extract from *After Strange Gods* by T. S. Eliot, copyright 1934 by Harcourt Brace Jovanovich Inc., renewed 1962 by T. S. Eliot, reprinted by permission of the publishers; Geoffrey Grigson for 'A Passionate Science' from *Poems and Poets* (Macmillan, 1969); Rupert Hart-Davis Ltd for an extract from *All in Due Time* by Humphry House; David Higham Associates Ltd for an extract from *Collected Essays in Literary Criticism* ('In Defence of Shelley and Other Essays') by Sir Herbert Read; Mrs Madeline House for 'A Note on Hopkins's Religious Life' by Humphry House from *New Verse* (April 1935); Hutchinson Publishing Group Ltd for an extract from Robert Bridges's introduction to a selection of Gerard Manley Hopkins's poems from *The Poets and Poetry of The Century*, vol. 8, ed. A. H. Miles; *The Month* for 'Father Gerard Hopkins' by Frederick Page, s.j., from *Dublin Review*, vol. 167 (1920), for 'Father Gerard Hopkins: His Character' by 'Plures' from *Dublin Review*, vol. 167 (1920), for 'The Unity of Incarnation' by Elizabeth Jennings from *Dublin Review*, vol. 234, for extracts by Harman Grisewood from *Dublin Review*, vol. 189 (1931), for extracts by Vincent Turner, S.J., from *Dublin Review*, vol. 431 (1944), for the 'Wreck of the *Deutschland*' by Bernard Kelly, from *The Mind and Poetry of Gerard Manley Hopkins* (St Dominic's Press, 1935), and for 'The Meaning of "Inscape"' by D. McChesney; Oxford University Press for extracts from *The Letters of Gerard Manley Hopkins to Robert Bridges* and *Further Letters of Gerard Manley Hopkins*, ed. C. C. Abbott, and for extracts from the Introduction by Charles Williams to the second edition of *The Poems of Gerard Manley Hopkins*; *Poetry* for 'Gerard Hopkins' by Edward Sapir from *Poetry* (September 1921); I. A. Richards for an article from *The Dial*, vol. 81 (September 1926); Routledge & Kegan Paul Ltd for 'The Windhover' by Dennis Ward from *Interpretations*, ed. John Wain; The Society of Authors as the literary representative of the Estate of John Middleton Murry for 'Essay on Hopkins' from *Aspects of Literature*; West Virginia University for 'The Paradox of Self' by Patricia A. Wolfe from *Victorian Poetry*, VI (1968) and for ' "Tom's Garland": Hopkins's Political Poem' by John Sutherland, *Victorian Poetry*, X (1972).

The Publishers have made every effort to trace the copyright holders, but if they have inadvertently overlooked any they will be pleased to make the necessary arrangement at the first opportunity.

GENERAL EDITOR'S PREFACE

Each of this series of Casebooks concerns either one well-known and influential work of literature or two or three closely linked works. The main section consists of critical readings, mostly modern, brought together from journals and books. A selection of reviews and comments by the author's contemporaries is also included, and sometimes comments from the author himsclf. The Editor's Introduction charts the reputation of the work from its first appearance until the present time.

The critical forum is a place of vigorous conflict and disagreement, but there is nothing in this to cause dismay. What is attested is the complexity of human experience and the richness of literature, not any chaos or relativity of taste. A critic is better seen, no doubt, as an explorer than as an 'authority', but explorers ought to be, and usually are, well equipped. The effect of good criticism is to convince us of what C. S. Lewis called 'the enormous extension of our being which we owe to authors'. This Casebook will be justified if it helps to promote the same end.

A single volume can represent no more than a small selection of critical opinions. Some critics have been excluded for reasons of space, and it is hoped that readers will follow up the further suggestions in the Select Bibliography. Other contributions have been severed from their original context, to which some readers may wish to return. Indeed, if they take a hint from the critics represented here, they certainly will.

A. E. DYSON

INTRODUCTION

'. . . but since, as Solomon says, there is a time for everything, there is nothing that does not some day come to be, it may be that the time will come for my verses.' So Hopkins wrote in 1881 to his friend Canon Dixon, who had been urging him to publish his poems. To Dixon's argument that one vocation should not be allowed to destroy another, and that he ought not to suppress, in obedience to his superiors, 'such gifts as have seldom been given by God to man', Hopkins reaffirmed his total loyalty to his commitment as a Jesuit priest. But the strong, resigned tone of his reply modulates finally into this tentative hope.

The time for Hopkins's poetry did indeed come, though with exceptional slowness. Robert Bridges, to whom the manuscript poems were entrusted after the death of Hopkins in 1889, considered it wise to withhold them from publication till 1918. The first edition of 750 copies was not exhausted for another ten years. Yet now the fame of Gerard Manley Hopkins is world-wide. His poems are read wherever English literature is studied. Recalcitrant though they must be to translation, many have been rendered into other languages. His journals, notebooks and correspondence have long since been given to the public. To the original canon, issued by Bridges, have been added his early poems and all the fragmentary verses that have come to light. Occasionally a letter, hitherto unnoted, turns up and is likely to provoke an exchange in the *Times Literary Supplement*. No item of Hopkinsiana is now too trifling to appeal to those who have fallen under the spell of his genius.

Book-length or briefer critical studies proliferate on both sides of the Atlantic. There are any number of detailed commentaries on specific poems; there are glossaries, concordances,[1] bibliographies. In London the Hopkins Society arranges annual lectures and commemorative sermons and publishes them, together with regular bibliographical check-lists.[2] Hopkins might be amazed by all this; but at least he has had his hope fulfilled. His originality, his passionate sincerity, his brilliant craftsmanship, have earned him a permanent place among the finest English poets.

It is not surprising that the poems of Hopkins have attracted a vast amount of exegesis and comment. The unorthodoxy of his language is only one element in their difficulty, but it is of course this feature that immeditaly challenges the newcomer, who often simply cannot construe the syntax or make out what the words mean – 'To-fro tender tram-beams truckle at the eye', or 'leaves me a lonely began'. He met with incomprehension from his friends Bridges and Patmore, both of whom were established poets with a real interest in innovatory techniques; and the encouragement which Canon Dixon gave him was often tinged with bewilderment. To meet their objections, Hopkins went so far as to suggest providing prose arguments to explain his more impenetrable poems. He did write a general introduction to his poems,[3] which was designed to explain his metrical experiments. Nor did he ever deny that his poetry demanded sustained intellectual effort from his readers, though he repeatedly stressed his conviction that if the verse were read aloud in a declamatory manner most of the difficulties would vanish.

The most intractable difficulty in the poetry of Hopkins is not so much a matter of language as of unfamiliar ideas, presented with an intense concentration of feeling and intellectual passion. Hopkins admitted to Bridges that sometimes he was endeavouring 'to express a subtle and recondite thought on a subtle and recondite subject in a subtle and recondite way, and with great felicity and perfection', and expressed his realisation that 'something must be sacrificed, with so trying a task, in the process';[4] that something being immediate intelligibility. The intricacy of his poetry remains a challenge to interpreters. He could be called the critic's poet, were it not that the impassioned beauty of his language can affect us powerfully even before we can construe its full meaning.

To understand why the poetic genius of Hopkins was so slow in winning recognition, it is helpful to have some documentation, such as this Casebook provides, of the rise of his reputation. The comments of the people with whom he corresponded, and the early reviews, remind us that the kind of literary analysis to which his poems are nowadays subjected had simply not been developed when they began to circulate. Greek and Latin texts, of course, were traditionally perused and annotated with the minutest attention to detail; Hopkins's own school notebooks testify to his training in this mode of scrutiny.[5] But the intensive reading of an English poetic text was pioneered in the twenties of this century. (It was already an established teaching method in French schools.) Laura Riding and Robert Graves were early exponents of this close reading, which was systematically developed by I. A. Richards and elaborated by William Empson. It is a method that can be applied with maximum effectiveness to closely textured poems like those of Hopkins. When we recall that the poet had to plead with Bridges, his dearest friend, to read 'The Wreck of the *Deutschland*' more than once, it is a reminder that the Victorians did not assume, as we do, that a strenuous effort on the reader's part is likely to be required before the riches of a poem become fully apparent.

Bridges may well have been right in supposing that poetry readers of the nineties would have been quite defeated by the obscurity of Hopkins's characteristic work. He did allow a few innocuous lyrics to be included in A. H. Miles's anthology, *Poets and Poetry of the Nineteenth Century*, introducing them by a less than enthusiastic account of his friend's life and talents (see p. 41). He also permitted some to appear in H. C. Beeching's *Lyra Sacra* (1895). In 1909 Father Joseph Keating, s.j., wanted the Jesuits to edit Hopkins's poems, but Bridges, who did not own the copyright, would neither relinquish the MSS. nor, at that point, make them public.[6] When in 1915 Bridges, as Poet Laureate, compiled *The Spirit of Man*, an anthology designed to strengthen and solace English readers in time of war, he included six items by Hopkins, some of them short edited excerpts. *The Spirit of Man* was widely read, but one of its features was that no author's name accompanied the passages cited; enquiring readers had to look this up at the back of the volume. Thus, though a few of Hopkins's poems had gained currency, his name was virtually unknown when in 1918 Robert Bridges prepared for the Oxford University Press a carefully edited and annotated text of the major poems. He did not write an introduction, but supplied a Preface to Notes, by way of preparing the reading public for the poems that had come into his keeping thirty years previously. This Preface (see p. 43) could almost be described in the words that he himself applied to 'The Wreck of the *Deutschland*' – 'a great dragon folded in the gate, to forbid all entrance'. It is so laced with cautionary remarks about the difficulty of Hopkins's style, and with censures of what he took to be faults of taste, that the praise he did mete out has a grudging air. Nevertheless, Bridges was a good editor. He included in the notes many illuminating comments from the letters he had received from Hopkins; and had he not carefully transcribed 'The Wreck of the *Deutschland*', when Hopkins lent him the manuscript, the master copy might have been lost. The discouraging tone of Bridges's commentary, with its emphasis on the extreme oddity and obscurity of Hopkins's verse, no doubt influenced the early reviewers. The prestige attached to the name of the Poet Laureate, however, lessened the chance that they would ignore the volume entirely.

Meanwhile, Hopkins's co-religionists, and especially the Jesuits, had shown some concern for his reputation. From time to time minor devotional poems had been printed in Catholic anthologies or religious periodicals, and as early as 1906 some extracts from his Journals appeared in the privately circulated Jesuit quarterly, *Letters and Notices*.[7] In 1920, after the publication of the *Poems*, *The Dublin Review* devoted twenty-six pages of its September issue to Gerard Manley Hopkins. Besides a critique of the poems, some further excerpts from the Journals were given, together with an anecdotal account of Hopkins as some of his fellow Jesuits remembered him (see p. 60).

Among the reviews of the first edition of the *Poems* should be noted the contribution of Edward Sapir to *Poetry* (Chicago) in 1921 (see p. 65). As early as 1914 the same remarkable 'little

review' had printed an appreciation by A. J. Kilmer of such
poems by Hopkins as he had come across. But more significant
than Sapir's perceptive notice was the article by I. A. Richards
in another influential American periodical, *The Dial*, in 1926
(see p. 69). Here he took 'The Windhover' as his central text.
The tensions in Hopkins's poetry, and the fusion of intellect
with passion, made it particularly attractive to Richards, who
had already formulated in *Principles of Literary Criticism* (1925)
an aesthetic theory stressing the importance of the equilibrium
of opposed impulses in both poets and readers of poetry, and the
superiority of complex to simple poetic language. He included
'Spring and Fall' as a specimen poem for analysis in his *Practical
Criticism* (1929);[8] and his influence as teacher as well as critic
carries over into William Empson's treatment of the same two
poems in *Seven Types of Ambiguity* (1930) (see p. 84). More in-
directly, it can be seen in the first book-length critique of
Hopkins,[9] E. E. Phare's survey and commentary on the poetry,
published in 1933.

Another early enthusiast for Hopkins who should not be for-
gotten was C. K. Ogden, Richards's associate in the whole
enterprise of Basic English and co-author of *The Meaning of
Meaning* (1923). Ogden contributed a long editorial and another
substantial article on Hopkins's prosody to *Psyche*.[10] Moreover,
he really did pay attention to the poet's plea that his verse must
be judged by its effect on the ear. In his house in Gordon Square
Ogden would declaim for the benefit of guests some of the most
vigorous passages from 'The Wreck of the *Deutschland*' and other
poems. 'The Soldier' was a particular favourite, the opening
line delivered in sergeant-major fashion.

Somewhat earlier, Laura Riding and Robert Graves, in their
Survey of Modernist Poetry (1928), devoted a few pages to Hopkins
which I would have liked to include in this volume had permission been forthcoming. In a chapter dealing with the plain
reader's dislike of any poetry that is not understandable at a
glance, they contended that any true poet is obliged to break
down stock responses and cliché-ridden diction if he is to
'remind people what the universe really looks and feels like,
that is, what language means'. Juxtaposing the Victorian poet

with E. E. Cummings, they noted Hopkins's extraordinary strictness in the use of words, and the unconventional notation he employed in setting them down, so that 'they had to be understood as he meant them to be, or understood not at all.' A few lines from the sonnet 'My own heart let me more have pity on . . .' analysed to show the aptness of the word-coinages and syntactical innovations, and the two poets defend against the censure of Bridges some of Hopkins's more far-fetched descriptions. That Hopkins should be included at all in a survey of modernist poetry is of course indicative of the impact he made in the twenties and thirties.

In 1930 the second edition of the *Poems* appeared, with a sensitively appreciative introduction by Charles Williams (see p. 81). This was very favourably received; and in the same year Father G. F. Lahey's biographical account of Hopkins was published, the first of its kind.[11] This too received a warm welcome. The great event of the decade, however, was the publication of letters and personal papers belonging to or connected with Hopkins. This gave a great impetus to the study of the man and the poet. In 1935 the *Letters* to Bridges and the *Correspondence* with Dixon were published by the Oxford University Press, both edited by C. C. Abbott. The first edition of the *Notebooks and Papers*, edited by Humphry House, followed in 1937, and *Further Letters*, including the correspondence with Coventry Patmore, came out in 1938 under Abbott's editorship. Henceforward there was ample material for critics to work on; and, more important, any reader attracted by the poems of Hopkins could now go on to become far better acquainted with his mind and spirit, as revealed in his private journals or in written discourse with his friends. Another twenty years elapsed before the expanded and revised edition of the *Journals and Papers* appeared, the work begun by Humphry House having been completed by Graham Storey (1959). In that year the Hopkins canon was completed by the publication of *The Sermons and Devotional Writings*, edited by Christopher Devlin, s.j., whose introductions are particularly useful to readers unfamiliar with the Catholic systems of thought which nourished Hopkins.

To return to the thirties – this was the decade in which Hopkins emerged decisively as a poet of major importance. His manner was being imitated by some of the poets of Auden's generation, notoriously by Rex Warner: but the critics dwelt less on his contemporaneity. In 1935 Geoffrey Grigson, the editor of *New Verse*, assembled for the April number a collection of essays on Hopkins, two of which are reproduced here (see pp. 109 and 113). F. R. Leavis's well-known appraisal in *New Bearings in English Poetry* (1932), antedates the surge of interest stimulated by the publication of the letters and notebook material. He devoted a chapter to an examination of Hopkins's characteristically energetic use of the English language in such major poems as 'The Wreck of the *Deutschland*' and 'Spelt from Sibyl's Leaves'. Far from stressing the oddity and outlandishness of Hopkins's diction, Leavis praised Hopkins for bringing poetry much closer to living speech than any other Victorian had done. It is a matter for regret that this important landmark in Hopkins criticism was not available for inclusion in this Casebook, but it can be found in G. H. Hartman's *Gerard Manley Hopkins: Twentieth Century Views* (1966), as well as in the revised edition of *New Bearings*.[12] It should certainly not be missed.

During the thirties Hopkins's poetic fame extended beyond England. Among his French critics was the Abbé Brémond, whose knowledge of English devotional poets of the seventeenth century gave him a good point of departure for the appreciation of Hopkins. Benedetto Croce contributed a long article to his literary review *La Critica* in 1937, which is an impressive testimony to the growth of Hopkins's international reputation. It includes many skilful prose renderings of the poems for the benefit of Croce's Italian readers.

In the mid-thirties, too, the work of one of the most comprehensive students of Hopkins began to appear. W. H. Gardner's essay on 'The Wreck of the *Deutschland*' was published in *Essays and Studies* in 1935, and in 1937 he contributed an article to *Scrutiny* on 'The Religious Problem in G. M. Hopkins'.[13] Gardner was later to edit the third edition of the *Poems* and to collaborate in editing the fourth.[14] He will also be remembered as author of one of the most generally valuable introductions

to the study of Hopkins's poetry. Though some of his interpretations have been challenged and bettered by more recent
critics, no newcomer can dispense with *Gerard Manley Hopkins:
A Study of Poetic Idiosyncrasy in Relation to Poetic Tradition*.[15] The
first volume of this appeared in 1944, the year that marked the
centenary of the poet's birth.

The occasion produced a large crop of critical essays and
commemorative tributes. An entire issue of *The Kenyon Review*
was devoted to Hopkins, and the articles were reprinted as a
volume by the Kenyon Critics in 1945, the English edition
dating from 1949. These essays constitute a brilliant collective
tribute. 'Analogical Mirrors', H. M. McLuhan's exegesis of
'The Windhover', first appeared in this context; and Arthur
Mizener's long essay on 'Victorian Hopkins' was the precursor
of many kindred studies. The American edition included an
article written by Dr Leavis for *Scrutiny* in 1944, but this was not
reproduced in the English edition. It can, however, be found
in F. R. Leavis, *The Common Pursuit* (1952).

A group of American Jesuits planned a centenary volume,
but as things turned out *Immortal Diamond*, edited by Norman
Weyand, did not appear until 1949. It contains a first-rate
essay on Sprung Rhythm by Walter J. Ong, and a useful
Glossary of difficult words in Hopkins's poetic vocabulary,
compiled by R. V. Schoder.[16]

Because Hopkins followed a vocation almost incomprehen-
sibly alien to the majority of his English readers, some of his
best interpreters have been those writing from within his own
religious tradition. Bridges had been handicapped in his response to Hopkins by a deep distaste for his theology and
religious sentiments. Most of the critics who launched Hopkins
as an exciting modernist poet were no more capable than
Bridges of imagining that the Jesuit yoke could be other than
damaging to so exquisite a poetic sensibility. At best, its pressure
could be seen as enforcing a peculiarly concentrated kind of
poetry.

It cannot be denied that Hopkins did suffer acutely from his
resolution to subordinate his creativity to the demands that his
religion made upon him (demands which his own scrupulosity

often exaggerated). There are heart-rending letters that bear witness to this, and the sonnet 'Thou art indeed just, Lord' epitomises his anguish. Yet what brought him near to despair was his inability to bring any of his enterprises to fruition. His pastoral work, his preaching, his university teaching, his scholarly projects – none of these had really prospered. Poets do write poems to lament the loss of their poetic power – Coleridge and George Herbert spring to mind – but this magnificent sonnet of Hopkins, along with the other poems of his latter years, are living proof that his poetic genius did not decline but increased. In his last sonnet, dedicated to Bridges, he complains that his 'lagging lines' do not express 'The roll, the rise, the carol, the creation' of inspired poetry; but with what mastery he makes his complaint!

Among the critical studies written from a theologically in-formed standpoint may be mentioned those of the Jesuits W. A. M. Peters, D. A. Downes and R. Boyle.[17] None of these books is easy reading; each is well-documented and closely argued; and all demonstrate how vitally important it is, in any interpretation of Hopkins, to be aware of the religious pre-suppositions on which most of his poetry rests. The *Spiritual Exercises* of St Ignatius Loyola permeated Hopkins's thinking. Humphry House summed up one important aspect of this in a footnote to the opening sentence, *Homo creatus est laudare*: 'No single sentence better explains the motives and direction of Hopkins's life than this, "Man was created to praise". He believed it as wholly as a man can believe anything; and when regret or sorrow over anything in his life comes to a critic's mind this must be remembered. To remember is not to share or advocate the belief; but it is essential to an intelligent reading of his work.'[18] The impact of Ignatian teaching on theme and metaphor is closly examined by both Downes and Boyle, and Peters pays much attention to the affinities between the doctrines of Duns Scotus and Hopkins's preoccupation with the value of idiosyncrasy and individuation. Detailed expositions of Scotist influence on Hopkins can also be found in articles contributed by Fr Christopher Devlin to *The Month*.[19]

Perhaps not surprisingly, no definitive life of the poet-priest has yet been written. The main difficulty stems less from lack of material than from an *embarras de richesses*. An attentive reading of the notebooks, journals and letters, besides illuminating the poems, leaves such a strong impression of the personality of Gerard Hopkins that any biographer would feel his work to be half accomplished already, in the sense that a Life that did not draw copiously on the personal documents would not be worth reading. Humphry House was working on a biographical study of Hopkins's youth, but this was left unfinished at his death.[20] Fr Anthony Bischoff, s.J., has for many years been accumulating material towards a definitive biography. Among the published biographical studies, John Pick's *G. M. Hopkins: Priest and Poet*, is informative and stimulating.[21] *Hopkins the Jesuit*, by Alfred Thomas, s.J.,[22] gives a painstaking account of the routine of Hopkins's life as a member of the Society of Jesus. Mention should also be made of a study of quite a different kind, J. G. Ritz's account of the friendship between Robert Bridges and Gerard Hopkins.[23] It is scrupulously fair, and does much to fill in the gaps sensed by any reader of the one-sided correspondence.

There is no need to expatiate on the more recent books on Hopkins, the most significant of which are listed in the Bibliography. Few of these are difficult to come by. But since most of Hopkins's critics err on the side of adulation, attention must be drawn to two who argue their cases against him with skill.

In 1949 the American critic Yvor Winters delivered two public lectures, sponsored by *The Hudson Review*, in which he accused Hopkins of emotional over-emphasis and 'violent assertiveness'. In his view too many of the poems were excited descriptions of landscapes or natural objects, with a perfunctory religious or moral sentiment tacked on. Hopkins 'hurls miscellaneous images at his subject from all sides'. His violations of grammar much offended Yvor Winters, who also disputed his metrics. The attack is not a mere outburst of petulance, but a case quite carefully made out by an able critic, whose mind was firmly rational and conventional.[24]

Donald Davie is another critic who has reservations about

Hopkins, though he rates him far higher as a poet than Winters did. A chapter in his *Purity of Diction in English Verse*[25] deals with 'Hopkins as a Decadent Critic'. Davie examines Hopkins's pronouncements on style, and concludes that they show 'self-regarding ingenuity' and an exaggerated regard for the systematic and the elaborate for their own sakes. Hopkins, he suggests, had the same arrogant disregard for the native qualities of the English language as his favourite poet Milton showed. 'His own poetry and criticism proceed from the single assumption that the function of poetry is to express a human individuality in its most wilfully uncompromising and provocative form.' This self-conscious singularity is what Davie stigmatises as decadent; and he thinks that Hopkins was wise to suspect a genuine clash between the Christian ideals of self-denial and self-sacrifice and his own vehemently individualistic poetic ideals.

There is, of course, substance in these charges. The singularity of Hopkins's style is extreme, and the liberties he took with the language are sometimes indefensible, though he never hesitated to defend them. The opening of his sonnet 'Henry Purcell', for example

> Have fair fallen, O far, fair have fallen, so dear
> To me . . .

remains thoroughly unidiomatic even when we have been told by the poet '*Have* is a singular imperative (or optative if you like) of the past, a thing possible and actual both in logic and grammar, but naturally a very rare one.'[26] But it is pointless to accuse a poet of eccentricity if he knows perfectly well what he is doing and why. Hopkins was a highly trained rhetorician, and to his mind English poets were usually deficient in their mastery of 'the common and teachable elements in literature, what grammar is to speech, what thorough-bass is to music, what theatrical experience gives to playwrights'.[27] His confident tone when explaining 'Henry Purcell' is another aspect of the quiet assurance with which he advised Coventry Patmore about his writings. People who are always prepared to back their own judgements are not, of course, always necessarily right, and Hopkins earned himself an amused reproof from Sir

Robert Stewart for his cocksureness in musical matters (see p. 38). Music was not, however, the field in which Hopkins had been trained. It is a fact that the explanations which he was able to supply for the obscurities in his poems do enlighten us. Even 'Tom's Garland', which required an exegesis of a couple of pages of prose to enable Bridges and Dixon to make head or tail of it, is not unintelligible or ineffective when the poet has expounded it.

Bridges perpetually took Hopkins to task for being obscure and affected in his diction. The first charge Hopkins was prepared to admit; the second he denied with some indignation. 'Obscurity I do and will try to avoid so far as is consistent with excellences higher than clearness at a first reading. . . . As for affectation I do not believe I am guilty of it; you should point out instances, but as long as mere novelty and boldness strike you as affectation, your criticism strikes me as – as water of the Lower Isis.'[28] Hopkins would truly have been guilty of affectation if he had adopted ready-made, conventional phraseology. Had he refrained from seeking an authentic language to express what was peculiar to his own way of seeing and feeling things, he would have violated the deepest of his convictions. His sense of uniqueness was extraordinarily developed; moreover, it came to be supported by a philosophical framework. 'When I consider my self being, my consciousness and feeling of myself, that taste of *I* and *me* above and in all things, which is more distinctive than the taste of ale or alum, more distinctive than the smell of walnut leaf or camphor, and is incommunicable by any means to another man . . .'.[29] So Hopkins wrote when meditating on God's creation of Man. Given that there is no possibility of conveying the innermost core of his self-being to others, the poet – any poet or artist – has to strive for an individual mode of utterance that will be as true as he can make it. This Hopkins did. He is, literally, an inimitable poet. He is also a poet who makes great demands on the intelligence of his readers. Yet because the quality of his mind and spirit was so exceptional, his poetry will surely never cease to fascinate, move and enrich those who are prepared to respond to it.

NOTES

1. A computerised *Concordance of the Poetry in English of G. M. Hopkins* was programmed by James Anderson and Angelo Triandafilou, and edited by A. Borrello (New Jersey, 1969).

2. The Hopkins Society, 114 Mount Street, London W1Y 6AH. See Bibliography for details of published lectures.

3. Printed as 'Author's Preface' in all editions.

4. C. C. Abbott (ed.), *Letters of G. M. Hopkins to R. Bridges* (Oxford, 1935) p. 265.

5. See T. K. Bender, *Gerard Manley Hopkins: the Classical Background and Critical Reception of his Work* (Baltimore, 1966).

6. See Preface to *The Journals and Papers of Gerard Manley Hopkins* (Oxford, 1959) p. xi.

7. Edited by Fr MacLeod, under the title 'The Diary of a Devoted Student of Nature' (April 1906, April 1907, October 1907).

8. The version Richards provided for his students was, however, incorrect. It lacked the third and fourth lines, gave 'unleafing' for 'unleaving' in the second line, thus spoiling the rhyme, and 'world' for 'worlds' in line 8. In A. H. Miles's anthology this unfortunate poem was also docked of lines 3 and 4, and the phrase in line 8 appears as 'world of wanhood'.

9. E. E. Phare, *The Poetry of G. M. Hopkins: A Survey and Commentary* (Cambridge, 1933).

10. C. K. Ogden, in *Psyche*, vol. 15 (1935) vol. 16 (1936).

11. G. F. Lahey, *Gerard Manley Hopkins* (London and Oxford, 1930).

12. F. R. Leavis, *New Bearings in English Poetry* (London, 1932; enlarged ed., 1950; Pelican ed., 1972).

13. W. H. Gardner, in *Essays and Studies of the English Association*, vol. xxi (1935); *Scrutiny*, vol. vi (June 1937).

14. W. H. Gardner (ed.), *Poems of Gerard Manley Hopkins*, 3rd ed. (Oxford, 1948); 4th ed., ed. with N. H. MacKenzie (Oxford, 1967).

15. W. H. Gardner, *Gerard Manley Hopkins: A Study of Poetic Idiosyncrasy in Relation to Poetic Tradition*, vol. 1 (London, 1944; New York, 1948) vol. 2 (London and New York, 1949); rev. ed. (London and Oxford, 1958).

16. For further details of these two collections, see Bibliography.

17. W. A. M. Peters, S.J., *G. M. Hopkins: A Critical Study* (London and Oxford, 1948); D. A. Downes, S.J., *G. M. Hopkins: A Study of his Ignatian Spirit* (New York, 1959, London, 1960); R. Boyle, S.J., *Metaphor in Hopkins* (Chapel Hill, N. Car., 1961).

18. *Notebooks and Papers* (Oxford, 1937) p. 416.

19. C. Devlin, s.j., in *The Month*, vol. i, new series (1949) and vol. iii (1950).

20. I am very grateful to Mrs Madeline House for letting me read the typescript.

21. John Pick, *G. M. Hopkins: Priest and Poet* (Oxford, 1942; 2nd ed., Oxford and New York, 1966).

22. Alfred Thomas, s.j., *Hopkins the Jesuit* (Oxford, 1969).

23. J. G. Ritz, *Robert Bridges and Gerard Manley Hopkins: A Literary Friendship* (Oxford, 1960).

24. Yvor Winters, lectures reprinted in G. H. Hartman (ed.), *Hopkins: a Collection of Critical Essays* (1966). See Bibliography.

25. Donald Davie, *Purity of English Diction* (London, 1952).

26. *Letters to Bridges*, p. 174.

27. C. C. Abbott (ed.), *Correspondence with Dixon* (Oxford, 1935) p. 141.

28. *Letters to Bridges*, p. 54.

29. Christopher Devlin, s.j., *Sermons and Devotional Writings* (Oxford, 1959) p. 123.

PART ONE

Contemporary and Early Criticism

1. EXTRACTS FROM THE NOTEBOOKS AND FROM LETTERS BY HOPKINS

The following extracts from Hopkins's notebooks and correspondence vividly illuminate the thinking that is embodied in his poetry.

I

God's utterance of himself in himself is God the Word, outside himself is this world. This world then is word, expression, news of God. Therefore its end, its purpose, its purport, its meaning, is God and its life or work to name and praise him. (7 August 1882)

II

Text of Exercises (*Principium sive Fundamentum*), Notes of G.M.H.

Man was created to praise, reverence and serve God Our Lord, and by so doing to save his soul. And the other things on the face of the earth were created for man's sake and to help him in the carrying out of the end for which he was created. Hence it follows that man should make use of creatures so far as they help him to attain his end and withdraw from them so far as they hinder him from so doing. For that, it is necessary to make ourselves indifferent in regard to all created things in so far as it is left to the choice of our free will and there is no prohibition; in such sort that we do not on our part seek for health rather than sickness, for riches rather than poverty, for honour rather than dishonour, for a long life rather than a short one; and so in all other things, desiring and choosing only those which may better lead us to the end for which we were created.

ON *Principium sive Fundamentum*

'Homo creatus est' – Aug. 20 1880: during this retreat, which I am making at Liverpool, I have been thinking about creation and this thought has led the way naturally through the exercises hitherto. I put down some thoughts. – We may learn that all things are created by consideration of the world without or of ourselves the world within. The former is the consideration commonly dwelt on, but the latter takes on the mind more hold. I find myself both as man and as myself something most determined and distinctive, at pitch, more distinctive and higher pitched than anything else I see; I find myself with my pleasures and pains, my powers and my experiences, my deserts and guilt, my shame and sense of beauty, my dangers, hopes, fears, and all my fate, more important to myself than anything I see. And when I ask where does all this throng and stack of being, so rich, so distinctive, so important, come from / nothing I see can answer me. And this whether I speak of human nature or of my individuality, my self being. For human nature, being more highly pitched, selved, and distinctive than anything in the world, can have been developed, evolved, condensed, from the vastness of the world not anyhow or by the working of common powers but only by one of finer or higher pitch and determination than itself and certainly than any that elsewhere we see, for this power had to force forward the starting or stubborn elements to the one pitch required. And this is much more true when we consider the mind; when I consider my self being, my consciousness and feeling of myself, that taste of myself, of *I* and *me* above and in all things, which is more distinctive than the taste of ale or alum, more distinctive than the smell of walnutleaf or camphor, and is incommunicable by any means to another man (as when I was a child I used to ask myself: What must it be to be someone else?). Nothing else in nature comes near this unspeakable stress of pitch, distinctiveness, and selving, this self being of my own. Nothing explains it or resembles it, except so far as this, that other men to themselves have the same feeling. But this only multiplies the phenomena to be explained so far as the cases are like and do resemble. But to me there is no resemblance: searching nature I taste *self* but at one tankard, that of my own being. The development, refinement, condensation of nothing shews any sign of being able to match this to me or give me another taste of it, a taste even resembling it. (1881–2)

III

The sun and the stars shining glorify God. They stand where he placed them, they move where he bid them. 'The heavens declare the glory of God.' They glorify God, *but they do not know it*. The birds sing to him, the thunder speaks of his terror, the lion is like his strength, the sea is like his greatness, the honey like his sweetness, they are something like him, they make him known, they tell of him, they give him glory, but they do not know they do, they do not know him, they never can, they are brute things that only think of food or think of nothing. This then is poor praise, faint reverence, slight service, dull glory. Nevertheless what they can, *they always do* . . .

. . . *But man can know God, can mean to give him glory*. This then is why he was made, to give God glory and to mean to give it, to praise God freely, willingly to reverence him, gladly to serve him. Man was made to give, and mean to give, God glory. (*Instructions*, 1883?)

SOURCE: the three extracts above are from C. Devlin (ed.), *The Sermons and Devotional Writings of G. M. Hopkins* (Oxford, 1959) p. 239.

IV

It seems to me that the poetical language of an age should be the current language heightened, to any degree heightened and unlike itself, but not (I mean normally: passing freaks and graces are another thing) an obsolete one. (Letter to Robert Bridges, 14 August 1879)

V

Why do I employ sprung rhythm at all? Because it is the nearest to the rhythm of prose, that is the native and natural rhythm of speech, the least forced, the most rhetorical and emphatic of all possible rhythms, combining, as it seems to me, opposite and one would have thought, incompatible excellences, markedness of rhythm – that is rhythm's self – and naturalness of expression. . . . My verse is less to be read than heard, as I have told you before; it is oratorical, that is the rhythm is so. (Letter to R.B., 21 August 1879)

VI

No doubt my poetry errs on the side of oddness. I hope in time to have a more balanced and Miltonic style. But as air, melody is what strikes me most of all in music and design in painting, so design, pattern or what I am in the habit of calling 'inscape' is what I above all aim at in poetry. Now it is the virtue of design, pattern or inscape to be distinctive and it is the vice of distinctiveness to become queer. This vice I cannot have escaped. (Letter to R.B., 15 February 1879)

VII

One of two kinds of clearness one should have – either the meaning to be felt without effort as fast as one reads or else, if dark at first reading, when once made out *to explode*. (Letter to R.B., 8 October 1879)

SOURCE: the four extracts above are from C. C. Abbott (ed.), *Letters of G. M. Hopkins to Robert Bridges* (Oxford, 1935) pp. 89, 46, 66, 90.

VIII

Poetry is speech framed for contemplation of the mind by the way of hearing or speech framed to be heard for its own sake and interest even over and above its interest of meaning. Some matter and meaning is essential to it but only as an element necessary to support and employ the shape which is contemplated for its own sake. (Lecture Notes: Rhetoric, 1873–4)

> SOURCE: from H. House and G. Storey (eds), *The Journals and Papers of G. M. Hopkins* (Oxford, 1959) p. 289.

IX

Every true poet . . . must be original and originality a condition of poetic genius; so that each poet is like a species in nature . . . and can never recur. (Letter to Coventry Patmore, 6 October 1886)

> SOURCE: from C. C. Abbott (ed.), *Further Letters of G. M. Hopkins* (Oxford, 1938) p. 222.

X

The effect of studying masterpieces is to make me admire and do otherwise. (Letter to Robert Bridges, 25 September 1888)

> SOURCE: from C. C. Abbott (ed.), *Letters of G. M. Hopkins to Robert Bridges* (Oxford, 1935) p. 291.

XI

The most inveterate fault of critics is the tendency to cramp and hedge in by rules the free movements of genius, so that I should say . . . the first requisite for a critic is liberality, and the second liberality, and the third, liberality. (Letter to Alexander Baillie, 6 September 1863)

> SOURCE: from C. C. Abbott (ed.), *Further Letters of G. M. Hopkins* (Oxford, 1938) p. 57.

2. EXTRACTS FROM LETTERS TO HOPKINS AND FROM CONTEMPORARY CORRESPONDENCE ABOUT HIM

RICHARD WATSON DIXON

I

Reverend and Most Dear Sir – I have your Poems and have read them I cannot say with what delight, astonishment, & admiration. They are among the most extraordinary I ever read & amazingly original. . . . It seems to me that they ought to be published. Can I do anything? I have said something of the institution of your Society in my next volume of Church History, which is not yet published. I could very well give an abrupt footnote about your poems, if you thought good. . . . You may think it odd for me to propose to introduce you in the year 1540, but I know how to do it. My object would be to awaken public interest & expectation in your as yet unpublished poems: or your recently published, if you think of publishing before that time. (Letter of 5 April 1879)

II

I return your Poems at last, having copied some, but not so many as I wished. I have so much writing in hand with the second volume of my History, that I have not been able to do all that I would. I have read them many times with the greatest admiration : in the power of forcibly & delicately giving the essence of things in nature, & of carrying one out of one's self with healing, these poems are unmatched. The Eurydice no one could read without the deepest & most ennobling emotion. The Sonnets are all truly wonderful: of them my best favourites are 'The Starlight Night', 'The Skylark', 'Duns Scotus' Oxford' and 'The Windhover'. I am haunted by the lines –

> And you were a liar, o blue March day,
> Bright, sunlanced fire of the heavenly bay',*

which seem to me more English-Greek than Milton, or as much so, and with more passion. The Deutschland is enormously powerful: it has however such elements of deep distress in it that one reads it with less excited delight though not with less interest than the others. I hope that you will accept the tribute of my deep and intense admiration. You spoke of sending me some more. I cannot in truth say what I think of your work.

Believe me ever your deeply attached friend. . . . (Letter of 1 March 1880)

III

. . . I hope that you are going on with poetry yourself. I can understand that your present position, seclusion and exercises would give to your writings a rare charm – they have done so in those that I have seen: something that I cannot describe, but know to myself by the inadequate word *terrible pathos* – something of what you call temper in poetry: a right temper which goes to the point of the terrible; the terrible crystal. Milton is the only one who has anything like it: & he has it in a totally different way: he has it through indignation, through injured majesty, which is an inferior thing in fact. I cannot tell whether you know what I mean. . . . (Letter of 26 October 1881)

IV

My dear, dear Friend, – Your letter touches & moves me more than I can say. I ought not in your present circumstances tease

* Hopkins points out in his answer (14 May 1880) that 'What I wrote was "Bright sun lanced fire in the heavenly bay, etc.", that is / a bright sun was darting fire from the bay of heaven, but that was of no avail, for did not a fatal north wind . . . and so on.' [Editor's Note]

you with the regret that much of it gives me: to hear of your
having destroyed poems, & feeling that you have a vocation in
comparison of which poetry & the fame that might assuredly be
yours is nothing. I could say much, for my heart bleeds: but I
ought also to feel the same: and do not as I ought, though I
thought myself very indifferent as to fame. So I will say nothing,
but cling to the hope that you will find it consistent with all
that you have undertaken to pursue poetry still, as occasion may
serve: & that in so doing you may be sanctioned & encouraged
by the great Society to which you belong, which has given so
many ornaments to literature. Surely one vocation cannot
destroy another; and such a Society as yours will not remain
ignorant that you have such gifts as have seldom been given by
God to man. . . . (Letter of 4 November 1881)

v

As to the first part of [your last letter], in which you speak of
your poetry, and its relation to your profession, I cannot but
take courage to hope that the day will come, when so health-
breathing and purely powerful a faculty as you have been gifted
with may find its proper issue in the world. Bridges struck the
truth long ago when he said to me that your poems more
carried him out of himself than those of any one. I have again
& again felt the same: & am certain that as a means of serving,
I will not say your cause, but religion, you cannot have a more
powerful instrument than your own verses. They have, of course
with all possible differences of originality on both sides, the
quality which Taine has marked in Milton: & which is more
to be noted in his minor poems than in the great ones, of
admiration – I forget Taine's expression, but it means admiration (or in you other emotions also) which reaches its fulness &
completeness in giving the exact aspect of the thing it takes: so
that a peculiar contentation is felt. . . . (Letter of 28 January
1882)

SOURCE: The foregoing five extracts are taken from
C. C. Abbott (ed.), *The Correspondence of G. M. Hopkins and
R. W. Dixon* (Oxford, 1935).

VI

He, Father Cormac, had a great opinion of Gerard, without, I think, knowing of his genius. He spoke of him as a most delightful companion, and as excellent in his calling, and so on, intimating at the same time that there was something unusual about him: that he was fond of pursuing niceties to an extent that stood in the way of his general usefulness. As that he dwelt on the niceties of the languages, in his classical lectures, in a way that rather stopped the progress of the classes. Also he was fond of taking up unusual subjects for himself. (Letter to Robert Bridges)

> SOURCE: James Sambrook, *A Poet Hidden: the Life of R. W. Dixon 1833–1900* (London, 1962) p. 96.

COVENTRY PATMORE

I

I have read your poems – most of them several times – and find my first impression confirmed with each reading. It seems to me that the thought and feeling of these poems, if expressed without any obscuring novelty of mode, are such as often to require the whole attention to apprehend and digest them; and are therefore of a kind to appeal only to the few. But to the already sufficiently arduous character of such poetry you seem to me to have added the difficulty of following *several* entirely novel and simultaneous experiments in versification and construction, together with an altogether unprecedented system of alliteration and compound words; – any one of which novelties would be startling and productive of distraction from the poetic matter to be expressed.

System and learned theory are manifest in all these experiments, but they seem to me to be *too* manifest. To me they often

darken the thought and feeling which all arts and artifices of
language should only illustrate; and I often find it as hard to
follow you as I have found it to follow the darkest parts of
Browning – who, however, has not an equal excuse of philo-
sophic system. 'Thoughts that *voluntary* move harmonious numbers' is, I suppose, the best definition of poetry that ever was
spoken. Whenever your thoughts forget your theories they do
so move, and no one who knows what poetry is can mistake
them for anything but poetry. 'The Blessed Virgin compared
to the Air we breathe' and a few other pieces are exquisite to
my mind, but, in these, you have attained to move about almost
unconsciously in your self-imposed shackles, and consequently
the ear follows you without much interruption from the surprise
of such novelties; and I can conceive that, after awhile, they
would become additional delights. But I do not think that I
could ever become sufficiently accustomed to your favourite
Poem 'The Wreck of the *Deutschland*' to reconcile me to its
strangeness. (Letter of 20 March 1884)

II

My dear Sir, – Your careful and subtle fault-finding is the
greatest praise my poetry has ever received. It makes me almost
inclined to begin to sing again, after I thought I had given over.
(Letter of 31 October 1883)

SOURCE: The two foregoing extracts are from C. C.
Abbott (ed.), *Further Letters of G. M. Hopkins* (Oxford,
1938).

III

To me [Hopkins's] poetry has the effect of veins of pure gold
embedded in masses of unpracticable quartz. He assures me
that his 'thoughts involuntarily moved' in such numbers, and
that he did not write them from preconceived theories. I cannot

understand it. His genius is however unmistakable, and is lovely and unique in its effects whenever he approximates to the ordinary rules of composition. (From a letter to Robert Bridges, 2 May 1884)

IV

I can well understand how terrible a loss you have suffered in the death of Gerard Hopkins – you who saw so much more of him than I did. I spent three days with him at Stonyhurst, and he spent a week with me here (Hastings); and that, with the exception of a somewhat abundant correspondence by letter, is all the communication I had with him; but this was enough to awaken in me a reverence and affection, the like of which I have never felt for any other man but one, that one being Frederick Greenwood, who for more than a quarter of a century has been the sole true and heroic politician and journalist in our de-graded land. Gerard Hopkins was the only orthodox and, as far as I could see, saintly man in whom religion had absolutely no narrowing effect upon his general opinions and sympathies. A Catholic of the most scrupulous strictness, he could nevertheless see the Holy Spirit in all goodness, truth and beauty; and there was something in all his words and manners which were at once a rebuke and an attraction to all who could only aspire to be like him. The *authority* of his goodness was so great with me that I threw the manuscript of a little book – a sort of 'Religio Poetae'* – into the fire simply because, when he read it, he said with a grave look, 'That's telling secrets.' This little book had been the work of ten years' continual meditations, and could not but have made a greater effect than all the rest I have ever written; but his doubt was final with me.

I am very glad to know that you are to write a memorial of him. It is quite right that it should be privately printed. I, as one of his friends, should protest against any attempt to share him with the public, to whom little of what was most truly

* *Sponsa Dei*. [Editor's Note]

characteristic in him could be communicated. (Letter to Robert Bridges, 12 August 1889)

> SOURCE: The two foregoing extracts are from Basil Champneys (ed.), *Memoirs and Correspondence of Coventry Patmore*, vol. 2 (London, 1900) pp. 247, 249.

SIR ROBERT STEWART

Indeed my dear Padre I *cannot* follow you through your maze of words in your letter of last week. I saw, ere we had conversed ten minutes on our first meeting, that you are one of the special pleaders who never believe yourself wrong in any respect. You always excuse yourself for anything I object to in your writing on music, so I think it is a pity to disturb you in your happy dreams of perfectability – nearly everything in your music was wrong – but you will not admit that to be the case. What does it matter? It will all be the same 100 Years hence. There's one thing I do admire – your hand-writing! I wish *I* could equal *that* – it is so scholarlike! (Letter of 22 May 1886)

> SOURCE: C. C. Abbott (ed.), *Further Letters*, p. 278.

C. N. LUXMOORE

[The letter opens with recollections of Hopkins as a schoolboy at Highgate, when Luxmoore was his contemporary.] Humanly speaking, he made a grievous mistake in joining the Jesuits, for on further acquaintance his whole soul must have revolted against a system which has killed many and many a noble soul; but what matters the means compared with the undoubted result. Any wood will do for the cross, when God's perfection is thereby reached. To get on with the Jesuits you must become

on many grave points a machine, without will, without conscience, and that in his nature was an impossibility. (Letter of 13
June 1890 to Arthur Hopkins, brother of the poet.)

SOURCE: C. C. Abbott (ed.), *Further Letters*, p. 249.

ANONYMOUS CONTEMPORARIES

I

One of his contemporaries writes:
My knowledge of Father Gerard Hopkins was almost entirely
confined to the time when we were studying theology together
at St. Beuno's. I shall always have a grateful and affectionate
remembrance of him. . . . What struck me most of all in him was
his child-like guilelessness and simplicity, his gentleness, tender-
heartedness, and his loving compassion for the young, the weak,
the poor, and all who were in any trouble or distress. Joined to
this and closely connected with it, was his purity of heart and
shrinking dread of anything that tended to endanger, especially
in the young, the angelic virtue.

Of this ability I need scarcely speak. He had a distinct dash
of genius. His opinion on any subject in Heaven and earth was
always worth listening to and always fresh and original. . . . He
was also most sensitive and this caused him to suffer much. I
have rarely known any one who sacrificed so much in under-
taking the yoke of religion. If I had known him outside, I should
have said that his love of speculation and originality of thought
would make it almost impossible for him to submit his intellect
to authority.

II

His mind was of too delicate a texture to grapple with the rough
elements of human life, but his kindness of heart and unselfish-

ness showed themselves in a thousand different ways, that gave full expression to the old words: 'Nil humani a me alienum puto.' The high order of his intellect was at once made evident to all who came into serious contact with him. . . .

SOURCE: quoted by G. F. Lahey, s.j., in *Gerard Manley Hopkins* (London and Oxford, 1930) pp. 133–40.

JOSEPH KEATING, S.J.

All that had met him knew him as a refined and cultured scholar, literary, musical, artistic, above all original. And he was loved by all who knew him as a man of a tender, self-devoted, sympathetic character, over-sensitive and delicate, perhaps, to face without much suffering the rough work of the world. But comparatively few outside the circle of his intimates, among whom his MSS. passed like Shakespeare's 'sugre'd sonnets', knew him as a poet of distinction, one who had contrived to preserve a certain individual spontaneity in an age when, seed being so abundant, most can raise the flower. Few men, as those friends can testify, had done more original work with less desire to make it known. . . .

[Father Keating notes that 'as a reversal of the common lot of poets', Hopkins's literary claims have gradually been gaining recognition. Mentioning the anthologies *Poets and Poetry* (ed. A. H. Miles) and *Lyra Sacra* (ed. H. C. Beeching), he continues]:

It may be that, thus bound up with blossoms from other soils, and appealing thus to a wider variety of tastes, the flowers of a single poetic mind have a greater chance of immortality than if they fashioned a bouquet of their own; still, it would seem that the time has now come for Father Hopkins's poems to appear in a collected form as a distinct and valuable addition to the literary heritage of the Catholic Church.

SOURCE: *The Month*, vol. CXIV (July 1909) p. 59.

3. EARLY CRITICISM

Robert Bridges

I

Hopkins's early verse shows a mastery of Keatsian sweetnesses, but he soon developed a very different sort of style of his own, so full of experiments in rhythm and diction that, were his poems collected into one volume, they would appear as a unique effort in English literature. Most of his poems are religious, and marked with Catholic theology, and almost all are injured by a natural eccentricity, a love for subtlety and uncommonness, well denoted by the Greek term τὸ περιττόν.[1] And this quality of mind hampered their author through life; for though to a fine intellect and varied accomplishments (he was both a draughtsman and a musician) he united humour, great personal charm, and the most attractive virtues of a tender and sympathetic nature, – which won him love wherever he went, and gave him zeal for his work – yet he was not considered publicly successful in his profession. . . .

The dated specimens below[2] are from all periods of his writing. The first two of these he would not have wished to be printed, but it is necessary to give them in proof that the unusual and difficult rhythms of his later work were consciously sought after, and elaborated from the common types which he set aside. Poems so far removed as his came to be from the ordinary simplicity of grammar and metre, had they no other drawback, could never be popular; but they will interest poets; and they may perhaps prove welcome to the critic, for they have this plain fault, that, aiming at an unattainable perfection of language (as if words – each with its two-fold value in sense and in sound – could be arranged like so many separate gems

to compose a whole expression of thought, in which the force
of grammar and the beauty of rhythm absolutely correspond),
they not only sacrifice simplicity, but very often, among verses
of the rarest beauty, show a neglect of those canons of taste
which seem common to all poetry.

SOURCE: from the Introduction contributed by Robert
Bridges to a selection of poems by Hopkins included in
A. H. Miles (ed.), *The Poets and Poems of the Century*, vol. 8
(London, 1894).

NOTES

1. τὸ περιττόν: 'over-subtle' or 'fine-spun'.
2. 'A Vision of the Mermaids' (selected lines), 'The Habit of
Perfection', 'The Starlight Night', 'Spring', 'The Candle Indoors',
'Spring and Fall', 'Inversnaid', 'To R.B., 1889'. [Editor's Notes]

11. 'Dedicatory Sonnet'

Our generation already is overpast,
And thy lov'd legacy, Gerard, hath lain
Coy in my home; as once thy heart was fain
Of shelter, when God's terror held thee fast
In life's wild wood at Beauty and Sorrow aghast;
Thy sainted sense trammel'd in ghostly pain,
Thy rare ill-broker'd talent in disdain:
Yet love of Christ will win man's love at last.

Hell wars without; but, dear, the while my hands
Gather'd thy book, I heard, this wintry day,
Thy spirit thank me, in his young delight
Stepping again upon the yellow sands.
Go forth; amidst our chaffinch flock display
Thy plumage of far wonder and heavenward flight!

SOURCE: *The Poems of Gerard Manley Hopkins*, 1st ed.
(Oxford, 1918).

III. *Notes on the Poetry of Hopkins*

Mannerisms. Apart from questions of taste – and if these poems were to be arraigned for errors of what may be called taste, they might be convicted of occasional affectation in metaphor, as where the hills are 'as a stallion stalwart, very-violet-sweet', or of some perversion of human feeling, as, for instance, the nostrils' relish of incense 'along the sanctuary side', or 'the Holy Ghost with warm breast and with ah! bright wings', these and a few such examples are mostly efforts to force emotion into theological or sectarian channels, as in 'the comfortless unconfessed' and the unpoetic line 'His mystery must be unstressed stressed', or, again, the exaggerated Marianism of some pieces, or the naked encounter of sensualism and asceticism which hurts 'The Leaden Echo and the Golden Echo', –

Style. Apart, I say, from such faults of taste, which few as they numerically are yet affect my liking and more repel my sympathy than do all the rude shocks of his purely artistic wantonness – apart from these there are definite faults of style which a reader must have courage to face, and must in some measure condone before he can discover the great beauties. For these blemishes in the poet's style are of such quality and magnitude as to deny him even a hearing from those who love a continuous literary decorum and are grown to be intolerant of its absence. And it is well to be clear that there is no pretence to reverse the condemnation of those faults, for which the poet has duly suffered. The extravagances are and will remain what they were. Nor can credit be gained from pointing them out: yet, to put readers at their ease, I will here define them: they may be called Oddity and Obscurity; and since the first may provoke laughter when a writer is serious (and this poet is always serious), while the latter must prevent him from being understood (and this poet has always something to say), it may be assumed that they were not a part of his intention.

Oddity and Obscurity. Something of what he thought on this subject may be seen in the following extracts from his letters. In Feb. 1879, he wrote:

All therefore that I think of doing is to keep my verses together in one place – at present I have not even correct copies –, that, if anyone should like, they might be published after my death. And that again is unlikely, as well as remote. . . . No doubt my poetry errs on the side of oddness. I hope in time to have a more balanced and Miltonic style. But as air, melody, is what strikes me most of all in music and design in painting, so design, pattern, or what I am in the habit of calling *inscape* is what I above all aim at in poetry. Now it is the virtue of design, pattern, or inscape to be distinctive and it is the vice of distinctiveness to become queer. This vice I cannot have escaped.

And again two months later:

Moreover the oddness may make them repulsive at first and yet Lang might have liked them on a second reading. Indeed when, on somebody returning me the *Eurydice*, I opened and read some lines, as one commonly reads whether prose or verse, with the eyes, so to say, only, it struck me aghast with a kind of raw nakedness and unmitigated violence I was unprepared for: but take breath and read it with the ears, as I always wish to be read, and my verse becomes all right.

   As regards Oddity then, it is plain that the poet was himself fully alive to it, but he was not sufficiently aware of his obscurity, and he could not understand why his friends found his sentences so difficult: he would never have believed that, among all the ellipses and liberties of his grammar, the one chief cause is his habitual omission of the relative pronoun; and yet this is so, and the examination of a simple example or two may serve a general purpose:

Omission of Relative Pronoun. This grammatical liberty, though it is a common convenience in conversation and has therefore its proper place in good writing, is apt to confuse the parts of speech, and to reduce a normal sequence of words to mere jargon. Writers who carelessly rely on their elliptical speech-forms to govern the elaborate sentences of their literary composition little know what a conscious effort of interpretation they often impose on their readers. But it was not carelessness in Gerard Hopkins: he had full skill and practice and scholarship in conventional forms, and it is easy to see that he banished these purely constructional syllables from his verse because they took up room which he thought he could not afford them: he needed in his scheme all his space for his poetical words, and he wished those to crowd out every merely grammatical colourless or toneless element; and so when he had got into the habit of doing without these relative pronouns – though he must, I suppose, have supplied them in his thought, – he abuses the licence beyond precedent, as when he writes (no. 17) 'O Hero savest!' for 'O Hero that savest!'.

Identical forms. Another example of this (from the 5th stanza of no. 23) will discover another cause of obscurity: the line 'Squander the hell-rook ranks sally to molest him' means 'Scatter the ranks that sally to molest him': but since the words *squander* and *sally* occupy similar positions in the two sections of the verse, and are enforced by a similar accentuation, the second verb deprived of its pronoun will follow the first and appear as an imperative; and there is nothing to prevent its being so taken but the contradiction that it makes in the meaning; whereas the grammar should expose and enforce the meaning, not have to be determined by the meaning. Moreover, there is no way of enunciating this line which will avoid the confusion; because if, knowing that *sally* should not have the same intonation as *squander*, the reader mitigates the accent, and in doing so lessens or obliterates the caesural pause which exposes its accent, then *ranks* becomes a genitive and *sally* a substantive.

Homophones. Here, then, is another source of the poet's obscurity; that in aiming at condensation he neglects the need that there is for care in the placing of words that are grammatically ambiguous. English swarms with words that have one identical form for substantive, adjective, and verb; and such a word should never be so placed as to allow of any doubt as to what part of speech it is used for; because such ambiguity or momentary uncertainty destroys the force of the sentence. Now our author not only neglects this essential propriety but he would seem even to welcome and seek artistic effect in the consequent confusion; and he will sometimes so arrange such words that a reader looking for a verb may find that he has two or three ambiguous monosyllables from which to select, and must be in

doubt as to which promises best to give any meaning that he
can welcome; and then, after his choice is made, he may be left
with some homeless monosyllable still on his hands. Nor is our
author apparently sensitive to the irrelevant suggestions that
our numerous homophones cause; and he will provoke further
ambiguities or obscurities by straining the meaning of these
unfortunate words.

Rhymes. Finally, the rhymes where they are peculiar are often
repellent, and so far from adding charm to the verse that they
appear as obstacles. This must not blind one from recognizing
that Gerard Hopkins, where he is simple and straightforward in
his rhyme is a master of it – there are many instances – but
when he indulges in freaks, his childishness is incredible. His
intention in such places is that the verses should be recited as
running on without pause, and the rhyme occurring in their
midst should be like a phonetic accident, merely satisfying the
prescribed form. But his phonetic rhymes are often indefensible
on his own principle. The rhyme to *communion* in 'The Bugler' is
hideous, and the suspicion that the poet thought it ingenious is
appalling; *eternal*, in 'The Loss of the *Eurydice*', does not correspond with *burn all*, and in 'Felix Randal' *and some* and *handsome*
is as truly an eye-rhyme as the *love* and *prove* which he despised
and abjured; – and it is more distressing, because the old-
fashioned conventional eye-rhymes are accepted as such without
speech-adaptation, and to many ears are a pleasant relief from
the fixed jingle of the perfect rhyme; whereas his false ear-
rhymes ask to have their slight but indispensable differences
obliterated in the reading, and thus they expose their defect,
which is of a disagreeable and vulgar or even comic quality. He
did not escape full criticism and ample ridicule for such things
in his lifetime; and in '83 he wrote: 'Some of my rhymes I
regret, but they are past changing, grubs in amber: there are
only a few of these; others are unassailable; some others again
there are which malignity may munch at but the Muses love.'

Euphony and Emphasis. Now these are bad faults, and, as I said,
a reader, if he is to get any enjoyment from the author's genius,
must be somewhat tolerant of them; and they have a real relation to the means whereby the very forcible and original effects

of beauty are produced. There is nothing stranger in these poems than the mixture of passages of extreme delicacy and exquisite diction with passages where, in a jungle of rough root-words, emphasis seems to oust euphony; and both these qualities, emphasis and euphony, appear in their extreme forms. It was an idiosyncrasy of this student's mind to push everything to its logical extreme, and take pleasure in a paradoxical result; as may be seen in his prosody where a simple theory seems to be used only as a basis for unexampled liberty. He was flattered when I called him περιττότατος,[1] and saw the humour of it – and one would expect to find in his work the force of emphatic condensation and the magic of melodious expression, both in their extreme forms. Now since those who study style in itself must allow a proper place to the emphatic expression, this experiment, which supplies as novel examples of success as of failure, should be full of interest; and such interest will promote tolerance.

The fragment, on a piece of music, No. 67, is the draft of what appears to be an attempt to explain how an artist has not free-will in his creation. He works out his own nature instinctively as he happens to be made, and is irresponsible for the result. It is lamentable that Gerard Hopkins died when, to judge by his latest work, he was beginning to concentrate the force of all his luxuriant experiments in rhythm and diction, and castigate his art into a more reserved style. Few will read the terrible posthumous sonnets without such high admiration and respect for his poetical powers as must lead them to search out the rare masterly beauties that distinguish his work.

SOURCE: from 'Preface to Notes', *The Poems of Gerard Manley Hopkins*, 1st ed. (Oxford, 1918).

IV. *Note on* 'The Wreck of the *Deutschland*'

The labour spent on this great metrical experiment must have served to establish the poet's prosody and perhaps his diction: therefore the poem stands logically as well as chronologically in the front of his book, like a great dragon folded in the gate to forbid all entrance, and confident in his strength from past success. This editor advises the reader to circumvent him and attack him later in the rear, for he was himself shamefully worsted in a brave frontal assault, the more easily perhaps because both subject and treatment were distasteful to him. A good method of approach is to read stanza 16 aloud to a chance company. To the metrist and rhythmist the poem will be of interest from the first, and throughout.

SOURCE: from Notes, *The Poems of Gerard Manley Hopkins*, 1st ed. (Oxford, 1918); reprinted in 2nd ed., ed. Charles Williams (Oxford, 1930).

NOTE

1. 'Prodigiously excessive.' [Editor's Note]

J. Middleton Murry

Modern poetry, like the modern consciousness of which it is the epitome, seems to stand irresolute at a crossways with no sign-post. It is hardly conscious of its own indecision, which it manages to conceal from itself by insisting that it is lyrical, whereas it is merely impressionist. The value of impressions depends upon the quality of the mind which receives and renders them, and to be lyrical demands at least as firm a temper of the mind, as definite and unfaltering a general direction as to be epic. Roughly speaking, the present poetical fashion may, with a few conspicuous exceptions, be described as poetry without tears. The poet may assume a hundred personalities in as many poems, or manifest a hundred influences, or he may work a single sham personality threadbare or render piecemeal an undigested influence. What he may not do, or do only at the risk of being unfashionable, is to attempt what we may call, for the lack of a better word, the logical progression of an *œuvre*. One has no sense of the rhythm of an achievement. There is an output of scraps, which are scraps, not because they are small, but because one scrap stands in no organic relation to another in the poet's work. Instead of lending each other strength, they betray each other's weakness.

Yet the organic progression for which we look, generally in vain, is not peculiar to poetic genius of the highest rank. If it were, we might be accused of mere querulousness. The rhythm of personality is hard, indeed, to achieve. The simple mind and the single outlook are now too rare to be considered as near possibilities, while the task of tempering a mind to a comprehensive adequacy to modern experience is not an easy one. The desire to escape and the desire to be lost in life were probably never so intimately associated as they are now; and it is a little preposterous to ask a moth fluttering round a candle-flame to see life steadily and see it whole. We happen to have been born into an age without perspective; hence our idolatry for the one living poet and prose writer who has it and comes, or appears to come, from another age. But another rhythm is possible. No doubt it would be mistaken to consider this rhythm as in fact wholly divorced from the rhythm of personality; it probably demands at least a minimum of personal coherence in its possessor. For critical purposes, however, they are distinct. This second and subsidiary rhythm is that of technical progression. The single pursuit of even the most subordinate artistic intention gives unity, significance, mass to a poet's work. When Verlaine declares 'de la musique avant toute chose', we know where we are. And we know this not in the obvious sense of expecting his verse to be predominantly musical; but in the more important sense of desiring to take a man seriously who declares for anything 'avant toute chose'.

It is the 'avant toute chose' that matters, not as a profession of faith – we do not greatly like professions of faith – but as the guarantee of the universal in the particular, of the *dianoia* in the episode. It is the 'avant toute chose' that we chiefly miss in modern poetry and modern society and in their quaint concatenations. It is the 'avant toute chose' that leads us to respect both Mr Hardy and Mr Bridges, though we give all our affection to one of them. It is the 'avant toute chose' that compels us to admire the poems of Gerard Manley Hopkins; it is the 'avant toute chose' in his work, which, as we believe, would have condemned him to obscurity to-day, if he had not (after many years) had Mr Bridges, who was his friend, to stand sponsor and

the Oxford University Press to stand the racket. Apparently
Mr Bridges himself is something of our opinion, for his intro-
ductory sonnet ends on a disdainful note: –

> Go forth: amidst our chaffinch flock display
> Thy plumage of far wonder and heavenward flight!

It is from a sonnet written by Hopkins to Mr Bridges that we
take the most concise expression of his artistic intention, for the
poet's explanatory preface is not merely technical, but is
written in a technical language peculiar to himself. Moreover,
its scope is small; the sonnet tells us more in two lines than the
preface in four pages.

> O then if in my lagging lines you miss
> The roll, the rise, the carol, the creation. . . .

There is his 'avant toute chose'. Perhaps it seems very like 'de
la musique'. But it tells us more about Hopkins's music than
Verlaine's line told us about his. This music is of a particular
kind, not the 'sanglots du violon', but pre-eminently the music
of song, the music most proper to lyrical verse. If one were to
seek in English the lyrical poem to which Hopkins's definition
could be most fittingly applied, one would find Shelley's
'Skylark'. A technical progression onwards from the 'Skylark'
is accordingly the main line of Hopkins's poetical evolution.
There are other, stranger threads interwoven; but this is the
chief. Swinburne, rightly enough if the intention of true song
is considered, appears hardly to have existed for Hopkins,
though he was his contemporary. There is an element of Keats
in his epithets, a half-echo in 'whorlèd ear' and 'lark-charmèd';
there is an aspiration after Milton's architectonic in the construction of the later sonnets and the most lucid of the fragments, 'Epithalamion'. But the central point of departure is the
'Skylark'. The 'May Magnificat' is evidence of Hopkins's
achievement in the direct line: –

> Ask of her, the mighty mother:
> Her reply puts this other
> Question: What is Spring? –
> Growth in everything –

> Flesh and fleece, fur and feather,
> Grass and greenworld all together;
> Starry-eyed strawberry-breasted
> Throstle above her nested
> Cluster of bugle-blue eggs thin
> Forms and warms the life within. . . .
> . . . When drop-of-blood-and-foam-dapple
> Bloom lights the orchard-apple,
> And thicket and thorp are merry
> With silver-surfèd cherry,
>
> And azuring-over graybell makes
> Wood banks and brakes wash wet like lakes,
> And magic cuckoo-call
> Caps, clears, and clinches all. . . .

That is the primary element manifested in one of its simplest, most recognisable, and some may feel most beautiful forms. But a melody so simple, though it is perhaps the swiftest of which the English language is capable without the obscurity which comes of the drowning of sense in sound, did not satisfy Hopkins. He aimed at complex internal harmonies, at a counterpoint of rhythm; for this more complex element he coined an expressive word of his own: –

But as air, melody, is what strikes me most of all in music and design in painting, so design, pattern, or what I am in the habit of calling *inscape* is what I above all aim at in poetry.

Here, then, in so many words, is Hopkins's 'avant toute chose' at a higher level of elaboration. 'Inscape' is still, in spite of the apparent differentiation, musical; but a quality of formalism seems to have entered with the specific designation. With formalism comes rigidity; and in this case the rigidity is bound to overwhelm the sense. For the relative constant in the composition of poetry is the law of language which admits only a certain amount of adaptation. Musical design must be subordinate to it, and the poet should be aware that even in speaking of musical design he is indulging a metaphor. Hopkins admitted this, if we may judge by his practice, only towards the end of his life. There is no escape by sound from the meaning of the posthumous sonnets, though we may hesitate to pronounce whether this directness was due to a modification of his poetical principles or to the urgency of the content of the sonnets, which, concerned with a matter of life and death, would permit no obscuring of their sense for musical reasons.

> I wake and feel the fell of dark, not day.
> What hours, O what black hours we have spent
> This night! what sights you, heart, saw; ways you went!
> And more must in yet longer light's delay.
>   With witness I speak this. But where I say
> Hours I mean years, mean life. And my lament
> Is cries countless, cries like dead letters sent
> To dearest him that lives, alas! away.

There is compression, but not beyond immediate comprehension; music, but a music of overtones; rhythm, but a rhythm which explicates meaning and makes it more intense.

Between the 'May Magnificat' and these sonnets is the bulk of Hopkins's poetical work and his peculiar achievement. Perhaps it could be regarded as a phase in his evolution towards the 'more balanced and Miltonic style' which he hoped for, and of which the posthumous sonnets are precursors; but the attempt to see him from this angle would be perverse. Hopkins was not the man to feel, save on exceptional occasions, that urgency of content of which we have spoken. The communication of thought was seldom the dominant impulse of his creative moment, and it is curious how simple his thought often proves to be when the obscurity of his language has been penetrated. Musical elaboration is the chief characteristic of his work, and for this reason what seem to be the strangest of his experiments are his most essential achievement. So, for instance, 'The Leaden Echo and the Golden Echo': –

>   Spare!
> There is one, yes, I have one (Hush there!);
> Only not within seeing of sun,
> Not within the singeing of the strong sun,

Tall sun's tingeing, or treacherous the tainting of the
    earth's air,
Somewhere else where there is, ah, well, where! one,
One. Yes, I can tell such a key, I do know such a place,
Where, whatever's prized and passes of us, everything
    that's fresh and fast flying of us, seems to us sweet
    of us and swiftly away with, done away with undone,
Undone, done with soon done with, and yet clearly
    and dangerously sweet
Of us, the wimpled-water-dimpled, not-by-morning-
    matchèd face,
The flower of beauty, fleece of beauty, too too apt to,
    ah! to fleet,
Never fleets more, fastened with the tenderest truth
To its own best being and its loveliness of youth. . . .

Than this, Hopkins truly wrote, 'I never did anything more
musical.' By his own verdict and his own standards it is therefore the finest thing that Hopkins did. Yet even here, where the
general beauty is undoubted, is not the music too obvious? Is
it not always on the point of degenerating into a jingle – as
much an exhibition of the limitations of a poetical theory as of
its capabilities? The tyranny of the 'avant toute chose' upon a
mind in which the other things were not stubborn and self-
assertive is apparent. Hopkins's mind was irresolute concerning
the quality of his own poetical ideal. A coarse and clumsy
assonance seldom spread its snare in vain. Exquisite openings
are involved in disaster: –

When will you ever, Peace, wild wood dove, shy wings
    shut,
Your round me roaming end, and under be my boughs?
When, when, Peace, will you, Peace? I'll not play hypocrite
To own my heart: I yield you do come sometimes; but
That piecemeal peace is poor peace. What pure
    peace. . . .

And the more wonderful opening of 'The Windhover' likewise
sinks, far less disastrously, but still perceptibly: –

I caught this morning morning's minion, kingdom of
    daylight's dauphin, dapple-dawn-drawn Falcon, in
    his riding
  Of the rolling level underneath him steady air, and
    striding
High there, how he rung upon the rein of a wimpling
    wing
In his ecstasy! then off, off forth on swing,
  As a skate's heel sweeps smooth on a bow-bend:
    the hurl and the gliding
  Rebuffed the big wind. My heart in hiding
Stirred for a bird, – the achieve of, the mastery of the
    thing!

We have no doubt that 'stirred for a bird' was an added excellence to the poet's ear; to our sense it is a serious blemish on
lines which have 'the roll, the rise, the carol, the creation'.

  There is no good reason why we should give characteristic
specimens of the poet's obscurity, since our aim is to induce
people to read him. The obscurities will slowly vanish and something of the intention appear; and they will find in him many of
the strange beauties won by men who push on to the border-
lands of their science; they will speculate whether the failure of
his whole achievement was due to the starvation of experience
which his vocation imposed upon him, or to a fundamental vice
in his poetical endeavour. For ourselves we believe that the
former was the true cause. His 'avant toute chose' whirling
dizzily in a spiritual vacuum, met with no salutary resistance
to modify, inform, and strengthen it. Hopkins told the truth of
himself – the reason why he must remain a poets' poet: –

    I want the one rapture of an inspiration.
    O then if in my lagging lines you miss
    The roll, the rise, the carol, the creation,
    My winter world, that scarcely yields that bliss
    Now, yields you, with some sighs, our explanation.

       SOURCE: *The Athenaeum* (June 1919); reprinted in
                Aspects of Literature (London, 1920).

Frederick Page, S.J.

Mr. Bridges is a poet of exquisite and usually right sensibility, unjust almost only to Catholics. He laughs at us – some of us – for preferring the least original of Father Gerard Hopkins' poems, which he excludes from his collection. The present writer is in a position to recognize the justice of Mr. Bridges' criticism, while still resenting the haughty urbanity with which he assures Catholics that we should not feel at home at this new feast he has spread. But when he deprecates the 'exaggerated Marianism' of some of the poems he now prints (and by implication, the 'exaggerated Marianism' of Catholic dogma) it is not our self-love which is hurt. We can but wonder how so fine a mind can see in the Mother of Our Lord the patroness of a fad, she the Destroyer of Heresies. . . .

This might be a false start in writing of the poetry of Gerard Hopkins, were it not that it easily leads to yet another Catholic divergence from this Protestant editor. Necessarily he is alive to the human import of these poems (if you tickle them, they laugh; if you prick them, they bleed), but except in his own beautiful prefatory sonnet, he prefers to speak of their author almost solely as a prosodist, we (the murder is out!) as a priest. Nor yet so much a priest, as a pastor, *Pastor in parochia*, who lays down his life for the sheep.

The prosody is as difficult as Mr. Bridges' own in his later and least welcome development. The difficulty of Browning's or Meredith's syntax is as nothing to the difficulty here from impermissible omissions and the clumsiest of inversions. The diction is as rough-hewn as Mr. Hardy's: the *Oxford Dictionary* would not have been large enough for Hopkins, but he must call in the *English Dialect Dictionary* to his aid. It is with malicious enjoyment that we note a Browningism in a *protégé* of Mr. Bridges, whose appreciation of Browning (we think Miss Mary Coleridge has told us) is confined to two lines. Gerard Hopkins, hesitating for, making shots at, the right word, the fitting

phrase, as every poet must, does not wait for them, but sets
down his hesitations, his pot-shots, as Browning may do legiti-
mately enough for his *dramatis personae*. But when Hopkins, in a
great religious lyric, writes as follows, we may enjoy it, yet find
it hard to justify:

> But how shall I . . . make me room there:
> Reach me a . . . Fancy, come faster –
> Strike you the sight of it? look at it loom there,
> Thing that she . . . there then! the Master.

It is only fair to say that, if another stanza from this same poem
reminds us also of Browning, it is chiefly of the ardour of
'Prospice', and of the divine close of 'Abt Vogler', not of the
queerness of 'Master Hugues':

> The frown of his face
> Before me, the hurtle of hell
> Behind, where, where was a, where was a place?
> I whirled out wings that spell
> And fled with a fling of the heart to the heart of the Host.
> My heart, but you were dove-winged, I can tell,
> Carrier-witted, I am bold to boast,
> To flash from the flame to the flame then, tower from the
> grace to the grace.

For the extenuation of Gerard Hopkins' too-learned perversi-
ties and self-indulged whims, I refer my reader to Mr. Bridges'
editorial notes, and now proceed to speak of that 'fatherliness',
that humanity, in Father Hopkins which we are sure Mr.
Bridges must see as some set-off to his friend's Romanism, and
which is for us the very essence of his sacerdotal character: we
have not here a priest who cannot be touched by a feeling of our
infirmities. He seems to have had a special feeling for children;
there are more than two or three poems evincing the same
tenderness, which yearns for the consecration of their innocence.
One little boy is exquisitely docile: and Father Hopkins is
anxious that his docility should be perfected. Another boy is
pathetically proud of his younger brother, and Father Hopkins
is touched by this 'radiance of Eden unquenched by the Fall' (to

use Patmore's words). He gives Holy Communion to a bugler boy, he administers Extreme Unction to a farrier, and it means as much to him as to them, their emotion is his, and is recollected in verse. His 'passion for souls' is the motive of many another poem. He notes a candle burning behind some window he passes, he watches a lantern moving through the dark, he remembers the hospitable cottages of Wales, in each case to yearn that the human actor may be worthy of the homely or mysterious or lovely scene. In 'The Candle Indoors' (and in another, unfinished, sonnet) he presses the point of his meditations home to his own bosom as who should say: 'A passion for souls? What then of your own?' It is with something of this same pastoral character that he envisages 'The Loss of the *Eurydice*' (a poem that offers a curious parallel to Cowper's 'The Loss of the *Royal George*' in that both seem intent to reproduce all the newspaper facts). There is pastoral responsibility here, but transferred to God:

> The Eurydice – it concerned thee, O Lord:
> Three hundred souls, O alas! on board,
> Some sleep unawakened, all unwarned, eleven fathoms deep,
> Where she foundered!

His own priesthood makes prayer for them. And so similarly with his longest and most ambitious poem, 'The Wreck of the *Deutschland*', 1875; for though the compelling occasion of this poem might seem to be the presence in the wreck of five German nuns expelled from Germany, yet the first part of the poem is (without any explicit reference to the shipwreck) a long, impassioned, and beautiful (though difficult) apostrophe to God, as the constrainer of men's wills, who has contrived this wreck for His own purpose as surely as Prospero contrived *his*. In the second part, where the wreck is narrated, one of the nuns (the Miranda of this tempest, and of the poet's love and wonder) becomes the interpreter and the mediatress of this purpose to the shipwrecked crew and passengers. The subject is still the salvation of souls.

'He calleth his own sheep by name': in 'The Loss of the *Eurydice*' it is 'Marcus Hare, high her captain', 'Sydney

Fletcher, Bristol-bred'; in other poems, Felix Randal, the farrier; the 'boy-bugler, born, he tells me, of Irish mother to an English sire' (how obviously a jotting from the notebook of a parish-priest!); the brothers Henry and John; the young child, Margaret ('grieving over Goldengrove unleaving'); Tom and Dick, the navvies; Harry, the ploughman. Even if these last are but the generic 'Tom, Dick and Harry', they yet bear witness to Father Hopkins' need to individualize his flock. Of great significance is the following confession. Passing 'the candle indoors':

> By that window, what task what fingers ply,
> I plod wondering, a-wanting, just for lack
> Of answer, the eagerer a-wanting Jessy or Jack,
> There God to aggrandise, God to glorify.

You have there, and throughout these poems, a double passion, the human affection for each Jessy and Jack, and the 'passion for souls': that they should glorify God. The theme is varied and developed in poems which express his love of, yet unsatisfaction with, beauty, and his imperious necessity of connecting it with God; and the beauty of the strength of manhood – a frequent theme, coinciding with Whitman. Of one such poem, 'a direct picture of a ploughman, without afterthought' – almost uniquely so in him – he writes: 'Let me know if there is anything like it in Walt Whitman, as perhaps there may be, and I should be sorry for that.' There *is*, and he should not have been sorry that at least sometimes this self-chartered libertine might coincide in feeling with a Jesuit father!

'To what serves mortal beauty?' he asks, and seems to answer that it endears goodness, and yet he is dissatisfied to leave us satisfied so, and bids us 'wish God's better beauty, grace'. He is much concerned with 'selves', but his æsthetic concern is reinforced or transubstantiated with a Pauline consideration that the 'self' lives not of itself, but Christ lives in it:

> . . . for Christ plays in ten thousand places,
> Lovely in limbs, and lovely in eyes not his
> To the Father through the features of men's faces.

'I lay down my life for my sheep': he is acutely conscious of the heavy sacrifice asked of him, and offered with so much resolution. From among his poems might be gathered a handful of sonnets (mostly), introspective in character, expressive of weariness, almost despair, at least unhopefulness, all but helplessness, longing, patience, fortitude, and that wisdom which is grateful for (what we may not call) small mercies. He disputes his sorrow like a man, but he also feels it as a man. He is perfect in both kinds. There could be nothing nobler than this disavowal of despair.

> Not, I'll not, carrion comfort, Despair, not feast on thee:
> Not untwist – slack they may be – these last strands of man
> In me, or, most weary, cry *I can no more*. I can;
> Can something, hope, wish day come, not choose not
>   to be.

I will not say that this poet's 'reading and writing', his theories of prosody, of which the reader has not seen the worst examples, appear when there is no need of such vanities, for at least they serve as foils to his essential simplicity. A poetic Unitarian, a mystical Broad Churchman – a Stopford Brooke, a George MacDonald – and, as we now discover, a curiously masculine Laureate – may speak to us of the Kingship of Christ, the Fatherhood of God, and we all but call the first windy, the second misty, and the third intellectual and not intelligent; but when Patmore is rarely tender – when Browning is rarely devotional (as in 'Saul' and 'The Arab Physician') or allegiant to Catholic doctrine (as in 'The Heretic's Tragedy' and 'Gold Hair') – when Gerard Hopkins is discerned to speak from the heart – we feel that their sincerity is guaranteed by what, in the first two, is more habitual, and what in the third is more apparent – by a not 'ingratiant' gaiety in Patmore; by a too-curious, too-active intellectuality in Browning; by a mad logicality in Father Hopkins which would carry to its extreme every privilege in every element of the technique of verse. Furthermore, what is lovely in them is supported by all its corollaries of dogma, whether these be harsh or sweet. I cannot put asunder the 'fatherliness' of Gerard Hopkins from his avowed discipleship to Duns Scotus, nor his love of Christ from his homage to 'the Mother of Christ and all His hallows'.

SOURCE: *Dublin Review*, vol. 167 (September 1920).

'Plures'

Thirty years have passed over his grave and Gerard Hopkins remains the elusive Jesuit, the obscure melodist, the lost Victorian. Only a gossamer web cut out of his shimmering life hangs in the memory of the few who remember. Of these the remembrance of the Laureate provokes comment, since he seems under the delusion that Jesuitry ruined his poetry (as Pascal would have prophesied) and that Gerard caged himself in a religious prison amid the political Yahoos and clerics of Dublin like some bright plumaged songster in a bat-tenanted belfry. Otherwise it is difficult to understand Mr. Bridges' curious impertinence or vulgar obtuseness, or to excuse his idiot shudder over the last 'terrible' and posthumous sonnets. The word 'terrible' has become terrible only in its meaninglessness. The late Master of Magdalene once assured his hearers that the most terrible text in the Bible was 'Ephraim is joined to idols: let him alone'. For thirty years Mr. Bridges has been thinking 'Hopkins is joined to idols: let him alone!' But he has not quite succeeded in doing so and it is necessary to add segments to the beautiful but broken arc which he has tried to describe.

His character and tastes survive ghostliwise in Diaries. He was alive to the minutest quaintness or beauty of sound, colour or phrase. He wrote down dreams, dialects, dippings into Irish or Welsh. He wished to learn Welsh to convert Wales, but abandoned it when he found his intention was not perfect. Perhaps he over enjoyed deriving a Welsh word for fairy from kidnapper, a discovery he recorded with pure joy. How happy, too, he was when 'The College watchman said, I will put on my shoon and let thee out.' He recorded ghosts, links with the past, such as his grandmother's memory in 1869 (she had heard her grandfather say he could remember an old man who had seen soldiers hunting the hedges for Charles I), the founderings of ships, which had an intense attraction for him, seeming to drag his imagination down into their gurgling wake. The Diary notes the *Captain* foundering in 1870, and his greatest poems were devoted to the disasters of the *Eurydice* and the *Deutschland*, the latter so strangely involved and wonderful that the *Month* no more dared to print it among its 'chaffinch' contributors than the *Dublin* dared record Francis Thompson's skylarking on Shelley amid its sparrowisms.

He described pictures, gems, cathedrals and sunsets with an impressionist's brush rather than the ink-quill. Comets, rainbows, the Tichborne Trial, and once even the House of Commons swarm into his iridescent glass (where the albino Lowe 'looked something like an apple in the snow'). His touch could be simplicity itself. 'Water is so clear in the still pools it is like shadowy air', or 'I see how chestnuts in bloom look like big-seeded strawberries'. He could count the octaves in the rainbow or smooth each orange feather of a golden-crested wren which flew into his room by night, whence he makes a novel wedding-present, 'Next morning I found many of them about the room and enclosed them in a letter to Cyril on his wedding day!' His compassion was extended to trees as, '(April 8th, 1873) The ash-tree growing in the corner of the garden was felled . . . a great pang and I wished to die and not to see the inscapes of the world destroyed any more.' And one remembers his dirge for the Binsey poplars felled in 1871:

> My aspens dear, whose airy cages quelled,
> Quelled or quenched in leaves the leaping sun,
> All felled, felled, are all felled;
> Of a fresh and following folded rank
>   Not spared but one
>   That dandled a sandalled
> Shadow that swam or sank . . .

Only those who live by the Thames and have their business in river waters know how perfect are those words whatever the metrist may make of their assonance. Nature carried him headlong into the supernatural. 'All nature', he wrote considering the breakers, 'is mechanical, but it is not seen that mechanics contain that which is beyond mechanics.' Nature's mechanics brought him to the Divine Mechanism. The mechanism of metre throbs through his poetry, and later through the dry mechanics of the Ignatian System he came to save his soul.

His sensitiveness gave him much pain but it added to his interest in life. In the refectory one day he writes that he tasted some yellow spoons to see if they were of brass. Soon afterwards, when told that the scarlet of flamingoes was due to a fine copper powder on their feathers, he found himself tasting brass. ('Unconscious cerebration, a bad phrase.') . . .

. . . This was the convert who at twenty-four years, finding himself the prey of his visual sensibilities, nervous to every sound of nature or art, with mind agape for colour, and being encumbered with much natural beauty himself, joined the rigid and pitiless Society of the Jesuits. He was not ill-advised when he laid his weakness upon the Ignatian pillow and harnessed his fancy to their shafts of iron. His beauty was made for crucifixion, but if the Society did not hinder him from following their cheerless road, they encouraged him to return to poetry and to attain his greatest as a poet under their roof. He had entered the Society over the ashes of his poems which he deliberately consumed. The Society had not bidden him burn them, nor can they have been responsible for the six-month penance of which there is a regretful hint among his nature-notes. 'But a penance I was doing from January 25th to July 25th prevented my seeing much that half year.' The lust of the eyes was quelled indeed. . . .

The Jesuit theory of obedience is exemplarized by the story of an Englishman ordered to go to China at twenty-four hours' notice for the rest of his life, whence possibly the word 'shanghaied'. But to send an English mystic compounded of Benjamin Jowett and Duns Scotus into Ireland is to launch him into a further and stranger country. It entails hopeless exile, and no one will deny the tragedy of Gerard Hopkins' Irish apostolate.

It takes more than the poetic temperament to face a forlorn hope, and Irish higher education was in a precarious situation. The work was hard and grinding. The conditions, though lightened by the society of a few brilliant fellow-sufferers, were insufferable. Into the rough and tumble of unendowed impromptu and the give and take of Anglo-Irish feud pitched Gerard Hopkins, by call of God a Jesuit and by His Grace no less a poet. The Greek chair was vacant and the Society believed that in placing him there they were playing a Hellenic ace out of their sleeves. They appreciated his Greek justly, but they knew not Hopkins.

Brilliant as had been his Greek learning, he could not, and even would not, teach it. Out of a quixotic justice to those who could not or would not hear him lecture, he would not allow his examination papers to refer to his lectures, so that students only came, to find out what would not be set. Interest must have lagged, for to illustrate the dragging of Hector he made a student lie on his back and be drawn through the room. His notes on Aeschylus show a scholarship soaring above unambitious aspirations for pass degrees. As an examiner he caused chaos by indecision in deciding single marks out of possible thousands. He marked each sentence down to halfs and quarters with unerring taste, but his mathematical powers were unfortunately not always equal to adding up the fractions. While the Examining Board were crying for his returns, he would be found with a wet towel round his head agonizing over the delivery of one mark. Perhaps he was not practical enough for a Jesuit, yet religion, fierce self-sacrificing religion, was the only backbone which ran the gamut of his dilettantism. He could not add, but he studied mathematical problems in relation to music. He composed music, but it could not be played, even by himself, since he wielded no instrument. The piano he approached with one finger and tapped out settings to 'Where is Sylvia?' Simple ballads and folk-songs appealed to him with their pathos of allusion. With freakish impulse he hunted for the odd and whimsical. The obvious he avoided like sin. He painted; he was a Ruskinian draughtsman. He wrote prose and in quiet secrecy poetry, of which the mass has been dragged out of his grave almost like the poems that poem-snatchers once took out of the hair of Rossetti's dead wife. It is no sacrilege to say that Gerard Hopkins would have buried his in the tomb of Christ and left their fragrance to be lost with the myrrh and spices for ever. . .

But Ireland added to his sorrow or, rather, it supplied material for his faculty of grief. Neurasthenia brought much introspective pain. The joy of living failed and only the power of the altar sustained him. In his human guise he wrote those piteous sonnets of his Dublin life which rose like the scent of a crushed flower, while the priest within him remained unshaken and sorrowless.

> I am in Ireland now . . .
>   only what word
> Wisest my heart breeds dark Heaven's baffling ban
> Bars or Hell's spell thwarts.

Six years brought his Dublin career within sight of the grave and he was leaving nothing save a submerged sheaf of poems to mark his richly-varied field. . . . He filled the Greek chair with distinction but little mark. . . . He did not live to see the time when University College, Dublin, would surpass all other colleges in Ireland together in distinctions. . . . He became an easy prey to typhoid, but his going was bright, for the call of the Society of Jesus, which he had not mistaken upon earth, seemed to echo from the next world and utterly absorb the suffering of this. If death is the test of vocation and of happiness, the test was not unfulfilled in the moment of exaltation with which Gerard Hopkins brought his religious passion to conclusion and peace, death's sting being only reserved for him, as with members of the Royal Family, in the pen of the Poet Laureate.

SOURCE: *The Dublin Review*, vol. 167 (September 1920).

Edward Sapir

. . . Hopkins is long in coming into his own; but it is not too much to say that his own will be secure, among the few that know, if not among the crowd, when many a Georgian name that completely overshadows him for the moment shall have become food for the curious.

For Hopkins' poetry is of the most precious. His voice is easily one of the half dozen most individual voices in the whole course of English nineteenth-century poetry. One may be repelled by his mannerisms, but he cannot be denied that overwhelming authenticity, that almost terrible immediacy of utterance, that distinguishes the genius from the man of talent. I would compare him to D. H. Lawrence but for his far greater sensitiveness to the music of words, to the rhythms and ever-changing speeds of syllables. In a note published in *Poetry* in 1914, Joyce Kilmer speaks of his mysticism and of his gloriously original imagery. This mysticism of the Jesuit poet is not a poetic manner, it is the very breath of his soul. Hopkins simply could not help comparing the Holy Virgin to the air we breathe; he was magnificently in earnest about the Holy Ghost that

> over the bent
> World broods with warm breast and with ah! bright wings.

As for imagery, there is hardly a line in these eighty-odd pages that does not glow with some strange new flower, divinely picked from his imagination.

Undeniably this poet is difficult. He strives for no innocuous Victorian smoothness. I have referred to his mannerisms, which are numerous and not always readily assimilable. They have an obsessive, turbulent quality about them – these repeated and trebly repeated words, the poignantly or rapturously interrupting *oh*'s and *ah*'s, the headlong omission of articles and relatives, the sometimes violent word order, the strange yet how often so lovely compounds, the plays on words, and, most of all, his

wild joy in the sheer sound of words. This phonetic passion of
Hopkins rushes him into a perfect maze of rhymes, half-rhymes,
assonances, alliterations:

> Tatter-tassel-tangled and dingle-a-dangled
> Dandy-hung dainty head.

These clangs are not like the nicely calculated jingling loveliness of Poe or Swinburne. They, no less than the impatient
ruggedness of his diction, are the foam-flakes and eddies of a
passionate, swift-streaming expression. To a certain extent
Hopkins undoubtedly loved difficulty, even obscurity, for its
own sake. He may have found in it a symbolic reflection of the
tumult that raged in his soul. Yet we must beware of exaggerat-
ing the external difficulties; they yield with unexpected ease to
the modicum of good will that Hopkins has a right to expect of
us.

Hopkins' prosody, concerning which he has something to say
in his preface, is worthy of careful study. In his most distinctive
pieces he abandons the 'running' verse of traditional English
poetry and substitutes for it his own 'sprung' rhythms. This new
verse of his is not based on the smooth flow of regularly recurring
stresses. The stresses are carefully grouped into line and stanza
patterns, but the movement of the verse is wholly free. The
iambic or trochaic foot yields at any moment to a spondee or a
dactyl or a foot of one stressed and three or more unstressed
syllables. There is, however, no blind groping in this irregular
movement. It is nicely adjusted to the constantly shifting speed
of the verse. Hopkins' effects, with a few exceptions, are in the
highest degree successful. Read with the ear, never with the eye,
his verse flows with an entirely new vigour and lightness, while
the stanzaic form gives it a powerful compactness and drive. It
is doubtful if the freest verse of our day is more sensitive in its
rhythmic pulsations than the 'sprung' verse of Hopkins. How
unexpectedly he has enlarged the possibilities of the sonnet, his
favourite form, will be obvious from the two examples that I am
going to quote. Meanwhile, here are two specimens of his more
smoothly flowing verse. The first is from 'The Leaden Echo and
the Golden Echo', a maiden's song:

How to keep – is there any any, is there none such, nowhere
   known some, bow or brooch or braid or brace, lace, latch
   or catch or key to keep
Back beauty, keep it, beauty, beauty, beauty, . . . from
   vanishing away?
Oh is there no frowning of these wrinkles, ranked wrinkles deep,
Down? no waving-off of these most mournful messengers, still
   messengers, sad and stealing messengers of grey?
No there's none, there's none – oh no, there's none!
Nor can you long be, what you now are, called fair –
Do what you may do, what, do what you may,
And wisdom is early to despair:
Be beginning; since, no, nothing can be done
To keep at bay
Age and age's evils – hoar hair,
Ruck and wrinkle, drooping, dying, death's worst, winding
   sheets, tombs and worms and tumbling to decay;
So be beginning, be beginning to despair.
Oh there's none – no no no, there's none:
Be beginning to despair, to despair,
Despair, despair, despair, despair.

This is as free as it can be with its irregular line-lengths and
its extreme changes of tempo, yet at no point is there hesitation
as the curve of the poem rounds out to a definite form. For long-
breathed, impetuous rhythms, wind-like and sea-like, such
verse as this of Hopkins' has nothing to learn from the best of
Carl Sandburg. My second quotation is from 'The Woodlark',
a precious fragment:

> *Teevo cheevo cheevio chee:*
> Oh where, where can that be?
> *Weedio-weedio:* there again!
> So tiny a trickle of song-strain;
> And all round not to be found
> For brier, bough, furrow, or green ground
> Before or behind or far or at hand
> Either left, either right,
> Anywhere in the sunlight.

> Well, after all! Ah, but hark –
> 'I am the little wood-lark.'

This is sheer music. The stresses fall into place with an altogether lovely freshness.

Yet neither mannerisms of diction and style nor prosody define the essential Hopkins. The real Hopkins is a passionate soul unendingly in conflict. The consuming mysticism, the intense religious faith are unreconciled with a basic sensuality that leaves the poet no peace. He is longing to give up the loveliness of the world for that greater loveliness of the spirit that all but descends to envelop him like a mother; but he is too poignantly aware of all sensuous beauty, too insistently haunted by the allurements of the flesh. A Freudian psychologist might call him an imperfectly sex-sublimated mystic. Girlish tenderness is masked by ruggedness. And his fuming self-torment is exteriorized by a diction that strains, and by a rhythmic flow that leaps or runs or stamps but never walks.

Here is 'The Starlight Night', one of his most characteristic sonnets – white-heat mysticism forged out of what pathos of sense-ecstasy!

> Look at the stars! look, look up at the skies!
> Oh look at all the fire-folk sitting in the air!
> The bright boroughs, the circle-citadels there!
> Down in dim woods, the diamond delves! the elves'-eyes!
> The grey lawns cold where gold, where quickgold lies!
> Wind-beat whitebeam! airy abeles set on a flare!
> Flake-doves sent floating forth at a farmyard scare! –
> Ah well! it is all a purchase, all is a prize.
>
> Buy then! bid then! – What? – Prayer, patience, alms, vows.
> Look look: a May-mess, like on orchard boughs!
> Look! March-bloom, like on mealed-with-yellow sallows!
> These are indeed the barn; within doors house
> The shocks. This piece-bright paling shuts the spouse
> Christ home, Christ and his mother and all his hallows.

'Ah well! it is all a purchase.' You cannot have it for the asking.

And, finally, this other sonnet, addressed to his own restless soul, 'with this tormented mind tormenting yet':

My own heart let me more have pity on; let
Me live to my sad self hereafter kind,
Charitable; not live this tormented mind
With this tormented mind tormenting yet.
I cast for comfort I can no more get
By groping round my comfortless, than blind
Eyes in their dark can day or thirst can find
Thirst's all-in-all in all a world of wet.

Soul, self; come, poor Jackself, I do advise
You, jaded, let be; call off thoughts awhile
Elsewhere; leave comfort root-room; let joy size
At God knows when to God knows what; whose smile
's not wrung, see you; unforeseen times rather – as skies
Betweenpie mountains – lights a lovely mile.

But how many 'lovely miles' could there have been on the long, rocky road traversed by this unhappy spirit?

In face of this agonising poem one can only marvel at the Poet Laureate's imperturbable exegesis of the word 'betweenpie': – 'This word might have delighted William Barnes if the verb "to pie" existed. It seems not to exist, and to be forbidden by homophonic absurdities.' From our best friends deliver us, O Lord!

SOURCE: *Poetry*, vol. XVIII (Chicago, September 1921).

I. A. Richards

Modern verse is perhaps more often too lucid than too obscure. It passes through the mind (or the mind passes over it) with too little friction and too swiftly for the development of the response. Poets who can compel slow reading have thus an initial advantage. The effort, the heightened attention, may brace the

reader, and that peculiar intellectual thrill which celebrates the
step-by-step conquest of understanding may irradiate and
awaken other mental activities more essential to poetry. It is a
good thing to make the light-footed reader work for what he
gets. It may make him both more wary and more appreciative
of his reward if the 'critical point' of value is passed.

These are arguments for some slight obscurity in its own right.
No one would pretend that the obscurity may not be excessive.
It may be distracting, for example. But what is a distraction in
a first reading may be non-existent in a second. We should be
clear (both as readers and writers) whether a given poem is to
be judged at its first reading or at its nth. The state of intellectual enquiry, the construing, interpretative, frame of mind, so
much condemned by some critics (through failure perhaps to
construe the phrase 'simple, sensuous, and passionate') passes
away once its task is completed, and the reader is likely to be
left with a far securer grasp of the whole poem, including its
passional structure, than if no resistance had been encountered.

Few poets illustrate this thesis better than Gerard Hopkins,
who may be described, without opposition, as the most obscure
of English verse writers. Born in 1844, he became a Jesuit priest
in 1868, a more probable fate for him then – he was at Oxford
– than now. Before joining the Order he burnt what verses he
had already written and 'resolved to write no more, as not
belonging to my profession, unless it were by the wish of my
superiors'. For seven years he wrote nothing. Then by good
fortune this wish was expressed and Hopkins set to work. 'I had
long had haunting my ear the echo of a new rhythm which now
I realized on paper. . . . However I had to mark the stresses . . .
and a great many more oddnesses could not but dismay an
editor's eye, so that when I offered it to our magazine . . . they
dared not print it.' Thenceforward he wrote a good deal, sending his poems in manuscript to Robert Bridges and to Canon
Dixon. He died in 1889 leaving a bundle of papers among
which were several of his best sonnets. In 1918 the Poet Laureate
edited a volume of poems with an introduction and notes of
great interest. From this volume comes all our knowledge of
his work.

Possibly their obscurity may explain the fact that these poems are not yet widely known. But their originality and the audacity of their experimentation have much to do with the delay. Even their editor found himself compelled to apologize at length for what he termed 'blemishes in the poet's style'. 'It is well to be clear that there is no pretence to reverse the condemnation of these faults, for which the poet has duly suffered. The extravagances are and will remain what they were . . . it may be assumed that they were not a part of his intention.' But too many other experiments have been made recently, especially in the last eight years, for this lofty tone and confident assumption to be maintained. The more the poems are studied, the clearer it becomes that their oddities are always deliberate. They may be aberrations, they are not blemishes. It is easier to see this to-day since some of his most daring innovations have been, in part, attempted independently by later poets.

I propose to examine a few of his best poems from this angle, choosing those which are both most suggestive technically and most indicative of his temper and mould as a poet. It is an important fact that he is so often most himself when he is most experimental. I will begin with a poem in which the shocks to convention are local and concern only word order.

'Peace'

When will you ever, Peace, wild wood dove, shy wings shut,
Your round me roaming end, and under be my boughs?
When, when, Peace, will you, Peace? I'll not play hypocrite
To own my heart: I yield you do come sometimes; but
That piecemeal peace is poor peace. What pure peace
    allows
Alarms of wars, the daunting wars, the death of it?

O surely, reaving Peace, my Lord should leave in lieu
Some good! And so he does leave Patience exquisite,
That plumes to Peace thereafter. And when Peace here does
    house
He comes with work to do, he does not come to coo,
    He comes to brood and sit.

Hopkins was always ready to disturb the usual word order of prose to gain an improvement in rhythm or an increased emotional poignancy. *To own my heart* = to my own heart; *reaving* = taking away. He uses words always as tools, an attitude towards them which the purist and grammarian can never understand. He was clear, too, that his poetry was for the ear, not for the eye, a point that should be noted before we proceed to 'The Windhover', which, unless we begin by listening to it, may *only* bewilder us. To quote from a letter: 'Indeed, when, on somebody's returning me the Eurydice, I opened and read some lines, as one commonly reads, whether prose or verse, with the eyes, so to say, only, it struck me aghast with a kind of raw nakedness and unmitigated violence I was unprepared for: but take breath and read it with the ears, as I always wish to be read, and my verse becomes all right.' I have to confess that 'The Windhover' only became all right for me, in the sense of perfectly clear and explicit, intellectually satisfying as well as emotionally moving, after many readings and several days of reflection. . . . [Richards here cites the poem in full; see p. 168 below for the text of the poem.]

The dedication [to 'Christ our Lord'] at first sight is puzzling. Hopkins said of this poem that it was the best thing he ever wrote, which is to me in part the explanation. It sounds like an echo of the offering made eleven years ago when his early poems were burnt. For a while I thought that the apostrophe, 'O my chevalier!' (it is perhaps superfluous to mention that this word rhymes strictly with 'here' and has only three syllables) had reference to Christ. I take it now to refer only to the poet, though the moral ideal, embodied of course for Hopkins in Christ, is before the mind.

Some further suggestions towards elucidation may save the reader trouble. If he does not need them I crave his forgiveness. *Kingdom of daylight's dauphin* – I see (unnecessarily) the falcon as a miniature sun, flashing so high up. *Rung upon the rein* – a term from the *manège*, ringing a horse = causing it to circle round one on a long rein. *My heart in hiding* – as with other good poets I have come to expect that when Hopkins leaves something which looks at first glance as though it were a concession

to rhyme or a mere pleasing jingle of words, some really important point is involved. Why in hiding? Hiding from what? Does
this link up with 'a billion times told lovelier, more dangerous,
O my chevalier!'? What is the greater danger and what the
less? I should say the poet's heart is in hiding from Life, has
chosen a safer way, and that the greater danger is the greater
exposure to temptation and error than a more adventurous,
less sheltered course (sheltered by Faith?) brings with it.
Another, equally plausible reading would be this: Renouncing
the glamour of the outer life of adventure the poet transfers its
qualities of audacity to the inner life. (*Here* is the bosom, the
inner consciousness.) The greater danger is that to which the
moral hero is exposed. Both readings may be combined, but
pages of prose would be required for a paraphrase of the result.
The last three lines carry the thought of the achievement
possible through renunciation further, and explain, with the
image of the ash-covered fire, why the dangers of the inner life
are greater. So much for the sense; but the close has a strange,
weary, almost exhausted, rhythm, and the word 'gall' has an
extraordinary force, bringing out painfully the shock with
which the sight of the soaring bird has jarred the poet into an
unappeased discontent.

If we compare those poems and passages of poems which
were conceived definitely within the circle of Hopkins' theology
with those which transcend it, we shall find difficulty in resisting
the conclusion that the poet in him was often oppressed and
stifled by the priest. In this case the conflict which seems to lie
behind and prompt all Hopkins' better poems is temporarily
resolved through a stoic acceptance of sacrifice. An asceticism
which fails to reach ecstasy and accepts the failure. All Hopkins'
poems are in this sense poems of defeat. This will perhaps become clearer if we turn to

'Spelt from Sibyl's Leaves'

Earnest, earthless, equal, attunable, vaulty, voluminous, . . .
　　stupendous,
Evening strains to be tímes's vást, womb-of-all, home-of-all,
　　hearse-of-all night.

Her fond yellow hornlight wound to the west, her wild hollow
    hoarlight hung to the height
Waste; her earliest stars, earl-stars, stárs principal, overbend
    us,
Fíré-featuring heaven. For earth her being has unbound, her
    dapple is at an end, as-
tray or aswarm, all throughther, in throngs; self ín self
    steepéd, and páshed – quite
Disremembering, dísmémbering áll now. Heart, you round me
    right
With: Óur évening is over us; óur night whélms, whélms and
    will end us.
Only the beak-leaved boughs dragonish damask the tool-
    smooth bleak light; black,
Ever so black on it. Óur tale, O óur oracle! Lét life, waned,
    ah lét life wind
Off hér once skéined stained véined varíety upon, áll on twó
    spools, párt, pén, páck
Now her áll in twó flocks, twó folds – black, white; right
    wrong; reckon but, reck but, mind
But thése two, wáre of a wórld where bút those twó tell, each
    off the óther; of a rack
Where, selfwrung, selfstrung, sheathe- and shelterless, thóughts
    agáinst thoughts ín groans grínd.

Elucidations are perhaps less needed. The heart speaks after
'Heart you round me right' to the end, applying in the moral
sphere the parable of the passing away of all the delights,
accidents, nuances, the 'dapple' of existence, to give place to
the awful dichotomy of right and wrong. It is characteristic of
this poet that there is no repose for him in the night of traditional morality. As the terrible last line shows, the renunciation
of all the myriad temptations of life brought no gain. It was all
loss. The present order of 'black, white; right, wrong' was an
afterthought and an intentional rearrangement; the original
order was more orthodox – *Let life, waned* – the imperative
mood carries through to the end, let life part, pen, pack, let
life be aware of. *All throughther* = each through the other.

I cannot refrain from pointing to the marvellous third and fourth lines. They seem to me to anticipate the descriptions we hope our younger contemporary poets will soon write. Such synaesthesis has tempted several of them, but this is, I believe, the supreme example. Hopkins' technical innovations reach out, however, into many fields. As a means of rendering self-consciousness, for example, consider this:

> Only what word
> Wisest my heart breeds dark heaven's baffling ban
> Bars or hell's spell thwarts. This to hoard unheard,
> Heard unheeded, leaves me a lonely began.

Or this:

> Soul, self; come poor Jackself, I do advise
> You, jaded, let be; call off thoughts awhile
> Elsewhere; leave comfort root-room; let joy size
> At God knows when to God knows what; whose smile
> 's not wrung, see you; unforeseen times rather – as skies
> Betweenpie mountains – lights a lovely mile.

My last quotations must be the sonnets which most I think, represent the poet's inner conflict.

Not, I'll not, carrion comfort, Despair, not feast on thee;
Not untwist – slack they may be – these last strands of man
In me or, most weary, cry *I can no more.* I can;
Can something, hope, wish day come, not choose not to be.
But ah, but O thou terrible, why wouldst thou rude on me
Thy wring-world right foot rock? lay a lionlimb against me?
> scan
With darksome devouring eyes my bruisèd bones? and fan,
O in turns of tempest, me heaped there; me frantic to
> avoid thee and flee?

Why? That my chaff might fly; my grain lie, sheer and clear.
Nay in all that toil, that coil, since (seems) I kissed the
> rod,
Hand rather, my heart lo! lapped strength, stole joy,
> would laugh, chéer.

Cheer whom though? the hero whose heaven-handling flung
     me, fóot tród
Me? or me that fought him? O which one? is it each one?
     That night, that year
Of now done darkness I wretch lay wrestling with (my God!)
     my God.

No worst, there is none. Pitched past pitch of grief,
More pangs will, schooled at forepangs, wilder wring.
Comforter, where, where is your comforting?
Mary, mother of us, where is your relief?
My cries heave, herd-long; huddle in a main, a chief
Woe, world-sorrow; on an age-old anvil wince and sing –
Then lull, then leave off. Fury had shrieked 'No ling-
ering! Let me be fell: force I must be brief.'

O the mind, mind has mountains; cliffs of fall
Frightful, sheer, no-man-fathomed. Hold them cheap
May who ne'er hung there. Nor does long our small
Durance deal with that steep or deep. Here! creep,
Wretch, under a comfort serves in a whirlwind: all
Life death does end and each day dies with sleep.

Few writers have dealt more directly with their experience
or been more candid. Perhaps to do this must invite the charge of
oddity, of playfulness, of whimsical eccentricity and wantonness. To some of his slighter pieces these charges do apply. Like
other writers he had to practise and perfect his craft. The little
that has been written about him has already said too much about
this aspect. His work as a pioneer has not been equally insisted
upon. It is true that Gerard Hopkins did not fully realize what
he was doing to the technique of poetry. For example, while
retaining rhyme, he gave himself complete rhythmical freedom,
but disguised this freedom as a system of what he called Sprung
Rhythm employing four sorts of feet ($-$,$-$ᵛ,$-$ᵛᵛ,$-$ᵛᵛᵛ). Since what
he called *hangers* or *outriders* (one, two, or three slack syllables
added to a foot and not counting in the nominal scanning)
were also permitted, it will be plain that he had nothing to fear
from the absurdities of prosodists. A curious way, however, of

eluding a mischievous tradition and a spurious question, to give them a mock observance and an equally unreal answer! When will prosodists seriously ask themselves what it is that they are investigating? But to raise this question is to lose all interest in prosody.

Meanwhile the lamentable fact must be admitted that many people just ripe to read Hopkins have been and will be too busy asking 'does he scan?' to notice that he has anything to say to them. And of those that escape this trap that our teachers so assiduously set, many will be still too troubled by the beliefs and disbeliefs to understand him. His is a poetry of divided and equal passions – which very nearly makes a new thing out of a new fusion of them both. But Hopkins' intelligence, though its subtlety with details was extraordinary, failed to remould its materials sufficiently in attacking his central problem. He solved it emotionally, at a cost which amounted to martyrdom; intellectually he was too stiff, too 'cogged and cumbered' with beliefs, those bundles of invested emotional capital, to escape except through appalling tension. The analysis of his poetry is hardly possible, however, without the use of technical language; the terms 'intellectual' and 'emotional' are too loose. His stature as a poet will not be recognized until the importance of the Belief problem from which his poetry sprang has been noticed. He did not need other beliefs than those he held. Like the rest of us, whatever our beliefs, he needed a change in belief, the mental attitude, itself.

SOURCE: *The Dial*, vol. 131 (September 1926).

PART TWO

Critical Appraisals, 1930–44

Charles Williams

FROM 'AN INTRODUCTION TO THE POETRY OF HOPKINS' (1930)

A good deal of attention has been paid to Gerard Hopkins's prosody, to his sprung-rhythms and logaoedic, his paeons and outrides; not so much has been spent in those habits, especially alliteration, to which English verse is more accustomed. Yet the alliteration so largely present in his poems is significant; especially if it be compared with that of another notable Victorian, Swinburne. It is of course a habit prevalent in all poets, but in general it is unintentionally disguised; the in-expert reader will not easily believe how much of it is in Shakespeare. But there have never been two poets who em-ployed it more than Hopkins and Swinburne; and the astonish-ing thing about Swinburne is not its presence but its uselessness, as the admirable thing about Hopkins is not its presence but its use. In verse after verse words beginning with the same letter hurry to Swinburne's demand; and all that can really be felt about them is that they do begin with the same letter. There is thought in Swinburne – more than it has of late been the fashion to admit – but the diction does not help it. The two things run almost parallel, so separate are they; they often divide at the opening of a poem, and when they come together it is by chance. The result is that Swinburne's alliteration will not usually stand close examination. Even the famous 'now folded in the flowerless fields of heaven' leaves the reader with the feeling that 'flowerless', which might – there – have been so remarkable an epithet was as a matter of fact an accidental one. He was the child of the English vocabulary.

But Gerard Hopkins was not the child of vocabulary but of

passion. And the unity of his passion is seen if we consider his alliteration: 'nor soul helps flesh more there than flesh helps soul.' The first stanza of the first poem, after the early ones, 'The Wreck of the *Deutschland*', may serve as an example. It is enough to suggest here that the curious reader might separate such almost inevitable 'poetic' alliterations as 'Lord of the living' from those in which the intense apprehension of the subject provides two or more necessary words almost at the same time. 'Thou has bound bones . . . fastened me flesh.' It is as if the imagination, seeking for expression, had found both verb and substantive at one rush, had begun almost to say them at once, and had separated them only because the intellect had reduced the original unity into divided but related sounds. A line like 'And cast by conscience out, spendsavour salt' ('The Candle Indoors') is one in which that intellect goes speeding to sound the full scope of the imaginative apprehension, and yet all the while to keep as close to its source as possible. It is true we cannot make haste when we are reading him, but that is what helps to make him difficult. The very race of the words and lines hurries on our emotion; our minds are left behind, not, as in Swinburne, because they have to suspend their labour until it is wanted, but because they cannot work at a quick enough rate. 'Cast by conscience out' is not a phrase; it is a word. So is 'spend-savour salt'. Each is thought and spoken all at once; and this is largely (as it seems) the cause and (as it is) the effect of their alliteration. They are like words of which we remember the derivations; they present their unity and their elements at once.

The work of the intellect is in the choice of the words. One may compare again 'Maiden and mistress of the months and years' with 'Why, tears! is it? tears; such a melting, a madrigal start' ('The Wreck of the *Deutschland*'). Madrigal is the last word expected, but it is justly chosen. So in 'Stigma, signal, cinquefoil token', 'lettering of the lamb's fleece', 'the gnarls of the nails', and many another. For all the art of the impulse and rush, 'the roll, the rise, the carol, the creation', it is very evident that the original impulse was to most careful labour as well as to apparent carelessness. The manuscripts confirm this by their numerous alterations, deletions, and alternative readings; they are what we might expect to find in the work-book of a good poet.

Of the same nature are his interior rhymes – as in 'The Lantern Out of Doors', 'heart wants, care haunts', 'first, fast, last friend', or the three last lines of the next poem; and his mere repetitions – 'and hurls for him, O half hurls earth for him', 'lay wrestling with (my God!) my God'. Alliteration, repetition, interior rhyme, all do the same work: first, they persuade us of the existence of a vital and surprising poetic energy; second, they suspend our attention from any rest until the whole thing, whatever it may be, is said. Just as phrases which in other poets would be comfortably fashioned clauses are in him complex and compressed words, so poems which in others would have their rising and falling, their moments of importance and unimportance, are in him allowed no chance of having anything of the sort. They proceed, they ascend, they lift us (breathlessly and dazedly clinging) with them, and when at last they rest and we loose hold and totter away we are sometimes too concerned with our own bruises to understand exactly what the experience has been.

It is arguable that this is not the greatest kind of poetry; but it is also arguable that the greatest kind of poetry might easily arise out of this. Robert Bridges has said that he was, at the end, abandoning his theories. But his theories were only ways of explaining to himself his own poetic energy, and if he were abandoning them it was because that energy needed to spend no more time on explanation, because, that is, it was becoming perfectly adequate to its business, 'without superfluousness, without defect'. While it was capable of producing lines like 'Or to-fro tender trambeams truckle at the eye', it may very well have felt that it ought to do a certain amount of explanation, though it did not (as it could not) explain that. It is perfectly possible to smile at the line, but hardly possible to laugh; or only sympathetically, as at the wilder images of the metaphysicals, the extremer rhetoric of Marlowe, the more sedate elegances of Pope, the more prosaic moralities of the Victorians, or the more morbid pedestrianisms of Thomas Hardy. Such things are the accidents of genius seriously engaged upon its own business, and not so apt as the observer to see how funny it looks.

The poet to whom we should most relate Gerard Hopkins, however, is perhaps none of these – not even the Metaphysicals nor the other Victorians – but Milton. The simultaneous consciousness of a controlled universe, and yet of division, conflict, and crises within that universe, is hardly so poignantly expressed in any other English poets than those two. Neither of them is primarily a mystic in his poetry, though Gerard Hopkins might easily have become one, or rather mysticism might very well have appeared in it. But such poems as 'The Blessed Virgin compared to the Air we breathe' hardly suffice to mark his verse with that infrequent seal, any more than the *Hound of Heaven* alone would seal Francis Thompson's. Both poets are on the verge of a mystical vision; neither actually seem to express it. But if the sense of division and pain, of summons and effort, make mysticism, then Hopkins was a mystic, but then also Milton was. The suffering in 'Thou art indeed just, Lord' is related to the suffering of Milton's *Samson Agonistes*, though Milton, under the influence of an austerer religious tradition, refused to 'contend' with God as Gerard Hopkins was free to do. Both their imaginations, nevertheless, felt the universe as divided both within them and without them; both realized single control in the universe; and both of them fashioned demands upon themselves and upon others out of what they held to be the nature of that control. This was the nature of their intellect.

Gerard Hopkins's experience of this is expressed largely in continual shocks of strength and beauty. Strength and beauty are in all of the more assured poets; it is therefore on the word 'shocks' that emphasis must be laid. Any poet when he is not at his greatest is preparing us for his greatest; it is by that approach to him that we can discern the elements which go to make up the unity of his achievements. We can find in this poet's work the two elements which have been mentioned: (*a*) a passionate emotion which seems to try and utter all its words in one, (*b*) a passionate intellect which is striving at once to recognize and explain both the singleness and division of the accepted universe. But to these must be added a passionate sense of the details of the world without[1] and the world within, a passionate consciousness of all kinds of experience. 'The Bugler's First Communion' is unsurpassed in its sense of the beauty of adolescence, as 'A Handsome Answer' or 'Brothers' of the beauty of childhood or 'Spring and Fall' of its sadness, as 'The Windhover' or 'The Starlight Night' are of the beauty of Nature, or certain of the sonnets of the extreme places of despair.

Yet perhaps, in the poems as we have them, the most recurrent vision seems to be that of some young and naked innocence existing dangerously poised among surrounding dangers – 'the achieve of, the mastery of the thing!' Had he lived, those dangers and that poise might have been more fully analysed and expressed. As it is, his intellect, startled at the sight, breaks now into joy, now into inquiry, now into a terror of fearful expectation, but always into song. Other poets have sung *about* their intellectual exaltations; in none has the intellect itself been more the song than in Gerard Hopkins. In this he was unique among the Victorians, but not because he was different from them in kind – as they indeed were not different in kind from us or from their predecessors – only because his purely poetic energy was so much greater.

His poetic tricks, his mannerisms, his explorations in the technique of verse, are not in the earlier poems and they are disappearing from the later. Had he lived, those tricks might have seemed to us no more than the incidental excitements of a developing genius. Since he did not live they will probably always occupy a disproportionate part of the attention given him. But that that attention must increase is already certain: poets will return to him as to a source not a channel of poetry; he is one who revivifies, not merely delights, equivalent genius. Much of his verse is described in that last line which in 'Felix Randal' brings in the outer world with such an overmastering noise of triumph over the spiritual meditation of the other lines; he himself at his poetry's 'grim forge, powerful amidst peers', fettled for the great gray drayhorse of the world 'his bright and battering sandal'. Some of his poems are precisely bright and

battering sandals. But some again are like another line – 'some
candle clear burns somewhere I come by'. He is 'barbarous in
beauty'. But he is also 'sweet's sweeter ending'. This again is
the result of and the testimony to his poetic energy. He is integral
to the beauty and storm without as to the beauty and storm
within. But it will take a good deal of patience in us before we
are integral to his own.

SOURCE: Introduction to *The Poems of Gerard Manley
Hopkins*, 2nd ed. (Oxford, 1930).

NOTE

1. He is usually so exact in his outward detail that one slip which is
certain to be remarked sooner or later by a student of such things
may as well be noted here. It will be observed that the stranger in
the lovely 'Epithalamion' – admirable fellow! – in preparing to
bathe, takes off his boots *last*.

William Empson

AMBIGUITIES IN HOPKINS (1930)

The meaning of an English sentence is largely decided by the accent, and yet one learns in conversation to put the accent in several places at once; it may be possible to read the poem so as to combine these two ways of underlining it.[1] . . . You may be intended, while reading a line one way, to be conscious that it could be read in another; so that if it is to be read aloud it must be read twice; or you may be intended to read it in some way different from the colloquial speech-movement so as to imply both ways at once. Different styles of reading poetry aloud use these methods in different proportions. . . . The following example from Hopkins shows the first case being forcibly included in the second.

> Margaret, are you grieving
> Over Goldengrove unleafing?
> So, for the things of man, you
> With your fresh thoughts care for, can you?
> Ah, as the heart grows older
> It will come to such sights colder
> By and by, nor spare a sigh
> Though world of wanwood leafmeal lie;
> And yet you will weep and know why.
> Now no matter, child, the name.
> Sorrow's springs are the same.
> Nor mouth had, no, nor mind express'd,
> What heart heard of, ghost guess'd:
> It is the blight man was born for,
> It is Margaret you mourn for.[2]

Will weep may mean: 'insist upon weeping, now or later', or 'shall weep in the future'. *Know* in either case may follow *will*, like *weep*, 'you insist upon knowing, or you shall know', or may mean: 'you already know why you weep, why you shall weep, or why you insist upon weeping,' or thirdly, may be imperative, 'listen and I shall tell you why you weep, or shall weep, or shall insist upon weeping, or insist upon weeping already'. Mr. Richards, from whom I copy this[3] considers that the ambiguity of *will* is removed by the accent which Hopkins placed upon it; it seems to me rather that it is intensified. Certainly, with the accent on *weep* and *and*, *will* can only be the auxiliary verb, and with the accent on *will* its main meaning is 'insist upon'. But the future meaning also can be imposed upon this latter way of reading the line if it is the tense which is being stressed, if it insists on the contrast between the two sorts of weeping, or, including *know* with *weep*, between the two sorts of knowledge. Now it is useful that the tense should be stressed at this crucial point, because it is these two contrasts and their unity which make the point of the poem.

It seems difficult to enjoy the accent on *are*, which the poet has inserted;[4] I take it to mean: 'Sorrow's springs, always the same, independent of our attitude to them and of our degree of consciousness of them, exist', permanently and as it were absolutely.

The two sorts of knowledge, intuitive and intellectual, form ambiguities again in the next couplet; this may help to show that they are really there in the line about *will*. *Mouth* and *mind* may belong to *Margaret* or somebody else; *what heart heard of* goes both forwards and backwards; and *ghost*, which in its grammatical position means both the profundities of the unconsciousness and the essentially conscious spirit, brings to mind both immortality and a dolorous haunting of the grave. 'Nobody else's mouth had told her, nobody else's mind had hinted to her, about the fact of mortality, which yet her own imagination had already invented, which her own spirit could foresee.' 'Her mouth had never mentioned death; she had never stated the idea to herself so as to be conscious of it; but death, since it was a part of her body, since it was natural to her organs, was known at sight as a portent by the obscure depths of her mind.' My point is not so much that these two are mixed up as that the poet has shown precisely by insisting that they were the *same*, that he knew they were distinguishable. . . .

An example of the seventh type of ambiguity, or at any rate of the last type of this series, as it is the most ambiguous that can be conceived, occurs when the two meanings of the word, the two values of the ambiguity, are the two opposite meanings defined by the context, so that the total effect is to show a fundamental division in the writer's mind. You might think that such a case could never occur and, if it occurred, could not be poetry, but as a matter of fact it is, in one sense or another, very frequent, and admits of many degrees. . . .

I shall end this chapter with a more controlled and intelligible example from George Herbert,[5] where the contradictory impulses that are held in equilibrium by the doctrine of atonement may be seen in a luminous juxtaposition. But in such cases of ambiguity of the seventh type one tends to lose sight of the conflict they assume; the ideas are no longer thought of as contradictory by the author, or if so, then only from a stylistic point of view; he has no doubt that they can be reconciled, and that he is stating their reconciliation. So I shall first consider a sonnet by Gerard Manley Hopkins, 'The Windhover: To Christ our Lord', as a more evident example of the use of poetry to convey an indecision, and its reverberations in the mind. . . .

[Empson cites the poem – with some serious misquoting;[6] for the correct text, see p. 168 below.]

I am indebted to Dr Richards for this case; he has already written excellently about it.[7] I have little to add to his analysis, and use it here merely because it is so good an example.

Hopkins became a Jesuit, and burnt his early poems on entering the order; there may be some reference to this sacrifice in the *fire* of the Sonnet. Confronted suddenly with the active physical beauty of the bird, he conceives it as the opposite of his patient spiritual renunciation; the statements of the poem appear to insist that his own life is superior, but he cannot decisively judge between them, and holds both with agony in his mind. *My heart in hiding* would seem to imply that the *more dangerous* life is that of the Windhover, but the last three lines insist it is *no wonder* that the life of renunciation should be the more *lovely*. *Buckle* admits of two tenses and two meanings: 'they do buckle here', or, 'come, and buckle yourself here', *buckle* like a military belt, for the discipline of heroic action, and *buckle* like a bicycle wheel, 'make useless, distorted and incapable of its natural motion'. *Here* may mean 'in the case of the bird', or 'in the case of the Jesuit'; *then* 'when you have become like the bird', or 'when you have become like the Jesuit'. *Chevalier* personifies either physical or spiritual activity; Christ riding to Jerusalem, or the cavalryman ready for the charge; Pegasus, or the Windhover.

Thus in the first three lines of the sestet we seem to have a clear case of the Freudian use of opposites, where two things thought of as incompatible, but desired intensely by different systems of judgments, are spoken of simultaneously by words applying to both; both desires are thus given a transient and exhausting satisfaction, and the two systems of judgment are forced into open conflict before the reader. Such a process, one might imagine, could pierce to regions that underlie the whole structure of our thought; could tap the energies of the very depths of the mind. At the same time one may doubt whether it is the most effective to do it so crudely as in these three lines; this enormous conjunction, standing as it were for the point of friction between the two worlds conceived together, affects one rather like shouting in an actor, and probably to many readers the lines seem so meaningless as to have no effect at all. The last three lines, which profess to come to a single judgement on the matter, convey the conflict more strongly and more beautifully.

The metaphor of the *fire* covered by ash seems most to insist on the beauty the *fire* gains when the ash falls in, when its precarious order is again shattered; perhaps, too, on the pleasure in that some movement, some risk, even to so determinedly static a prisoner, is still possible. The *gold* that painters have used for the haloes of saints is forced by alliteration to agree with the *gash* and *gall* of their self-tortures; from this precarious triumph we fall again, with *vermilion*, to bleeding.[8]

Source: *Seven Types of Ambiguity*, 1st ed. (London, 1929).

NOTES

1. Empson has been discussing Donne's 'The Apparition'. [Editor's Note]
2. Line 3 should read *Leaves, like the things of man, you*. In line 8 *world* should read *worlds*. [Editor's Note]
3. I. A. Richards, *Practical Criticism* (London, 1929).
4. Hopkins has inserted a good many other accents – or rather, stress-marks – not referred to by Empson. [Editor's Note]
5. The critic has been discussing a verse from Crashaw's 'Dies Irae'. He goes on to examine Herbert's 'The Sacrifice'. [Editor's Note]
6. Empson's quoting of the poem omits *rolling* before *level* in line 3; and in line 5 he gives

> *In his ecstasy. Then back, back forth on a swing*

instead of

> *In his ecstasy! then off, off forth on swing*

Besides misquoting, the critic ignores the poet's punctuation and alignment throughout the sonnet. [Editor's Note]
7. See pp. 72–3 above. [Editor's Note]
8. In the second edition of *Seven Types of Ambiguity* (revised and reset, 1947), Empson adds the following footnote: 'Nearly all this analysis is only putting in the background; the text is *buckle*. What would Hopkins have said if he could have been shown this analysis! It is, perhaps, the only really disagreeable case in the book. If I am right, I am afraid he would have denied with anger that he had meant "like a bicycle wheel", and then after much conscientious self-torture would have suppressed the whole poem.' [Editor's Note]

Harman Grisewood

THE IMPACT OF G. M. HOPKINS
(1931)

The appreciation of Hopkins' poetry has become more than the curious interest of literary scholarship appraising one last candidate who might have qualified for Victorian poet-hood. Indeed, the critic may well be discouraged from this way of scrutiny by the example of those with whom the attempt has usually ended in the safety-first admonition, 'a poet's poet'. It is with this phrase that the critic, on finding the work too exacting for his taste, has protected his own inadequate understanding against the prying of those outside his hastily drawn pentacle. Certainly Hopkins is exacting.

> Brute beauty and valour and act, oh, air, pride, plume, here
> Buckle! AND the fire that breaks from thee then, a billion
> Times told lovelier, more dangerous, O my chevalier!
> No wonder of it: shéer plód makes plough down sillion
> Shine, and blue-bleak embers, ah my dear,
> Fall, gall themselves, and gash gold-vermilion.

But it is one of his most excellent qualities that he made poetry difficult at a time when it had become deadly easy. 'Il y a trop peu d'écrivains obscurs en français; ainsi nous nous habituons lâchement à n'aimer que des écritures aiseés et bientôt primaires.'[1] It was during the prevalence of a similar *lâcheté* in England that Hopkins was writing those 'obscurities' and 'oddities' which made his friend Robert Bridges so uneasy.

That shrewd observer, Sir Edmund Gosse, in an address

delivered in 1913, in speaking of the Future of Poetry, said:

If we could read his [the modern poet's] verses which are still un-written, I feel sure that we should consider them obscure. That is to say, we should find that in his anxiety not to repeat what has been said before him, and in his horror of the trite and the superficial, he will achieve effect and attach interest – *obscuris vera involvens* – wrapping the truth in darkness. . . . He will be tempted to draw farther and farther away from contact with the world. He will wrap his singing robes not over his limbs only, but over his face and treat his readers with exemplary disdain.

It is significant that what is in some ways a far-seeing forecast of poetry now, serves also as something of an explanation of Hopkins' poetry that had been written thirty years before. And it is, in fact, the poets of to-day, the heirs of this predicted obscurity, who are the natural companions of Hopkins. Much poetry, and his with it, has had to wait till our times for poets to justify and again insist upon the necessary quality of troub-ling the reader.

'Poetry cannot be entirely the work of the poet. It must be or should be in part the conception of the reader.' For, as Mr. Sitwell goes on, recalling Ronsard: 'Poetry is the conversation of Gods through the medium of Man.'[2] This is in considerable contrast, if not wholly irreconcilable, with the opinion of Dr. Hake, a critic respected at the time when Hopkins wrote, who says: 'Poetry that is perfect poetry ought never to subject any tolerable intellect to the necessity of searching for its meaning.' Since Hopkins and the poetry of to-day have at least the charge of obscurity in common, it may be interesting so to consider them, that together they may make each other a little less strange.

Living poets have not remained untouched by the fitness of this association. The *Anthology of Twentieth-Century Poetry* in-cludes as much Hopkins as T. S. Eliot, and, commenting on such an inclusion in his preface, Mr. Harold Monro says: 'On the same lines, it might be argued that the magnificent Gerard Manley Hopkins should have no room. But chronology may now be dropped, he belonging temperamentally and techni-cally to the Twentieth Century, not to the Nineteenth.'

One aspect of this technical likeness may be illustrated by comparing the end of James Joyce's 'Anna Livia Plurabelle':

Can't hear with the waters of. The chittering waters of. Flittering bats, fieldmice bawk talk. Ho! Are you not gone ahome? What Tom Malone? Can't hear with bawk of bats, all the liffeying waters of. . . . Night now! Tell me, tell me, tell me, elm! Night night! Telmetale of stem or stone. Beside the rivering waters of, hither-andthithering waters of. Night!

with, for instance, the sestet of Hopkins' sonnet, 'Harry Ploughman':

> He leans to it, Harry bends, look. Back, elbow, and liquid
> waist
> In him, all quail to the wallowing o' the plough; 's cheek
> crimsons; curls
> Wag or crossbridle, in a wind lifted, windlaced –
>   See his wind-lilylocks-laced;
> Churlsgrace, too, child of Amansstrength, how it hangs or
> hurls
> Them – broad in bluffhide his frowning feet lashed! raced
> With, along them, cragiron under and cold furls –
>   With-a-fountain's shining-shot furls.

Or with this from 'The Wreck of the *Deutschland*':

> And the sea flint-flake, black-backed in the regular blow,
> Sitting Eastnortheast, in cursed quarter, the wind;
>   Wiry and white-fiery and whirlwind-swivélled snow
> Spins to the widow-making unchilding unfathering deeps.

Or:

> What hours, O what black hours we have spent.

Or:

> Sees the bevy of them, how the boys
>   With dare and with downdolphinry and bellbright
>   bodies huddling out,
> Are earthworld, airworld, waterworld thorough hurled, all
>   by turn and turn about.

These will illustrate sufficiently Hopkins' technique, and the reader may see in them, too, other affinities with modern methods than this 'Revolution of the Word' which is being formed into a doctrine around the body of James Joyce's later work.

M. Paul Bourget[3] insists on a distinction between literature which is *actual* and literature which is *historical*: which implies, as Mr. Herbert Read says of this distinction, that for the existing state of affairs certain authors have no immediacy, no impelling influence, no sympathetic power. 'We can learn from them, but we cannot be inspired by them.'[4] But Hopkins has immediacy. . . .

Mr. Charles Williams, in the preface to his excellent second edition of Bridges' original edition of 1918, makes a sensible distinction in saying: 'Other poets have sung *about* their intellectual exaltations; in none has the intellect itself been more the song than in Gerard Hopkins. In this he was unique among the Victorians.' And it is this quality which associates him naturally with poets to-day. Hopkins would have agreed with Rimbaud that 'poetry will no longer sing of action; it will be in advance'. 'There will be such poets! . . .' Rimbaud goes on. Hopkins was one. And it is perhaps in this quality of being 'in advance', this quality, not of celebrating, but of being itself the most extreme limit of the consciousness of living, being 'in advance' of life, that most surely links Hopkins to the Rimbaud succession and to its present developments.

Poetry 'in advance' may not be easy. It must, however, be sincere. And we can learn from the notes in this edition how natural it was for him to write in this difficult manner. Mr. Williams, has added examples of his early work which show that he could make fine use of traditional styles. Even when he was developing his later technique he could write, for instance, the poem 'May Magnificat'; but this was not the poetry he wrote to please himself, and in comment on it Hopkins says, 'A May piece in which I see little good'. Of his sonnet in honour of St. Alphonsus Rodriguez, he says, 'The sonnet (I say it snorting) aims at being intelligible.'

Father Lahey's *Life of Gerard Manley Hopkins* – an *apéritif* –

quotes enough of his letters to show that Hopkins was very far from desiring to make converts to any new school of experiment. He showed his work only to a small group of friends: Robert Bridges, Coventry Patmore and Canon Dixon. And one cannot but admire with what charm he preserved himself technically aloof from these poets and yet never lost sympathy with their writing in the least degree. His style was purely the outcome of his poetic sensibilities, and, in the nature of things, entirely above the suspicion of desiring to attract attention. It is characteristic that he stretched the sonnet form to its utmost rather than broke it, that he invented a new, though not a rebellious, system of prosody rather than denied prosodicality. And it is the inevitability of his new and strange phrases and the certainty that here at least is no literary humbug that compels the attention of the reader, who may feel the style a rebuff. For Hopkins is one who not so much turns his back upon but simply avoids the thinning ends of the Romantic and Humanist tradition. . . .

His vocation and faith tended to set Hopkins apart from these perplexities. His natural perception was of a purity and keenness which one can compare with the original founts of romanticism. With Keats he might have written, 'If a Sparrow comes before my Window, I take part in its existence and peck about the gravel.' For him, as for Shelley, 'life like a dome of many-coloured glass stains the white radiance of Eternity', but his faith allows him even more than a Wordsworthian delight in the consequent variegation of colour, for

Christ plays in ten thousand places.

. . . Yet though he retrieved all the first romantics' keenness of perception, he knew there could be no copying their method of rendering this perception in art. Where Shelley writes:

> Sound of vernal showers
> On the twinkling grass,
> Rain-awakened flowers,
> All that ever was
> Joyous, and clear, and fresh, thy music
> Doth surpass.

Or Wordsworth:

> Up with me! Up with me, into the clouds!
> For thy song, lark, is strong;
> Up with me, up with me, into the clouds!
> Singing, singing,
> With all the heavens about thee ringing.

Hopkins has:

> Left hand, off land, I hear the lark ascend,
>> His rash-fresh re-winded new-skeinèd score
>> In crisps of curl off wild winch whirl, and pour
> And pelt music, till none's to spill nor spend.

And aside from the mainstream of literary development he made a method fit for his own insight.

Among the new influences that tended to free art from its false position in the moral order was Pater's remark that all art aspires to the condition of music – a suspicious beckoning towards Symbolism. . . .

Hopkins says of his writing 'The Wreck of the *Deutschland*': 'I had long had haunting my ear the echo of a new rhythm which now I realized on paper', but in the result there is no aspiring to the condition of music as in Swinburne; there is nothing '*mallarméen*' about this or anything Hopkins wrote. But there is a hitherto unachieved luxury of sound-effects. No poet in the English language has worked more satisfactorily in this field. His artistic sensibility, however, warned him off the more dangerous ground.

There is a sketch for a poem of Hopkins beginning:

> *TEEVO cheevio cheevio chee:*
> O where, what can that be?
> *Weedio-weedio:* there again!

and ending:

> Through the velvety wind V-winged
> To the nest's nook I balance and buoy
> With a sweet joy of a sweet joy,
> Sweet, of a sweet, of a sweet joy
> Of a sweet – a sweet – sweet – joy

that shows Steinish leanings. But Hopkins never finished this poem and goes no further down that road. This method, however, produced some extremely fine work, as can be seen from the quotations above. A good example can be taken from his sonnet 'The Windhover'. . . .

About 1884 his work, enormously enriched by technical experiment and discovery, becomes deeper and more certain. An example is the sonnet beginning:

> Tom – garlanded with squat and surly steel
> Tom; then Tom's fallowbootfellow piles pick
> By him and rips out rockfire homeforth – sturdy Dick

where this last line compresses both the sound and the sight of a gang of workmen going home, the nails of their boots striking fire from the flinty road. Yet this image dexterously serves the effect of the whole poem, which gives an insight clear into the happening itself.

There is less luxuriating in the use of Pure Sound. Corresponding with this change, it is in our present times, when music is no longer in its former iatric relation to poetry, that we are to look for a further statement in poetic theory in advance of Pater's dictum. It is to be found in the Abbé Brémond's discourse 'Pure Poetry', delivered before the French Academy in October 1925.

His address ends with the words that all poetry aspires not to the condition of music but of prayer. In his book, consequent on the address, he presents the poet as a mystic *manqué*. The Abbé uses the word mystic to stress the importance he attached to the intuition.

It is the intuition – M. Claudel's 'Anima', Herr Wust's 'Vernunft' – that is more constantly Hopkins' poetical material than anything else. 'Such divination of the spiritual in the things of sense, which also will express itself in the things of sense, is what we properly call Poetry.' Here M. Maritain is speaking not only of art; the Abbé Bremond, too, is writing not so much about the art of poetry, but about that faculty of intuition of poets, also called poetry, by which they divine,

perceive, are inspired. Hopkins puts it thus in his sonnet to
Robert Bridges:

> The fine delight that fathers thought; the strong
> Spur, live and lancing like the blowpipe flame,
> Breathes once and, quenchéd faster than it came,
> Leaves yet the mind a mother of immortal song.
> Nine months she then, nay years, nine years she long
> Within her wears, bears, cares and combs the same:
> The widow of an insight lost she lives, with aim
> Now known and hand at work now never wrong.

This insight is what is important for Hopkins as a poet. He had
written in 1879: 'But as air, melody, is what strikes me most of
all in music and design in painting, so design, pattern, or what
I am in the habit of calling *inscape*, is what I above all aim at in
poetry.' Hopkins' insistence on the perceptive faculty of 'insee-
ing inscape' is most in accord with the work and discussion of
T. E. Hulme and the imagists, to whom modern poetry owes
so much. It was this group, followers of Bergson in his revolt
against Descartes, that recovered and insisted on the faculty of
intuition; who, in pressing further the symbolist doctrine, set
the poet to render the image.

Hopkins agrees that the object for poetry is not the thing seen
but the seeing of it. His poetry does not describe the thing or
even describe the perception. But, in his way of speaking,
poetry *in*scribes it. Poetry does not impart conceptual or rational knowledge, but 'real' knowledge, 'infused' wisdom.

Hopkins brings words together so that from their condition
there may leap out whole and clear that 'insight' which is the
very essence of poetry. Of the ellipses, usage of strange words and
spellings that may be necessary to this result, Mr. Robert Graves
says: '. . . if the mood reaches a point in fantasia where grammar becomes frayed and snaps, then it can dispense with
grammar. In structure it is Protean; there is no architectural
preconception; the growth is organic. In imagery it is only
bound by the preference of the individual author for imagery
of a particular kind.'[5]

It is the work of the original poet to pass sentence on what is trivial, trite, or lax, and to recall the reader to the elementary definitions of Poetry. It was some such task which confronted Blake coming at the end of the Age of Reason, who says: 'When the sun rises, do you not see a round disc of fire somewhat like a guinea? O no, no, I see an Innumerable company of the Heavenly host crying: "Holy, Holy, Holy, is the Lord God Almighty!" I question not my corporeal or vegetative eye any more than I would question a window concerning my Sight. I look through it and not with it.'[6]

SOURCE: *Dublin Review*, vol. 189 (October 1931).

NOTES

1. Rémy de Gourmont, *De Stéphane Mallarmé*.
2. Osbert Sitwell, *Who Killed Cock Robin?* (London, 1921).
3. Paul Bourget, *Quelques Temoignages* (Paris, 1928).
4. Herbert Read, *Phases of English Poetry* (London, 1918) preface, p. 1.
5. Robert Graves, *Another Future of Poetry* (London, 1926).
6. William Blake, *Catalogue to an Exhibition, 1810*.

Herbert Read

CREATIVITY AND SPIRITUAL TENSION (1933)

In Hopkins's poetry, as perhaps in the work of other poets, we can distinguish (1) poetry which is the direct expression of religious beliefs, (2) poetry which has no direct or causal relation to any such beliefs at all, and (3) poetry which is not so much the expression of belief in any strict sense but more precisely of doubt. All Hopkins's poems of any importance can be grouped under these three categories. When this has been done, I think that there would be general agreement that in poetic value the second and third categories are immensely superior to the first. Indeed, so inferior are such strictly religious poems as 'Barnfloor and Winepress', 'Nondum', 'Easter', 'Ad Mariam', 'Rosa Mystica', and one or two others, that Robert Bridges rightly excluded them from the first edition of the *Poems*. Of the *Poems* published by Dr. Bridges, one or two might conceivably be classified as poems of positive belief, like the exquisite 'Heaven-Haven' and 'The Habit of Perfection'. 'The Wreck of the *Deutschland*', the long poem which Hopkins himself held in such high regard, is a poem of contrition, of fear and submission rather than of the love of God:

> Be adored among men,
> God, three-numberèd form;
> Wring thy rebel, dogged in den,
> Man's malice, with wrecking and storm.
> Beyond saying sweet, past telling of tongue,
> Thou art lightning and love, I found it, a winter and warm;
> Father and fondler of heart thou hast wrung:
> Hast thy dark descending and most art merciful then.

This is the beauty of terror, the 'terrible pathos' of the phrase in which Canon Dixon so perfectly defined Hopkins's quality.

Of the poetry which has no direct or causal relation to beliefs of any kind, poems such as 'Penmaen Pool', 'The Starlight Night', 'Spring', 'The Sea and the Skylark', 'The Windhover', 'Pied Beauty', 'Hurrahing in Harvest', 'The Caged Skylark', 'Inversnaid', 'Harry Ploughman', and the two 'Echoes', the poetic force comes from a vital awareness of the objective beauty of the world. That awareness – 'sensualism', as Dr. Bridges calls it – is best and sufficiently revealed in original metaphors such as 'mealed-with-yellow sallows', 'piece-bright paling', 'daylight's dauphin', 'a stallion stalwart, very violet-sweet', and many others of their kind, in which the poet re-forges words to match the shape and sharpness of his feelings. Dr. Bridges [Notes to the *Poems*], speaks of 'the naked encounter of sensualism and asceticism which hurts "The Leaden Echo and the Golden Echo" ' – a phrase I cannot in any sense apply to the poem in question; for while I appreciate the magnificent sensualism of this poem, I fail to detect any asceticism in the ordinary secular meaning of the word. But that in general there was a conflict of this sort in Hopkins is revealed, not only by the fact that he destroyed many of his poems which he found inconsistent with his religious discipline, but most clearly in his curious criticism of Keats:

. . . Since I last wrote, I have re-read Keats a little, and the force of your criticism on him has struck me more than it did. It is impossible not to feel with weariness how his verse is at every turn abandoning itself to an unmanly and enervating luxury. It appears too that he said something like 'O, for a life of impressions instead of thoughts'. It was, I suppose, the life he tried to lead. The impressions are not likely to have been all innocent, and they soon ceased in death. His contemporaries, as Wordsworth, Byron, Shelley, and even Leigh Hunt, right or wrong, still concerned themselves with great causes, as liberty and religion; but he lived in mythology and fairyland, the life of a dreamer: nevertheless, I feel and see in him the beginnings of something opposite to this, of an interest in higher things, and of powerful and active thought. . . . His mind had, as it seems to me, the distinctly masculine powers in abundance, his character the manly virtues; but, while he gave himself up to dreaming and self-indulgence, of course they were in abeyance. Nor do I mean that he would have turned to a life of virtue – only God can know that – but that his genius would have taken to an austerer utterance in art. Reason, thought, what he did not want to live by, would have asserted itself presently, and perhaps have been as much more powerful than that of his contemporaries as his sensibility or impressionableness, by which he did want to live, was keener and richer than theirs.

The implication of this criticism is that the poet, by nature a dreamer and a sensualist, only raises himself to greatness by concerning himself with 'great causes, as liberty and religion'. In what sense did Hopkins so sublimate his poetic powers? In a poem like 'Pied Beauty' we see the process openly enacted. After a catalogue of dappled things, things which owe their beauty to contrast, inconsistency and change, Hopkins concludes by a neat inversion – an invocation to God who, fathering forth such things, is Himself changeless. In 'Hurrahing in Harvest' again we have an extended metaphor: the senses glean the Saviour in all the beauty of Summer's end. 'The Windhover' is completely objective in its senseful catalogues: but Hopkins gets over his scruples by dedicating the poem 'To Christ our Lord'. But this is a patent deception. It does not alter the naked sensualism of the poem; and there is no asceticism in this poem; nor essentially in any of the other poems of this group. They are tributes to God's glory, as all poetry must be; but they are tributes of the senses; and a right conception of God and of religion is not hurt by such tributes.

In the third section, poems expressive not so much of belief as of doubt, I would place those final sonnets, Nos. 40, 41, 44, 45, 46, 47 and 50 in the published *Poems*.[1] These all date from the last years of Hopkins's life – the first six from 1885, the other from 1889, the actual year of his death. But even earlier poems express at least despair: 'Spring and Fall' – the blight man was born for; the 'Sibyl's Leaves' – the self-wrung rack where thoughts against thoughts grind. But the sonnets themselves are complete in their gloom, awful in their anguish. I need only quote that last terrible sonnet:

Thou art indeed just, Lord, if I contend
With thee; but, sir, so what I plead is just.
Why do sinners' ways prosper? and why must
Disappointment all I endeavour end?

    Wert thou my enemy, O thou my friend,
How wouldst thou worse, I wonder, than thou dost
Defeat, thwart me? Oh, the sots and thralls of lust
Do in spare hours more thrive than I that spend,
Sir, life upon thy cause. See, banks and brakes
Now, leavèd how thick! lacèd they are again
With fretty chervil, look, and fresh wind shakes
Them; birds build – but not I build; no, but strain,
Time's eunuch, and not breed one work that wakes.
Mine, O thou lord of life, send my roots rain.

Is there any evidence in the known facts of Hopkins's life
which throws light on this state of mind? Father Lahey, in his
memoir of Hopkins, speaks of the three sorrows of his last years.
The first two were due to external causes and do not concern
us here; but Father Lahey then writes:

Of Hopkins's third sorrow it is more difficult to speak. It sprang
from causes which have their origin in true mysticism. Hopkins,
smiling and joyful with his friends, was at the same time on the
bleak heights of spiritual night with his God. All writers on mysticism – St. Teresa, St. John of the Cross, Poulain, Maumigny, etc. –
have told us that this severe trial is the greatest and most cherished
gift from One Who has accepted literally His servants' oblation.
Hopkins was always remembered by all who met him as essentially
a priest, a deep and prayerful religious. With the fine uncompromising courage of his initial conversion, he pursued his never-
ending quest after spiritual perfection. The celebrated 'terrible'
sonnets are only terrible in the same way that the beauty of Jesus
Christ is terrible. Only the strong pinions of an eagle can realise the
cherished happiness of such suffering. It is a place where Golgotha
and Thabor meet. Read in this light his poems cease to be tragic.

The relation of doubt to belief is another and a profounder
question than the one which concerns us now. No one who has
thought about such matters fails to realise the paradoxical

significance of the cry of the dumb child's father: 'Lord, I believe; help Thou mine unbelief.' As Father Lahey points out, this absence of spiritual complacency is of the very essence of Christian mysticism. An absence of spiritual complacency may also well be of the very nature of poetic sensibility.

Of that psychological aspect of creativity in the poet I have dealt at length in my essay on *Form in Modern Poetry*. I will only say here, by way of résumé, that we are born with sensibility and come into a world of ready-formulated ideas. As we develop, we may either adapt our sensibility to receive these ideas; or we may painfully create ideas (disciplinary dogmas) which the freely expanding personality can hold in tension. In the latter case the space between self and dogma is *bridged* – there is a bridge, not an abysm of despair – by doubt. My contention is, that a creative gift or poetic sensibility is only consistent with such a state of spiritual tension and acuity. True originality is due to a conflict between sensibility and belief; both exist in the personality, but in counter-action. The evidence is clear to read in all genuine mysticism and poetry; and nowhere more clearly than in the poetry and mysticism of Gerard Hopkins.

The terrible sincerity of the process of Hopkins's thought inevitably led him to an originality of expression which rejected the ready-made counters of contemporary poetics. His originality in this respect is both verbal and metrical, and perhaps the innovations he introduced into metre prevent more than anything else the appreciation of his poetry. Except for a few early poems, which need not be taken into account, practically every poem written by Hopkins presents rhythmical irregularities. The poet himself attempted a theoretical justification of these, and it is an extremely ingenious piece of work. But there can be no possible doubt – and it is important to emphasise this – that the rhythm of Hopkins's poems, considered individually, was intuitive in origin –

> Since all the make of man
> Is law's indifference.

The theory was invented later to justify his actual powers.

It makes its first appearance in his correspondence in 1877, and in his letters to Bridges and Dixon, Hopkins shows that he understood the technique of English poetry as no poet since Dryden had understood it – Dryden whom he describes so well in one of these letters as 'the most masculine of our poets; his style and his rhythms lay the strongest stress of all our literature on the naked thew and sinew of the English language'. Such a description looks innocent enough, but it implies the great realisation that poetry must start from the nature of a language – must flow with a language's inflexions and quantities, must, in a word, be *natural*. Such was the secret of Greek poetry, and of Anglo-Saxon poetry; and it is the virtue of most of our poets that they instinctively reject Italianate rhythms, and other foreign impositions, and fall into this natural rhythm, which Hopkins called sprung rhythm.

Source: *English Critical Essays, Twentieth Century* (Oxford, 1933).

NOTE

1. 1st and 2nd editions. [Editor's Note]

T. S. Eliot

A NOTE ON HOPKINS (1934)

At this point, having called attention to the difficulties experienced by Mr. Pound and Mr. Yeats through no fault of their own, you may be expecting that I shall produce Gerard Hopkins, with an air of triumph, as the orthodox and traditional poet. I wish indeed that I could; but I cannot altogether share the enthusiasm which many critics feel for this poet, or put him on a level with those whom I have just mentioned. In the first place, the fact that he was a Jesuit priest, and the author of some very beautiful devotional verse, is only partially relevant. To be converted, in any case, while it is sufficient for entertaining the hope of individual salvation, is not going to do for a man, as a writer, what his ancestry and his country for some generations have failed to do. Hopkins is a fine poet, to be sure; but he is not nearly so much a poet of our time as the accidents of his publication and the inventions of his metric have led us to suppose. His innovations certainly were good, but like the mind of their author, they operate only within a narrow range, and are easily imitated though not adaptable for many purposes; furthermore, they sometimes strike me as lacking inevitability – that is to say, they sometimes come near to being purely *verbal*, in that a whole poem will give us *more* of the same thing, an accumulation, rather than a real development of thought or feeling.

I may be wrong about Hopkins's metric and vocabulary. But I am sure that in the matter of devotional poetry a good deal more is at issue than just the purity and strength of the author's devotional passion. To be a 'devotional poet' is a limitation: a saint limits himself by writing poetry, and a poet who confines himself to even this subject matter is limiting himself too. Hopkins is not a religious poet in the more important sense in which I have elsewhere maintained Baudelaire to be a religious poet; or in the sense in which I find Villon to be a religious poet; or in the sense in which I consider Mr. Joyce's work to be penetrated with Christian feeling. I do not wish to depreciate him, but to affirm limitations and distinctions. He should be compared, not with our contemporaries whose situation is different from his, but with the minor poet nearest contemporary to him, and most like him: George Meredith. The comparison is altogether to Hopkins's advantage. They are both English nature poets, they have similar technical tricks, and Hopkins is much the more agile. And where Meredith, beyond a few acute and pertly expressed observations of human nature, has only a rather cheap and shallow 'philosophy of life' to offer, Hopkins has the dignity of the Church behind him, and is consequently in closer contact with reality. But from the struggle of our time to concentrate, not to dissipate; to renew our association with traditional wisdom; to re-establish a vital connexion between the individual and the race; the struggle, in a word, against Liberalism: from all this Hopkins is a little apart, and in this Hopkins has very little aid to offer us.

SOURCE: *After Strange Gods* (London, 1934).

Humphry House

A NOTE ON HOPKINS'S RELIGIOUS LIFE (1935)

The Society of Jesus is an active and not a contemplative order; its members are missionaries and teachers; its discipline is military rather than monastic. The *Spiritual Exercises* were intended by St. Ignatius primarily as a means of testing the vocation of novices, or deepening the sense of their vocation in Jesuits of longer standing. The book was to be used normally in retreat. The late Fr. Joseph Rickaby, one of Hopkins's early friends in the Society, wrote: 'The end of the Spiritual Exercises is such amount and quality of self-denial as shall bring you to do the work given you by obedience or by Providence, wholly, steadily, intelligently, courageously, cheerfully. We make retreats either to find out our vocation or to enable us better to do the work of our vocation.'[1]

Hopkins worked through the exercises annually for his twenty-one years in the Society, and began to write a commentary on them. The Directory to the Exercises makes it clear that the chief aim of a Jesuit's continued use of them is that he may be equipped to give retreats to laymen; but this Hopkins rarely, if ever, did. His special application to the Exercises was more probably for his own purposes and seems to indicate an ever-tender anxiety about his vocation; and in particular it is likely that according to the suggestion of the Directory (ch. x., § 13) he meant to govern much of his life by the Ignatian methods of election, and that all his major decisions – whether to continue writing poetry, whether to make attempts to publish it, whether to learn Welsh etc. – were deliberately made by them.

'The exercises', it has been said, 'are not a manual of perfection, but a manual of election.' They are a discipline designed for the practical guidance of missionaries and teachers. They are in no sense a school of mysticism. Hopkins was not a mystic; he was not in the narrower sense a contemplative. His vocation in the Society was a practical one, and he knew this when he joined it. The difficulty for him and for his superiors was to find the specific work he was to do. The continual changes in his appointments – Roehampton, London, Oxford, Liverpool, Stonyhurst and finally Dublin – show this uncertainty only too well. One of his contemporaries in Dublin said of him: 'Never was a squarer man in a rounder hole.' A similar lack of success is found in the many articles, essays and books which he planned to publish, but never apparently finished. He did not know what his vocational work was to be. The letters show how commonly and how bitterly he felt disappointment and failure. His practical life was lived in an almost perpetual state of crisis. Yet in spite of all this he had a persistent and passionate devotion to the Society. To regret his membership of it is as useless as to regret the early death of Keats. 'There is death in that hand.'

He was not by training likely to become a mystic: nor by nature. There is nothing in the poems to show that he felt that immediate and personal *presence* of God, a consciousness of which is common to the mystics and those who can achieve the more advanced states of contemplative prayer. There is nothing of that disturbing intimacy in the love of God which is the mark of St. Theresa or St. John of the Cross. His awareness of God is meditated in happiness by man or nature or the details of Catholic dogma; in unhappiness by the feeling of alienation, which can be overcome only by activity of his own: 'I feel thy finger and find thee.' Nothing in the letters is more moving than his confession to Bridges about 'The Wreck of the *Deutschland*': 'I may add for your greater interest and edification that what refers to myself in the poem is all strictly and literally true and did all occur; nothing is added for poetical padding.'

It is God's terror and majesty which is chiefly localised. 'Thou knowest the walls, altar and hour and night.' The physical pain of that moment is chiefly remembered. There is no familiar acceptance of God's presence: 'His mystery must be instressed,

stressed. . . .' Faith is sustained by an effort of intellect and will. In all this his experience, intense though it was, is the common experience of Christians; its central points are the conflict between the fear of God and the love of God, and the attempt to interpret an inscrutable will.

It is surprising that many Catholic critics have drawn an analogy between the 'terrible' sonnets and the 'dark night of the soul' of St. John of the Cross. The dark night is a defined period in a long and specialised life of contemplative prayer. The experience behind these sonnets is more elementary and universal: there is nothing of the hunger which follows on the withdrawal of unique favours. Unique favours have never been granted. Dixon's phrase 'terrible pathos' could never have been applied to the mystics; and indeed the pathos, though not non-Christian, is not specifically Christian. It is nearer in temper, as poem 50 explicitly states, to Jeremiah or to Job. And also it is worse than useless to wish that the experience behind these poems had never been: it is to wish him all undone, relegated to an unremitting rural gaiety.

In one vitally important way his Ignatian devotions intensified an already existing habit. Even as an undergraduate and an Anglican he was in morals over-scrupulous; and this scrupulosity must have been accentuated by the practice of the 'particular examen', the detailed method of self-examination which St. Ignatius designed for his followers. The examen is guarded about with cautions against this very fault; and it is precarious without the evidence of the lost spiritual diary to guess how far and how often under the guidance of these cautions Hopkins was able after minute self-examination to achieve a confidence that he was forgiven. But it is known that he frequently performed long and exacting penances imposed not by his director, but by himself; and many of the poems have across them a shadow of guilt, while others (like the sonnets on Patience and Peace) show the opposing passion for the means to evade it. In this also his experience was of a conflict common to all Christians, certainly directed and heightened by the Jesuit discipline, but neither artificially fostered by it nor absent without it.

These items in his religious experience, the acute sense of sin and resulting conflict between love and fear; the feeling of alienation from a majestic and transcendent God with a correlative deep and sudden tenderness at its removal; the sense of failure to interpret the will of God in practical life with a proportionate anxiety to be able to do so – these items are not all by any means; but they are the most simple, they are those which his discipline brought into greatest prominence, and they were the direct origin of some of his greatest poems.

SOURCE: *New Verse* (April 1935).

NOTE

1. Joseph Rickaby, s.j., *Waters that Go Softly* (London, 1906) ch. VII, p. 75.

Christopher Devlin, S.J.

HOPKINS AND DUNS SCOTUS (1935)

Gerard Hopkins at one period of his life, 1875–9, drew his poetry almost entirely from Nature. In this he appears to have been aided by Scotus, for in 1875 he wrote 'I was flush with a new enthusiasm. Whenever I took in an inscape of the sea or sky, I thought of Scotus. . . .' To anyone who has taken in an inscape and then opened a page of Scotus this remark should come as a shock. For Scotus presents at first nothing but a mass of bristling syllogisms. Nevertheless behind this barrier savagely guarded is the sleeping beauty. That is why Scotus is not served in the ordinary course of scholastic philosophy. Scholastic philosophy must not go beyond what the average man with the unaided use of reason can attain; for a scholastic to appeal to private inspiration would be ludicrous. Actually Scotus knew this and never does appeal beyond reason. But he achieves his effect by hiatuses – as one might draw from all angles any number of lines correct but meaningless till you step back and see a radiant figure shaped not by the lines but by the points where they stop. Knowledge ceases on the threshold that Desire may enter in: he warns you about that at the beginning of his book. Hence as an intelligent everyman's guide to a harmonious solution of all intellectual problems, he is greatly inferior to St. Thomas Aquinas. Yet to a poet so interwoven with the beauty of earth that heaven would seem agony without it, he might well be what he was to Hopkins, in 1879 'he who of all men most sways my spirits to peace', even if it was not peace with victory in theological examinations.

One ought really to approach this dramatically, showing by effect how to Hopkins through the murky air of the mediaeval lecture-room there dawned the revelation. But in the space available all one can do is to indicate some of the points where the minds of Scotus and Hopkins found themselves in unison. A convenient standpoint is the Scotist formal distinction between the Nature in a thing and its Individuality. Each man's nature is the Nature of all the world, elemental, vegetative, sensitive, human. But one man differs utterly from another because by his Individuality he possesses the common nature in an especial degree. The individual degree is the degree in which he lacks the Infinite, it knits together in the one man all his natural activities, animal, rational etc., and gives them direction Godwards. The effect of this metaphysical lack of the Infinite when felt physically by sympathy, seems to be the 'stress' of the opening verses of 'The Wreck of the *Deutschland*' – the 'touch' of God upon the very centre of the being: 'over again I feel Thy finger and find Thee': cf. also poem no. 73. Hence also the idea in sonnets 16 and 35, that only through man can earth go back to its Creator. It is important to note that according to Scotus, Christ as Man possesses His created Nature in the highest possible degree summing up all other degrees. Fittingly therefore the sonnet on individualities, no. 34, ends up with

> Christ – for Christ plays in ten thousand places
> Lovely in limbs, and lovely in eyes not His,
> To the Father through the features of men's faces.

This must lead on to a description however inadequate of the Scotist theory of knowledge. The source and the object of all knowledge in man is the common nature which he possesses: it is that which gives colour, warmth, meaning etc., in response to external excitations of the nervous system. Every distinct act of knowing which takes in the adapted world of habit and practical necessity, has been preceded by a first act wherein sense and intellect are one, a confused intuition of Nature as a living whole, though the effect of the senses is to contract this intuition to a particular 'glimpse', which is called the 'species specialissima'. Ordinarily, no sooner has the glimpse occurred than conation enters in and by abstraction adapts knowledge to suit needs. But if the first act is dwelt on (by 'instress'?) to the exclusion of succeeding abstractions, then you can feel, see, hear or somehow experience the Nature which is yours and all creation's as 'pattern, air, melody, – what I call *inscape*'. And if you can hold that, then you have a poem 'in petto' to which with the abstractive intelligence you must return in order to express it. That seems to be why Hopkins's images so tumble over each other intertwining so as to keep pace with and capture a single 'species' which has broken from his consciousness – 'How a lush-kept plush-capped sloe Will, mouthed to flesh-burst, Gush! . . . Brim, in a flash, full!' The vividness of the 'glimpse' depends upon its nearness to the individual degree; and its fertility depends upon the kindred 'species' which it arouses to be re-experienced in the memory. The more perfect the harmony between sensation and memory the more fully will one glimpse Nature. Hopkins could justify himself when he 'knew the beauty of our Lord by a bluebell', and in the flight of a windhover, because in Christ is the fulness of Nature.

Scotus's theory of knowledge has been adapted for mystical and for ascetic purposes. The mystical adaptation must be passed over in silence except to opine that it does not support the late Abbé Brémond's thesis in *Prayer and Poetry* though he quotes it as doing so. But the ascetic adaptation is one which seems to have had a very marked influence on Hopkins's poetry. Holding, as sonnet 52 shows him to have done, an inspirational view of poetry, he seems to have connected Scotus's 'first act' with that artistic inspiration which under differing names will be familiar to all who know the aesthetic theories of various 19th and early 20th century psychologists. A useful résumé of them is given by Professor Stewart[1] in the second part of his book on Plato's Ideas where he is trying to explain the ἐξαίφνης κατόψεταί τι τὸ καλόν in current terminology. Now according to Scotus, this act being a spontaneous expression of Nature, is good but neither right nor wrong. To make it 'right' the individual will must step in and direct it to God by an act of love. Only thus can natural beauty be transformed into supernatural – 'God's better beauty, Grace'. This is the whole point of the poem (67) 'How all's to one thing wrought': he praises the inspiration as a masterpiece of Nature, but mourns that it may have no more immortal value than 'sweet the golden glue that's builded by the bee'. And frequently one notes the same distrust of natural inspiration – perhaps because it really is as Bergson says akin to the hypnotic trance. In his unfinished poems, e.g. 'Moonrise', 'Ashboughs', 'The Woodlark', he abandons himself to it swaying in unison with nature. But in finished poems such as 'The Leaden Echo and the Golden Echo', 'Spelt from Sibyl's Leaves', 'The Windhover', there is a deliberate intervention of the will-guided intelligence to give 'beauty back to God – beauty's self and beauty's giver'. And a terror lest natural beauty fade unharvested is the dominant note of all his poems on people. With such startling clearness did he realise that only through man's mind is Nature made transitorily beautiful – 'quench this clearest-selved spark' and '*both* are in an unfathomable dark drowned' – yet only in Christ by man's free will can both be made beautiful for ever.

How God the Son 'personifies' nature, is in the world yet not of it, Scotus strives to explain. Passages about Matter and the source of Light suggest that in such lines as 'lovely-asunder starlight wafting Him out of it' Hopkins was aiming at truth rather than fancy; and passages in the book on the Blessed Sacrament make the 'Hurrahing in Harvest' sonnet much less and much more than 'affectation in metaphor'.

But they meet, philosopher and poet, rather as fellow-pilgrims than as master and disciple. Both were trying in their different languages to express the vision of St. Francis of Assisi. Perhaps they failed. It is difficult to say because at the end of both their lives failure in expression fulfilling the philosopher's tenet, became achievement in the will.

SOURCE: *New Verse* (April 1935).

NOTE

1. J. A. Stewart, *Plato's Doctrine of Ideas* (Oxford, 1909). The Greek may be rendered 'a sudden apprehension of the beautiful'. [Editor's Note]

Bernard Kelly

'THE WRECK OF THE
DEUTSCHLAND' (1935)

It is useless to read 'The Wreck of the *Deutschland*' with a mind unprepared for the profound power of its spiritual movement. Meditate first for a fortnight on the Passion of our Lord. The exercise will not guarantee an understanding of the poem, but will put you in touch with it. The meaning, the movement, the poetic depth (always in Hopkins the same thing with the spiritual depth of mind searched, probed, made lucid by the august theology of the Church) of this, the longest and most powerful of his poems, is Christianity integral and absolute, Christianity splendid and entire in its accepted sacrifice. Its place is beside and among the liturgies of Holy Week that culminate in the Host's return to the altars made bare for His Passion.

I propose to treat separately as two movements of the poem what are in fact two sides or aspects of the same movement, a movement which is the substance, the form, the force, the maker of life in the poem itself. This I propose to do on account of the difficulty of the speculative thought which, though it deepens and quickens the significance of the poem, is far from explicit in the text, whereas the main act is explicit as far as will suffice for an adequate poetic understanding of it. By the *act* I do not mean the mere physical fact of shipwreck, but a more profound spiritual act to which the shipwreck is material or fuel only, and of which the poem is utterance.

A first part of ten stanzas is prefixed not as a prologue in the sense of a thing apart introducing the theme but not entering into the turmoil; it is a flying start, a beginning of the movement itself in its full force, which overtakes the shipwreck, the so-called merely narrative part, carrying that forward with its own velocity.

> Thou mastering me
> God! giver of breath and bread;
> World's strand, sway of the sea;
> Lord of living and dead;
> Thou hast bound bones and veins in me, fastened me flesh,
> And after it almost unmade, what with dread,
> Thy doing: and dost thou touch me afresh?
> Over again I feel thy finger and find thee.

> I did say yes
> O at lightning and lashed rod;
> Thou heardest me truer than tongue confess
> Thy terror, O Christ, O God;
> Thou knowest the walls, altar and hour and night:
> The swoon of a heart that the sweep and the hurl of Thee trod
> Hard down with a horror of height;
> And the midriff astrain with leaning of, laced with fire of stress.

> The frown of his face
> Before me, the hurtle of hell
> Behind, where, where was a, where was a place?
> I whirled out wings that spell
> And fled with a fling of the heart to the heart of the Host.
> My heart, but you were dovewinged, I can tell,
> Carrier-witted, I am bold to boast,
> To flash from the flame to the flame then, tower from the grace to the grace.

Powerfully, in the fulness of his mastery of an itself masterful rhythm, Hopkins uncovers the depths like the bed of the sea in which the poem is to move; the swell of a North Sea storm. And 'sprung rhythm' is the rhythm of a deep-sea swell. Stanzas 2 and 3 overshadow in the mind of the poet what is to be enacted later on deck, when

> . . . the inboard seas run swirling and hawling;
> The rash smart sloggering brine

    Blinds her; but she that weather sees one thing, one;
Has one fetch in her: she rears herself to divine
    Ears, and the call of the tall nun
To the men in the tops and the tackle rode over the storm's
    brawling.

They overshadow, too, in a way marvellously complete, the later spiritual life of the poet himself, a life of stress and terror and the rare joy of consolation, that we understand clumsily, but the saints know perfectly, and with great gladness.

Into the threatened storm, storm of the spiritual life that now takes up the action of the hurricane and the storm at sea, travel five Franciscan nuns to their drowning, exiles by the Falk laws, aboard the *Deutschland*.

[Having quoted copiously from stanzas 13, 14, 15 and 17, the writer continues]: What mastery, what superb rhythm! The wreckage, the helplessness, the hurl and the romp of a murderous sea; they are here. . . . Never was there such a poet. And the pity of it, and the piercing of that pity in the heroic figure of the tall nun, touch the heart of the poet, and he calls aloud to his own heart.

    Ah, touched in your bower of bone,
    Are you! turned for an exquisite smart,
  Have you! make words break from me here all alone,
    Do you! – mother of being in me, heart.
O unteachable after evil, but uttering truth,
  Why, tears! is it? tears; such a melting, a madrigal start!
    Never-eldering revel and river of youth,
What can it be, this glee? the good you have there of your own?

Here and throughout the poem, in the first three stanzas quoted and in the end, the poet is the celebrant. It is he who offers through the vehicle of his hands, of his mind, a sacrifice of which the victim, other than he, is he also by participation. Hopkins is the priest of poetry; he is also the poet of the priesthood. The sufferings of shipwreck, terrible in words, profound in the feeling of the poem, are an offering, an oblation, and an oblation received.

. . . but thou art above, thou Orion of light;
Thy unchancelling poising palms were weighing the worth,
    Thou martyr-master: in thy sight
Storm flakes were scroll-leaved flowers, lily showers – sweet
heaven was astrew in them.

If the shipwreck had been merely narrative, the poem merely
pictorial in its narration, then these lines have turned it inside
out like an old coat lined with incredible jewels. Suffering, the
cruellest torment, becomes sacrifice, becomes in that act of
oblation sweet heaven astrew in flowers.

And the tall nun:

She to the black-about air, to the breaker, the thickly
Falling flakes, to the throng that catches and quails
    Was calling 'O Christ, Christ, come quickly':
The cross to her she calls Christ to her, christens her wild-worst
Best.

      The majesty! what did she mean?
    Breathe, arch and original Breath.
  Is it love in her of the being as her lover had been?
    Breathe, body of lovely Death.
They were else-minded then, altogether, the men
Woke thee with a *We are perishing* in the weather of
    Gennesareth.
    Or is it that she cried for the crown then,
The keener to come at the comfort for feeling the combating
keen?

No. Comfort was not her meaning. It is weariness, it is time's
tasking, not danger, electrical horror, that calls for comfort,
asks for ease. Nor was it the force of her distress that made the
haven of it more brightly appealing. These meanings, that a
mind less pitilessly direct would have rested in, the poet sweeps
aside. They are the half-way houses, the less perfect. Relentlessly
he strips them off from the naked, the stark perfection of the act
which follows; and his mind staggers and cries at the coming of
it.

[Stanzas 28, 29 and 30 are quoted.] I do not pretend to

analyse and expound the meaning of each word. I feel that I
understand, but Hopkins only could explain, if he would,
exactly what he meant by the third line of the 29th stanza.
(Read the unshapeable shock night.) The first thing, admirable
always, terrifying in him, is his directness. All that would have
softened the poem to timid ears he gloriously refuses. If we are
to have our joy, we who dare to wear the insignia of Christ, we
are to have it in the majesty of its conquest, in the shattering
beauty of the crucified Incarnate God. Comfort he flings aside.
We are dazed, dazzled, wonderfully elated in the high heart of
the tall nun.

He was to cure the extremity where He had cast her. For
Christ was that extremity. He in the storm met joy for His joy
of the harvest. Reason, breathless, lagging, big with stupendous
truths, is consumed in vision. Pain has become sacrifice, has
become joy. Christ the priest; Christ the victim; Christ the joy
of the accepted sacrifice. Everywhere one face only. Behind,
exact, a glacial pregnant monument, the mystery of the
Immaculate Conception, dominates the last four lines of the
30th stanza.

> (Feast of the one woman without stain.
> For so conceived, so to conceive thee is done;
>   But here was heart-throe, birth of a brain,
> Word, that heard and kept thee and uttered thee outright.)

Read the lovely poem, 'The Blessed Virgin compared to the
Air we breathe', and come back for the significance of these
lines. In this climax, the 'problem of human suffering' receives
its only tolerable solution. And when St. Francis said to his
spiritual child, 'Friar Leo, little lamb of God . . .', what else did
he mean by 'lamb'?

[Stanzas 32 and 25 are quoted, and the author concludes this
section by remarking 'All the music that poetry demands rests
in this prodigious last chord, prodigiously appeased.']

What I propose to deal with as a second movement of the
poem is an intellectual probing, that everywhere searches out
the first movement, and is itself sometimes so vitally the form
of that movement that the distinction I have made will often

seem a violent one. I made it in order to separate what is very
difficult indeed from what is intellectually less difficult, in such
a way that the poem in both its aspects could be considered
entire. To this second enquiry must be prefaced the fact of
Hopkins's discipleship of Duns Scotus. . . . Even the type of
adjective he so loved, *rash-fresh*, has a peculiar importance to
the admiration of Scotus that was so constant in his mind. Of
his first enthusiasm he wrote: 'It may come to nothing, or it may
be a gift from God. But just then when I took in any inscape of
the sky or sea I thought of Scotus.' It did not come to nothing.
He wrote in his diary later, 'I do not think I have ever seen anything more beautiful than the blue-bell I have been looking at.
I know the beauty of Our Lord by it. Its inscape is mixed of
strength and grace like an ash-tree.' A further significant
(?diary) extract from Father Lahey's book 'God's utterance of
Himself in Himself is God the Word, outside Himself is this
world. Therefore its end, its purpose, its purport, its meaning, is
God, and its life and work to name and praise Him', links in a
surprising way with the note on the Purcell sonnet 'Sake is a
word I find it convenient to use . . . I mean by it the being a
thing has out of itself, as a voice by its echo, a face by its reflection, a body by its shadow, a man by his name, fame or memory,
and also that in the thing by virtue of which it has this being
abroad, and that is something distinctive, marked, . . . as for
voice and echo clearness.' . . . *Inscape*, too, lovely delicate indefinable word, denotes with him a character of distinctiveness, and a man's mind is much revealed in his favourite words,
especially if he invents them himself.

The Scotist *v.* Thomist debate engaged on one of its battle-
fronts upon the perfections of created things, and how these are
verified in God. . . . On both sides subtlety . . . but on the side of
Scotus, rash-freshness, an excitement in dialectic ingenuity, a
passion for close intellectual, almost physical, encounter. The
value of this attitude of mind may be guessed from later
Scotism, but must be sought originally in Duns Scotus himself;
the effect of it on Hopkins's thought is evident and profound.

[Stanzas 5, 6, 7 and 8 are quoted.] There is a passionate
mysteriousness of thought here of which the poet has taken care

to give his warnings; but it is important thought, for in it the intimacy of Christ's appealing in the beauty of this world is vitally apprehended by the mind in the white-hot clarity of its creative excitement. And this clarity, subjectively speaking, is one which the purely metaphysical world will not easily understand; one too which many modern theorists of poetry tend to stultify.

The apprehension of beauty (I mean of the tangible beauty of the world) means in the mind of the beholder a simultaneous delight of the intelligence and the senses. Not two delights at once, but one, a delight in which the senses and the mind are integral in one act. This is the delight towards which Hopkins's poetry moves, and in the pursuit of it he does not refine away to nothing the sensible and emotional qualities of beauty. Rather he renders them more fecund, more vitally themselves, than any poetry can which rests in emotion and the senses alone. He tends to a fusion of all that words can utter; of their intelligibility, of their sound, of the power they have on emotion, of the meaning they have to desire. And this fusion is living and intimate, a fusion made in the pain of poetic creation, lit by the clarity of a rare mind. But more than this. He is not content to rest delightfully in the object of poetic experience. The whole force of his mind and of his nature drives him further. As in the conclusion of the sonnet 'Ashboughs' he says

> . . . it is the old earth's groping towards the steep
> Heaven whom she childs us by

opening, as it were, a window in created beauty to look through on the Uncreated, so again and sometimes by the neat structure of the verse, as in 'Pied Beauty', but often by the direct drive and grappling of the mind into the very object of his poetic experience, he seeks from the heart of things that secret word of praise which is their link with their Creator.

'The beautiful is a delight, an experience of a complete good, *that which pleases the mind.* It has the nature of an end in itself . . .' says Fr. Thomas Gilby, O.P., in *Poetic Experience.*[1] . . . But created beauty is not the end of man. It is a peace, a delight, a rest, a momentary fruition. '*Selves,* goes itself, *myself* it speaks and spells.' The beautiful delivers itself immediately and wholly; as beautiful it does not deliver more. It gives peace, but not a final peace. It has the flavour of the earthly paradise in the very integration of powers it achieves, but the flavour is poignant and a reminder of loss, for our experience of beauty is in the natural order, while the integrity of the earthly paradise was rooted in the supernatural. Our beauty is no less beauty but our faith is veiled. Nothing less than the Beatific Vision in which all things will be visible in the splendour of God, their Creator, will satisfy us for the loss of that vision which was man's in the beginning – *fides occulata*, a faith with eyes.

But the appealing of natural beauty is not for nothing. It is to bring man 'To hero of Calvary, to Christ's feet'. How can this be if the beautiful 'has the nature of an end in itself'? Hopkins has already said, 'This world is then word, expression, news of God.' *News* says more than to indicate the formal proof of metaphysics, for to them the world is only evidence. It says, in fact, that the being and substance of the world is God's meaning, God's external utterance, God's information. And the world is not an *Encyclopedia Britannica*, nor yet a *Daily Mail*. It is a telegram, reply paid, addressed to a particular person, man.

> I kiss my hand
> To the stars, lovely-asunder

Upon the lines quoted here these further lines from the sonnet 'Hurrahing in Harvest' are a significant comment.

> I walk, I lift up, I lift up heart, eyes,
> Down all that glory in the heavens to glean our Saviour.

Our Saviour precisely, since through Him only can our senses be lifted to the supernatural; since it is He, the Eternal Lord, whose meaning lies under the beauties of the world.

> These things, these things were here and but the beholder
> Wanting; which two when they once meet,
> The heart rears wings bold and bolder
> And hurls for him, O half hurls earth for him off under his feet.[2]

The poet's meaning, in the four stanzas (5–8) I have quoted above, would seem to be that the Incarnation and Redemption, which have gladdened the destiny of man, have also profoundly affected his relation to the beauty of the world. For if the world is news of God, it is also news from an Incarnate God; not that the truths of the Christian faith are revealed by the world, rather that a message of divine love becomes loaded with divine sacrifice. A character in Claudel's *L'Annonce faite à Marie* calls the skylark 'la petite croix véhémente!' Beauty is signed with the cross, and is an invitation to the cross. And this is not an intellectual or devotional construction put upon the world by the faithful, but is of the very nature of the world and of beauty, for the world is news of God.

> Not first from heaven (and few know this)
> Swings the stroke dealt –

Perhaps even now we had better be content, with the rest of the faithful, to 'waver and miss'. Certainly he does mean that.

The call of Christ in the beauty of the world is a call from the cross, and this is a key to the intellectual vitality of very nearly all the mature poetry of Gerard Hopkins; a vitality not going at a cross purpose to his 'pure poetry', but making that poetry; not crushing the life of the emotions and senses, but giving them the very juice and life and direction of their own nature.

SOURCE: *The Mind and Poetry of Gerard Manley Hopkins, S.J.*
(1935).

NOTES

1. Thomas Gilby, O.P., *Poetic Experience* (n.d.).
2. 'Hurrahing in Harvest'.

Vincent Turner, S.J.

'MANY A POEM THAT BOTH BREEDS AND WAKES' (1944)

The distinction between what a piece of literature is and what it is about is a difficult one. . . . But if subject-matter – that is, what the subject means to the writer in his ordinary intellectual and emotional experience – is relevant to what a poem is and must itself, in one way or another, be responded to, then criticism of Hopkins begins to find itself in an impasse. At any rate, there is a dragon in the way, a hydra difficult to circumvent and impossible to kill.

For what are these poems about and what is the experience they communicate? And what is the poet counting on – what does he presuppose in us if from us is to be elicited a total response similar in quality to his own experience and emotion? And if what he is counting on is not there, and we cannot understand what he is at, or are affected by what he says in a fashion quite different from that in which he is himself affected; if the central line of communication is cut, can we really have the proper aesthetic enjoyment of all those grandeurs and subtleties of form and texture that are modes of expressing we know not what? But surely, one might say, there is no mystery here and no occasion for fuss. What these poems are about is pretty clear: Hopkins may be difficult, but he is never vague; his obscure passages are almost always 'the midnight that is charged with the mysteries of veiled luminaries and budding morrows'. Yet some element of distortion has intruded itself between reader and poet when a critic like Mr. W. J. Turner can write that

Hopkins's poetry, fine as it is, remains, in a sense, minor poetry. His range is very limited. His work has no philosophical or intellectual content; it is purely physical and verbal. He remains always on the sensuous surface of things. Nor is he a profound imaginative poet as Wordsworth is. He never conveys any sense of the mystery in things. Perhaps as a Roman Catholic he was inhibited from conceiving of any since the whole truth had, once for all, been revealed to mankind. Yet Dante in the Paradiso is creative on the grand scale, but I suspect that to Dante his religion was something added to him, on the principle that he who has much shall have more, whereas with Hopkins was it possibly a case of he who has little shall lose even the little that he hath?[1]

What is it that is distorting the view?

If subject-matter counts in literature, and if to respond adequately to a poem you must to some extent know what the poet is talking about, it would seem to follow that in certain circumstances it is impossible to respond adequately to certain poets. This is the dragon. The differences of intellectual and emotional habits of mind between the poet and audience may be so extreme that the audience just does not know what the poet is saying, or (but this is only to put it in another way) marks a theme but spontaneously feels about it quite differently from the way in which the author feels; so that the minimum of common belief and feeling that a poet must inevitably pre-suppose is completely to seek. If a man, for instance, is so habituated that all love between the sexes is nothing but more or less disguised physical appetite, then Donne's love poems, the earlier no less than the later, are surely a closed book to him; and if Donne cannot 'get across' what he has in mind, then there can be no aesthetic delight in his mode of expressing it. Now Gerard Manley Hopkins is a religious poet, and a religious poet of a special kind; but many of his readers are not religious men, or are religious men of quite a different kind. But can a poet whose subject-matter is controlled and informed and inspired by a certain set of religious beliefs communicate what he has in mind to a reader to whom those beliefs are moonshine or (and this is really more important) who not only disbelieves them but is so far estranged from their atmosphere that he does not know what it would feel like to believe them? It is

a question that critics discuss – though perhaps they rarely face
it in its bleakness – and some, like the critic I have been quoting,
implicitly suppose that it is a sham question. On the whole, they
incline to say that in these circumstances communication does
not present much difficulty, granted a good measure of sympathy and 'a willing suspension of disbelief'. For reasons that
have been hinted at, it is not, I think a satisfactory answer; but
in some instances it is at the present moment a plausible one.
It is plausible to argue that an unbeliever, and even (perhaps)
a man who cannot imagine what it would feel like to believe,
could divine what Crashaw was at, or Herbert or Vaughan; at
any rate, these poets would probably not shock him. For their
poetry can be construed (not that it is rightly construed) as
religious poetry in the sense of a distillation of the aspiring
spirit of man; and in a time when Christianity is conceived and
felt as a sort of disincarnate spiritual essence such a construction
will escape a reader's own notice: indeed, it is the spectacles
through which he sees.

But the religion of Hopkins's verse stubbornly and obtrusively
resists such a construction: it cannot be imperceptibly liberal-
ized. It is not a religion of the spirit, but historical and dogmatic
and institutional Christianity. If anything, it is conflict with the
spirit of man:

That night, that year

Of now done darkness I wretch lay wrestling with (my God!)
  my God.

As Mr. Gardner has written, Hopkins 'may almost be said to
struggle with the Holy Ghost as with an incubus: the pangs of
surrender are physical no less than spiritual; his midriff is
astrain, his whole being laced with the terrific "stress" of Pente-
costal fire'. Compared with Hopkins, John Donne, even, is
almost languid.

Inspired as it is by dogmatic beliefs that have entered into the
very texture of his mind and give their 'selfbeing' to his feelings,
there is something, I think, in Hopkins's poetry that is outside
the compass of many a reader's apprehension and sensibility;
and there is much that baffles and shocks and alienates. There

was a great deal that alienated Bridges. This is an honest reaction, with which one has great sympathy; however much he regretted Hopkins's theology, he never pretended that it was not really there. It is possible, too, and not unreasonable, to turn a blind eye to the disconcerting in a poet whom otherwise one admires and loves, and in the beginning it was easily possible. Many poems are masterpieces of nature-poetry in which theology is 'unobtrusive', and to a lover of great verse the impact of Hopkins is terrific: the fierce strength and packed beauty and the stress of him take a reader captive, and in the 'twenties his novelties of rhythm and diction and form were overwhelming. He seemed, indeed, to be a very modern poet. But this phase now belongs to yesterday. Today much criticism of him appears to be coloured by one or other answer to the 'problem' of Hopkins the poet and Hopkins the devoted Jesuit priest. How has this come about?

His verse, even in its darkest passages, is not obscure from fumbling or faltering. It is, moreover, successful artistic work, a substantival thing with its own being, to the experience and comprehension of which information about its author is, strictly speaking, either a luxury or an irrelevance. None the less, there is a sense in which it belongs to a culture remote from our contemporary world; it may call, therefore, for a measure of explanation. It is a habit of the mind, to which sufficient attention is rarely paid, to perceive and experience through its own dominant patterns, to interpret the unfamiliar in terms of the familiar, and this quite subconsciously; we tend to think that a proposition, say, means what we should have meant by it had we uttered it, and we may be pulled up sharp by the discovery, out of a man's biography or letters, that for him it meant something rather different or had a different emotional aura. Even for the literary criticism of Milton it may be necessary to have a *Preface to Paradise Lost*, and for the literary criticism of Hopkins it may be necessary to have his letters and the note-books.

It is not that they throw new light on the subject-matter of his verse; but they force it even more closely on our attention. They revealed a man who was all of a piece: his own unique signature is written over everything that he thought or said or did. And it emerged very clearly that if any man ever gave himself wholeheartedly and without reserves to the life that he had chosen it was Fr. Hopkins. But the life that he had chosen was that of a Roman Catholic priest and Jesuit – and this (be it observed) is a life and not a profession: it was not for him a job for certain working hours of the day, but a life lived with his entire self and all the astonishing endowment of his natural faculties. In all his poetic work, it appeared more and more vividly the more these letters and note-books were read, there was unity of pattern and of inspiration, and the essence of this unity lay in his spiritual and intellectual and emotional life as a Jesuit priest. . . .

. . . Yet there are many who are bothered, and with reason, by what the letters have revealed, an apparent undercurrent of anxiety in Hopkins lest after all his love of and admiration for human beauty be only by a self-deception on his part assumed into his love and praise of God; they are bothered because they do not find the same kind of anxiety about his response to non-human beauty. We must not exaggerate here, but passages of letters come to mind. He wrote to Baillie: 'You know I once wanted to be a painter. But even if I could I wd. not I think, now, for the fact is that the higher and more attractive parts of the art put a strain upon the passions which I shd. think it un-safe to encounter.' But this passage he wrote on February 12, 1868, about seven months before he entered the Jesuit noviciate and hardly eighteen months after he had become a Catholic; at a time, therefore, when in his devotional and ascetical out-look he was still close to Liddon and to Pusey and not at all affected by 'Jesuit spirituality'. The note-books and letters re-mind us of what the deferred publication of his work and his recent fame make us forget, that he was indeed born a hundred years ago and grew up and lived in Victorian England. But more particularly do they remind us that the religious Oxford in which he grew to manhood was amongst other things an atmosphere charged with the spirit of the great Tractarians. Of this spirit one component was a stern, unbending asceticism of a type whose flavour is caught in Pusey's resolution, sanctioned by Keble, 'to drink cold water at dinner as only fit to be where there is not a drop "to cool this flame" '; an asceticism, more-over, whose accompaniment would seem to be an 'either–or' type of spiritual and devotional outlook (there are examples of it throughout Newman), in which the first and quasi-instinctive reaction to 'creatures' is that they are competitors with God in a world where the only realities that count are the transcendent God and the individual soul.

> Be shelléd, eyes, with double dark
>   And find the uncreated light:
> This ruck and reel which you remark
>   Coils, keeps, and teases simple sight.

This is Hopkins in his pre-Jesuit days.

Dispositions formed in a man's university years usually linger for long, and sometimes for ever. But reflection on the philo-sophy and theology that he was taught, on Duns Scotus, on the *Spiritual Exercises* of St. Ignatius, allayed in Hopkins this fear of the senses and released all the glory of his 'nature-poetry'. None the less, in a letter to Bridges in 1879, he wrote: 'I think then no one can admire beauty of the body more than I do, and it is of course a comfort to find beauty in a friend or a friend in beauty. But this kind of beauty is dangerous.' Dangerous? Does the word still betray an 'unresolved tension'? Hopkins firmly believed two things: that any creature is genuinely most loved and admired when it is loved and admired as the 'image' of God and 'for the sake of' God, and that to love something as the 'image' of God and 'for His sake' is genuinely to love *it* for what it is in itself and is not to use it as a means for the release of the love of God. But he knew that though ideally love for a creature (human beauty, say) and love of God are not competi-tive loves, yet self-deception is possible and that in human love, for instance, there *may* be a siren-voice that beguiles a man into such an absorbed predilection and choice of it for its *exclusive* self as is incompatible with God's will as otherwise known. Hence, as he says, such love is 'dangerous'. This is plain sense. Perhaps, indeed, Victorian as he was, he was timid – but who shall judge? And in any case this is a matter not of principle but of emphasis.[2] On the positive side, we may transpose here what

Hopkins wrote in his Comments on the *Spiritual Exercises* concerning grace: so far as grace 'is looked at *in esse quieto* it is Christ in his member on the one side, his member in Christ on the other. It is as if a man said: That is Christ playing at me and me playing at Christ, only that it is no play but truth; That is Christ *being me* and me being Christ.'

> I say more: the just man justices;
>   Keeps grace: that keeps all his goings graces:
> Acts in God's eye what in God's eye he is –
>   Christ – for Christ plays in ten thousand places,
> Lovely in limbs, and lovely in eyes not his
>   To the Father through the features of men's faces.

So far as his sensibility is concerned, then, Hopkins's experience as a Jesuit both released his poetic endowment and kindled it to fresh fire. As for his intelligence, his professional studies opened to him rare pastures to feed in and a whole universe of discourse to bite on, and leisure to bite on it. But who runs may read, and if any be tempted to think of a mind in chains or dulled by repression let them reflect on his account of personality in the Comments on the Spiritual Exercises,[3] a superb specimen of analysis. Nor were his interests narrowed or confined. His output of literary criticism is considerable, and towards the end of his life there is his growing interest in music ('I am at work on a great choral fugue! I can hardly believe it' – in December, 1887),[4] and his strange but exhilarating excursions into Egyptology. Even the frightful routine of teaching in Dublin was no bar to his ranging wide into Greek metric or the structure of Greek choral odes.

No doubt, of course, it may be thought that the 'hard discipline' of the Society of Jesus will inevitably crush or mangle the flowering of a genius so rare and intense and individual and sensitive as his; it may even be thought that no religious order or closely organized celibate body of men is a proper *milieu* for the development of anyone so extraordinarily endowed by nature. But behind this thought there lurks, I think, the belief that genius is inevitably a sensitive plant that cannot flourish except in very specially prepared soil, and even that a poet ought to be so sheltered that he is free simply to write. Remy de Gourmont praised Flaubert as the very examplar of the creative writer because he devoted his entire self to his craft and refused to be distracted by the mere business of living. But so far was Gerard Hopkins from believing this that he thought that other things were more important than poetry – and so he became a Jesuit. And it never crossed his mind to doubt this even when, on the missions, he sighed for leisure to write.

But in fact the answer to all these wonderings is surprisingly simple. One might think, for instance, in consequence of them, that in his Jesuit *milieu* Hopkins must have felt terribly alone and apart and unhappy, though of course one might well go on to add that a man such as he would have felt like this anywhere. Did he not, after all, pour out his soul in letters? (But can we imagine him flourishing in the household of his dear Bridges?) Yet in truth during the years when he was most closely subjected to Jesuit discipline, up to his ordination and a little beyond, there is no indication anywhere that that was what he felt. His was indeed, as all the evidence goes to show, a very robust soul, and one too keenly interested in other people and things ever to shiver in an isolation of the common sort. His letters during all this period are wide-eyed and breezy, and these years are his most prolific years as a poet. To this time belongs his 'nature-poetry', poems like 'Pied Beauty', 'The Starlight Night', 'God's Grandeur', 'The Caged Skylark', 'The Windhover', in which his eyes are no longer 'shelléd' but open to praise and reverence God in the vividly observed particularities of creation. There is no unresolved tension here; yet its very absence appears to mislead many of his critics. Where Hopkins in one single vision sees 'the own scape' of natural beauties proclaiming the glory of God and sings of it (therefore) for what it is in itself, they miss this centralizing insight of his and think that these poems bear witness merely to the poet's amazing sensuous awareness – an awareness externally related to the praise of God by a species of dutiful afterthought. It is odd to watch the burden of a Jesuit's poetry being misheard through the puritanism of his readers.

But this season of 'rustling calm and tendrilous poetic apprehension' was not to last. Behind the great last sonnets (four of which 'came like inspirations unbidden and against my will') lay months and years of terrible suffering and torment. The sonnets are lucid – terrifyingly so; but besides this Hopkins has on not a few occasions revealed both the depth and the nature of this appalling suffering in letters. But a strange reluctance to accept his own account of himself has kicked up a dust and called it an undisclosed tragedy, and once again an irritated pity at the crucifixion of a genius (a pity that Hopkins himself would have despised) has intruded itself between a poet and his audience.

To what Hopkins himself has said of these years there is really little to add. None the less, it has not been sufficiently remarked, I think, that it is precisely the very quality that is the essence of his genius which is perhaps the main contributory factor to the agony of his last years. Take a passage from his Journal, of July 20, 1868.

Walked down to the Rhone glacier. It has three stages – first a smoothly moulded bed in a pan or theatre of thorny peaks, swells of ice rising through the snow-sheet and the snow itself tossing and fretting into the sides of the rock walls in spray-like points: this is the first stage of the glaciers generally; it is like bright-plucked water swaying in a pail; second, after a slope nearly covered with landslips of moraine, was a ruck of horned waves steep and narrow in the gut: now in the upper Grindelwald glacier between the bed or highest stage was a descending limb which was like the rude and knotty bossings of a strombus shell; third the foot, a broad limb opening out and reaching the plain, shaped like the fan-fin of a dolphin or a great bivalve shell turned on its face, the flutings in either case being suggested by the crevasses and the ribs by the risings between them, these being swerved and inscaped strictly to the motion of the mass. Or you may compare the three stages to the heel, instep, and ball or toes of a foot. The second stage looked at from nearer appeared like a box of plaster of Paris or starch or tooth-powder, a little moist, tilted up and then struck and jarred so that the powder broke and tumbled in shapes and rifts.

I have quoted this early passage in full (it could be abundantly paralleled), because it exemplifies a character of Hopkins's observation so radical that it is also a character of his personality. You have a description that is unstrained indeed but is in its every phrase endeavouring to grasp and state the 'thisness' of a particular scene (Hopkins knew what *ecceitas* was before he read Duns Scotus); unstrained, it is 'stressed' and 'strung', and comes of an intense concentration of awareness. Compare with it a passage written some twelve years later: 'Nothing else in nature comes near this unspeakable stress of pitch, distinctiveness, and selving, this selfbeing of my own.' You have here a mind that can take no refuge in the general, but is taut all the time to the fresh, unstaled experience of what things are in the impact of their individual self-hoods. Nothing is thought or felt at second-hand; and he no more grows into conventions that shield the mind any more than into visual commonplaces that film the senses. This is the mainspring of his poetic genius (as also of much of his criticism); it is the reason, too, why his verse is so tightly packed with strength upon strength that the reader is inclined to cry 'Mercy' and to ask for breathing-space in a relaxed line. It is the reason why 'he is too greedy as poet and prosodist, and too anxious to "load every rift with ore" '. It is the source of his originality as also of his singularity and eccentricity both as poet and as man.

But not only did this fierce intensity of concentration make him an eccentric, in spite of himself; it strung him to a tense, relentless, minute-to-minute effort to strive after the best that he could see. 'This is that chastity of mind which seems to lie at the very heart and be the parent of all other good, the seeing at once what is best, the holding to that, and the not allowing anything else whatever to be even heard pleading to the contrary.' But an intensity like this can lead to an anguish that we should call unendurable did we not know that it can in fact be somehow endured. It did. He felt himself to be Time's eunuch, and even to be patient was still further to torment himself.

> Soul, self; come, poor Jackself, I do advise
>   You, jaded, let be; call off thoughts awhile
> Elsewhere; leave comfort root-room; let joy size
>   At god knows when to God knows what; whose smile
> 'S not wrung, see you; unforeseen times rather – as skies
>   Betweenpie mountains – lights a lovely mile.

But there were aggravating circumstances, all interacting with one another. His health grew steadily worse and deteriorated into a chronic nervous prostration; a rack 'where, selfwrung, selfstrung, sheathe- and shelterless, thoughts against thoughts in groans grind'. As the poems and letters of his early priesthood show, the sight of physical and moral evil and of the contrast between the beauty of nature and grace and the evil that he met in human nature not only caused him unspeakable suffering but also, I think, went some way to shattering his health. In Dublin he felt a stranger and alone, 'at a third remove'. His scrupulousness increased till it got out of hand.

'Out of hand' – but it had always been there. Earlier on I tried to convey something of the flavour of the 'either–or' spirituality of the Tractarians; it is a spirituality that easily engenders a restless scrupulosity in a rich and many-sided nature; for instead of making for a calm inner detachment from the pursuits and interests that his gifts inspire, it is all too liable to goad a man into a sheer severance of them, in the belief that only so can he sincerely serve God 'and Him alone'. Hopkins's ascetical training in the Society of Jesus did something to restore a balance and to take the edge off such a scrupulosity. But much remained. . . .

. . . He seems to have wanted an order of obedience (though even about this he was timid) to publish work of the existence of which his superiors were ignorant and which he thought it self-willed to bring to their notice. In other ways, too, as in his agonies over examination papers, he appears, in the fearful prostration of his body, to have reverted at the end of his life to the 'either–or' asceticism of his pre-Jesuit days, and the quality of his scrupulousness recalls Hurrell Froude's anxious self-accusations that he may be making the attempt to do something for another a mere excuse for sheer self-assertion and self-satisfaction. But whereas Froude's spirit was one of swift gaiety, Hopkins's was no longer so. On April 24, 1885, he wrote to Baillie:

The melancholy I have all my life been subject to has become of late years not indeed more intense in its fits but rather more distributed, constant, and crippling. One, the lightest but a very inconvenient form of it, is daily anxiety about work to be done, which makes me break off or never finish all that lies outside that work. It is useless to write more on this: when I am at the worst, though my judgement is never affected, my state is much like madness.

> We hear our hearts grate on themselves: it kills
> To bruise them dearer.

It is a horrifying story. But Hopkins would have said that this story is merely the outside record of events through which Christ, the Master, was touching him with a finger of infinite love, a 'heaven-handling', and that the inside story is one of spiritual dereliction in which the shipwreck is a harvest. The utter desolation of his 'winter world' he regarded as a privilege.[5] But so to welcome suffering does not in the least anaesthetize it: it does not entail that agony of mind ceases to be frantic agony of mind or that one sees the point of it.

> No worst, there is none. Pitched past pitch of grief,
> More pangs will, schooled at forepangs, wilder wring.

In the blackest days of August or September, 1884, Hopkins wrote in a note-book: 'Man was created to praise etc. . . . And the other things on earth – take it that weakness, ill health, every cross is a help. Calix quem Pater meus dedit mihi non bibam illud?'[6] This he believed 'as wholly as a man can believe any-thing'; but in desolation the belief does not lighten the blackness, and the mind still hangs over 'cliffs of fall Frightful, sheer, no-man-fathomed'.

But this is where so many of his readers 'fable and miss', as Hopkins knew they must. We are back where we started from. Even in 1942 critics were still writing of the weakening of Hopkins's 'faith', on the evidence of these Dublin sonnets. This is to miss completely what they are about, as also what much of 'The Wreck of the *Deutschland*' is about. It is natural, if after patient study of the poems and the relevant documents and after the effort of imaginative sympathy a man cannot divine what it feels like to be as Hopkins was, communication does indeed appear to be impossible. It is not that it is essential to share his beliefs, though without them it is perhaps doubtful whether the emotional and even the aesthetic response will be qualitatively quite the same as what they would be if the beliefs were shared; but it is essential, I think, that there should be a certain homogeneity of religious and moral outlook in Hopkins and his readers, for otherwise his work is either incomprehensible or else evocative of a distorted response. What the bounds of this homogeneity are is obscure, but the history of Hopkins criticism shows that simply to prescribe a willing suspension of disbelief is not to settle the question but to shelve it or to fob oneself off with a sham.

'Surely one vocation cannot destroy another', Dixon had said, and Hopkins replied that he feared lest his purpose be frayed by the 'secret solicitations' of the world: he would be passive, for 'if our Lord chooses to avail Himself of what I leave at His disposal He can do so with a felicity and with a success which I could never command'. In principle and in its context (the letter is that of December 1, 1881) this may betray an 'exaggerated scrupulosity'. But the fame that alarmed him found out the poetry that made him anxious, and half a century afterwards broadcast his name and his faith; and the priest who called himself Time's eunuch 'has defeated Time with many a poem that both breeds and wakes'.

SOURCE: 'Gerard Manley Hopkins, 1844–1944', *Dublin Review*, vol. 215 (October 1944).

NOTES

1. W. J. Turner, *The Spectator* (14 July 1944).
2. It is astonishing that, unless my memory tricks me, one of the finest of Hopkins's scholars has, in unpublished MSS. and in conversation, thought it necessary to bring 'homosexuality' into his explanation of Hopkins's mind on this matter. This seems to me to be blunting Occam's razor and to find no support in the evidence.
3. Humphry House, *Notebooks and Papers* (Oxford, 1937) pp. 322–8. Quoted, p. 28 above.
4. I think there is much to be said for Professor Abbott's suggestion that in these years he was turning from poetry to music, and that 'music would have absorbed him had he lived'. Lord David Cecil

has suggested that several passages in his poetry appear to start from an experience shaped not verbally but musically, and it may well be that he had reached a stage (as Mr Eliot perhaps has) when what he had it in him to say could no longer be adequately said in verse.

5. *Poems*, 40, 45, 46. Compare the letter to Bridges of 29 April 1869 (C. C. Abbott, ed., *Letters of G. M. Hopkins to Robert Bridges*, Oxford, 1935, xxiii) and to Dixon of 3 July (?)1886 (C. C. Abbott, ed., *The Correspondence of G. M. Hopkins and R. W. Dixon*, Oxford, 1935, pp. 117–18).

6. House, *Notebooks and Papers*, p. 416. Hopkins is referring to the beginning of the *Spiritual Exercises*.

Humphry House

IN PRAISE OF HOPKINS (1944)

Hardly a poet who began writing between the wars was not directly influenced by Gerard Hopkins. His elaborate metres and highly-wrought control helped restore to English verse both a firmness and a freedom of movement it was in danger of losing. He showed perhaps more clearly than any poet since the seventeenth century that the passion and music of verse can belong with highly conscious and informed intellectual activity. But when we read Hopkins now, it is not his subtlety and quaintness which most come home. It is the very things he sometimes thought himself to lack – 'the roll, the rise, the carol, the creation' of his verse; the terrible pathos of his feeling for man and for the ultimate being of things; the solemn construction of his poems, built with careful thought like a piece of music by Purcell, whom he loved, through the intricacy of numbers, to the greater glory of the God in whose service he lived and died.

SOURCE: *The Listener* (22 June 1944); reprinted in *All in Due Time* (London, 1955) p. 163.

PART THREE

Modern Studies

A PASSIONATE SCIENCE (1953)

The poetry of Gerard Manley Hopkins might be called a 'passionate science'. Like other poets and like painters of his era, this poet delighted in the observation and grasping of nature. With the greatest delicacy, strength, and intelligence he possessed his environment, making it the intimate vehicle for the passionate praises of his belief.

Hopkins is 'strange'; and for a long while his poems, which were first published in 1918, twenty-nine years after his death, had to be excused or grudged or argued about. Yet the strangeness of Hopkins is only concentrated in the excess and force of his qualities; there was nothing peculiar about his turn to a strong naturalism, to a passionate science, at his particular time in the nineteenth century; he was born five years after Cézanne, four years after Thomas Hardy, a year after Henry James. The scientific mind had slowly formed, slowly extroverted itself on to nature, and at an even slower rate the concerns of the artist had moved in the same direction, at least outwardly. The process had already known its phases and varieties. A being and a personality had been ascribed to nature; some artists had been pantheists, some nature-drunkards. Passionate emotions declined to an easy, popular sentiment about nature; poets and painters then corrected themselves by looking carefully at its select details.

In the 1860s, at home and at school in London, at the university in Oxford, Hopkins was familiar with the poems of Tennyson, Browning, Coventry Patmore, with the prose of Ruskin, and with the careful painting of the Pre-Raphaelites. Nature, he could well detect, had become something to employ:

the selected details were presented almost for themselves, or else as ornaments of a moral tale. Tennyson in the sixties was talking about Irish landscape: 'I saw wonderful things there: twenty different showers at once in a great expanse – a vast yellow cloud with a little bit of rainbow stuck on one corner.' William Allingham, who put this on record, says that Tennyson swept his arm round for the cloud and gave a nick in the air with his thumb for the bit of rainbow; and then added, 'I wish I could bring these things in'. Or again, Allingham and Tennyson talked of the kinship between white lilies and white peacocks; Allingham quoted Browning on a passage in Tennyson's *Princess*: 'Tennyson', said Browning, 'has taken to white peacocks. I always intended to use them. The Pope has a number of white peacocks.'

Browning intended to *use* white peacocks; Tennyson has *taken* to them, Tennyson wanted to *bring in* those things which he noticed so delicately. Hopkins, coming after them, more intelligent, more passionate, did not select details, and add them up. He did not make rhetorical gestures towards nature; no wave of an arm for the yellow cloud, no nick of a thumb for the rainbow. A central fact of his poems is their birth in a science of empathy, carried so far that it distinguishes him from other English poets.

The journals he kept from 1868 to 1875 help to an understanding of Hopkins and nature. They are not very long, and occasionally they are difficult to read because Hopkins observes so closely and has to find peculiar language for the peculiar. Although he is personal and though he selects, one notices not so much his immediate passion, as a certain more or less scientific neutrality; this observer is free from most of our common associative poetic preferences.

In 1871 Hopkins put down an observation on the leaves of wood-sorrel, a common enough European and English plant. 'The half-opened wood-sorrel leaves,' he wrote, 'the centre or spring of the leaflets rising foremost and the leaflets dropping back like ears, leaving straight-chipped clefts between them, look like some green lettering.' That is easy for the reader to take. Though wood-sorrel is not a species like rose or columbine or iris or lily in the tradition of aesthetic preference, a poet of the mid- or later nineteenth century may be expected to like an organism so crisp and delicate; and the accuracy of the description is quite obvious, the analogue is not immediately too peculiar. This comparison of the tiny, crisp leaves to green lettering by itself delimits the leaves and gives their colour its correct sharpness.

In 1872, on a Holy Saturday warm with thunder, Hopkins observed 'odd tufts of thin-textured very plump round clouds something like' – and the convincing analogue is less expected – 'something like the eggs in an opened ant-hill'. Clouds, as well, are poetic properties of the century for other English poets, Patmore or Tennyson, or Barnes, or Bridges; yet now the explicative object is more peculiar, the clouds are like ants' eggs in the opened nest, they are different altogether from Tennyson's clouds in water-colour; and the nature of the Hopkins science is more revealed. The more excessive peculiarity begins to demand extra knowledge and attention; although in his poems Hopkins does check too much eccentricity of observation, too much intrusion of peculiar things which are outside the likely experience of readers. The journal was for himself alone.

In 1870, concerned with the beauties and severities of the winter and neutrally alive to things as much in one place as another, Hopkins observed that 'the slate slabs of the urinals even are frosted with graceful sprays'. Or in Lancashire in 1873 he watched a dying sheep under a stone hedge, making of it an entirely matter-of-fact record without sentiment: 'There ran slowly from his nostrils a thick flesh-coloured ooze, scarlet in places, coiling and roping its way down, so thick that it looked like fat.'

Here, with letter-leaves, ant's egg clouds, roping ooze, and frost-sprayed urinals, we are divorced from the averagely fine poetic detection of the nineteenth century. Here – and almost everywhere in Hopkins – we knock our sensibilities against exactitudes and starknesses which may still repel or dismay either those who live aesthetically in older, gentler modes or those who do not require to live outwardly at all. The peculiarity goes further, in one respect. In these notes out of the journal Hopkins uses 'like' – *like* fat, *like* ants' eggs in the opened nest, *like* green lettering. In his greater intensities 'like' disappears: adjectives, compound adjectives, compound nouns, active and embracing and characterizing verbs, take its place; words have been as starkly and freshly scrutinized and possessed as any other relevant part or property of the poet's environment, until the selected words are as close an equivalent as they can be to the things and the actions and the states which they convey. Thus pigeons go 'strutting and *jod-jodding* with their heads'. 'Jod' is a rare verb, yet its revival and adaptation are not frigid or eccentric. One acknowledges quickly, after surprise, that pigeons do behave exactly so.

In the acceptance of his poems, in the critical unravelling of their verbal knots, in the general consideration of Hopkins as a poet of his time who was yet absolutely distinct, this peculiar science of his does not receive enough attention. To know this poet one does not need dictionaries alone, or a fine recognition of ambiguities alone, or only a knowledge of the Ignatian Exercises or of Duns Scotus, 'Of realty the rarest-veined unraveller': one must also have or must also cultivate some equivalence of pure sensation, some of Hopkins's own accurate empathic cognition of the plants, trees, fruit, metals, skies, clouds, sunsets, birds, water, surfaces, grains, activities, perfumes of all the phenomena at which he stared or to which he opened his senses, precisely of

> Landscape plotted and pieced – fold, fallow and plough;
>   And áll trádes, their gear and tackle and trim.

> All things counter, original, spare, strange;
>   Whatever is fickle, freckled (who knows how?)
>   With swift, slow; sweet, sour; adazzle, dim.

A story is told of one of the Jesuit fathers at Stonyhurst pointing out the young Hopkins to the gardener and telling him that Hopkins was a very fine scholar. The gardener replied that he had seen him hanging round and staring at a piece of glass on one of the paths: he had taken him for a 'natural'. But staring at glass among the gravel may involve the meanings, causes and principles of things.[1]

II

Hopkins was received by John Henry Newman into the Roman Catholic Church in 1866, while he was still an undergraduate. Nearly two years later, in 1868, he joined the Society of Jesus, and destroyed much of his poetry. He was then twenty-four. A long preparation now followed for his service and self-dedication as a priest, during which the making of more poems was abandoned as (his own word in later circumstances) a luxury. A total personality, though, cannot be changed, and the run of the journal which Hopkins kept from 1868 to 1875 proves the continuation, development, and enrichment of his particularizing science. In the last days of 1875 he returned to poetry with the grandeur and grimness of his memorial poem to the nuns drowned in the wreck of the *Deutschland*. . . . He was thirty-one; and it is the voice now of the man who has been active, dismayed, and exultant in a spiritual contest. In 1877 Hopkins was moving to the end of his preparation and was coming to a May-like crest in his life. His senses were exultantly and ecstatically open to his environment around the hill-perched St. Beuno's College above the Vale of Clwyd, in his purple and pastoral Wales. For a while he allowed himself the hours required for composition, and poem followed on poem. His world now was 'charged with the grandeur of God', stars sat like fire-folk in the air, weeds were shooting 'long and lovely and lush', pied beauty was fathered-forth by that deity he served, the kestrel stood to the gale with pride and valour and act and fire. Summer ended, but stooks of harvest rose around, 'barbarous in beauty', and the hills of Wales also rose around, 'azurous hung', the 'world-wielding shoulder' of his saviour,

Majestic – as a stallion stalwart, very-violet-sweet! –

all in a poem which he made as 'the outcome of half an hour of extreme enthusiasm', on 1 September of that year. On 23 September Hopkins was ordained priest.

Alternating between gladness and dejection, Hopkins now made poems on and off until he died of enteric fever in 1889, the three richest seasons being this year of his ordination, the year 1879, in which he returned for a while to Oxford, where he wrote 'Duns Scotus's Oxford', 'Binsey Poplars', 'Henry Purcell', and 'Peace'; and the dejected Irish year of 1885, of which the bitter, strong, and wonderful consequences were 'Carrion Comfort', 'No worst, there is none', and probably the sonnet in which he says that he wakes and feels 'the fell of dark, not day', in which he says

> I am gall, I am heartburn. God's most deep decree
> Bitter would have me taste: my taste was me.

Added to the poems, these few details of his life help to answer the debate about the effects of religious discipline on Hopkins as a poet. Did it make him a poet? Did it reduce the range, the strength, the quantity of his art? Unprofitable questions either way. As a strong poet in spite of himself, self-ripened, he wrote for some thirteen years, joining in that time the English company of Herbert and Donne. His nature, one would affirm, ordained his development, his choice of calling, his submission to religious rules. His religious meditation on the meanings, causes, and principles of things then conferred – whatever misgivings he retained, whatever restrictions he imposed – the highest sanction on his pursuit and interests as a poet; and livened them with the greatest glint, fullness, and flush.

III

This will be more apparent if one looks for a moment at the poet in his earliest days, before Newman, and before he began to tread the hard discipline of the Jesuit Order, which would bring him, declared Newman, to heaven. His earliest poems and diaries show two characteristics, the boy 'hanging around words and listening to what they say', and this boy so in love with words reacting with an already individual acuteness and consciousness to everything else around him. In a diary of 1863 – Hopkins was nineteen – both characteristics are clear. For example, he picks up words with gr- and cr- sounds and listens to them discriminately and as kin to each other:

Grind, gride, gird, grit, groat, grate, greet, κρούειν, *crush, crash,* κροτεῖν, *etc.* Original meaning to *strike, rub,* particularly *together.* That which is produced by such means is the *grit,* the *groats* or crumbs, like *fragmentum* from *frangere, bit* from *bite. Crumb, crumble* perhaps akin. To *greet,* to strike the hands together (?). *Greet,* grief, wearing, *tribulation. Grief* possibly connected. *Gruff,* with a sound of two things rubbing together.

Then a page away he catches carefully at the active facts of water coming through a lock, or he particularizes the blue-green of wheat: it suggests silver, is the 'exact complement of carnation', and nearest of any green he knows to emerald, 'the real emerald *stone*'.

The year before, during the Christmas holidays of 1862, Hopkins had completed the poem he called 'A Vision of the Mermaids'. As Robert Bridges remarked, it was Keatsian, but it also involved fashionable interests and extroversions of the time which Hopkins liked. Sunsets – these were an interest which was to last him all his life. Already he tries to grasp their forms and colours:

> Plum-purple was the west; but spikes of light
> Spear'd open lustrous gashes, crimson-white . . .
> And thro' their parting lids there came and went
> Keen glimpses of the inner firmament.

In the fifties able naturalists had discovered and popularized by their books an aesthetic of sea pools and sea margins, of the delicate shapes and the fungal gemmy brilliance of their creatures. Hopkins had stared into the pools, he had examined, so one would think, books by the high (or low) priest of the mania, P. H. Gosse. His brothers followed the pursuit and kept marine aquariums. So Hopkins decorated the Keatsian mermaids of his poem with marine-biological adornments, *Nautilus, Strombus, Glaucus, Eolis* –

                                metal-lustered
       With growths of myriad feelers, crystalline
       To shew the crimson streams that inward shine,[2]
       Which, lightening o'er the body rosy-pale,
       Like shiver'd rubies dance or sheen of sapphire hail –

– and with sea-anemones, which he names 'flesh-flowers of the
rock'.

He tells a story reminding one a little of Keats covering his
tongue and throat with cayenne-pepper (according to Haydon)
so as to appreciate the coldness and glory of claret. One mer-
maid in the *Vision* had been diadem'd with the anemones. 'I
thought it would look strikingly graceful, etc.', Hopkins said
soon afterwards, in a letter in which he referred to the poem,
'to wear sea-anemones round my forehead. . . . So I put a large
one on in the middle, and it fixed itself correctly. Now one has
heard of their stinging, but I had handled them so often un-
harmed, and who could have imagined a creature stinging with
its – base, you call it in sea-anemones? But it did, loudly, and
when the pain had ceased a mark remained, which is now a
large scar.'

'I have particular periods of admiration', he wrote in this
same letter of 1863, 'for particular things in Nature; for a certain time I am astonished at the beauty of a tree, shape, effect,
etc., then when the passion, so to speak, has subsided, it is con-
signed to my treasury of explored beauty, while something new
takes its place in my enthusiasm. The present fury is the ash,
and perhaps barley and two shapes of growth in leaves and one
in tree boughs and also a conformation of fine-weather cloud.'

                                        IV

Such was the exploration Hopkins began as a child and continued, though cautiously, after he had become a Jesuit and
indeed for all his life. One must consider also his exploration of
himself, a self individual, strong, originating, in some sense
sceptical as well as proud. The young Hopkins had intellectual
and sensual pride, yet little blindness, little deafness or dumb-

ness. All must be examined afresh, nature, language, poetry and poetics, and religion. Dustiness must be blown off to reveal the solid. All that is too easily, too lazily accepted must be scrutinized and tested for truth. Accepted Tennyson, then the emperor of poetry, he examined and 'began to doubt', as he confided in 1864 to his friend of the story of the sea-anemones, discovering that Tennyson himself was Tennysonian, that he wrote chiefly in the average or lower poetic language which Hopkins (always liking to mint his own critical concepts and terms) named 'Parnassian'.

Accepted religion he examined, as if that as well were too 'Parnassian'. And accepted self: that also must be cleared and sifted. Rapidly, one may conclude, the young Hopkins came on guard against his own intellectual impatience, his own elastic steeliness, his own sensuality. As a boy at school, seeming slight and gentle, he withstood a headmaster 'whose logic was comprised in the birch'. There was no fight in him, another of the boys recalled, 'unless he was unjustly used or attacked, and in that he was godlike, for it sprang from his love of justice or truth'.

Here there were dangers. More than twenty years later the musician Sir Robert Stewart, who loved him as a priest and a man and attempted to instruct him in music, wrote to his 'darling padre' that he was impatient of correction when he had made up his mind on any point – 'I saw, ere we had conversed ten minutes on our first meeting, that you are one of those special pleaders who never believe yourself wrong in any respect. You always excuse yourself for anything I object to in your writing or music so I think it a pity to disturb you in your happy dreams of perfectibility – nearly everything in your music was wrong – but you will not admit that to be the case.' He could not always forgo the artist's self-certainty. Yet in his long correspondence with Robert Bridges (who destroyed his side of the exchange), love and self-examination had to fight an intellectual impatience with Bridges' shortcomings, which in another man would have become intellectual contempt.

Most of all it was the danger of a sensualism out of hand, the danger of the attractions of 'mortal beauty', even when checked and tasted and observed strictly, and of mortal beauty in part in his personal relationships, that Hopkins finely understood. 'To what serves mortal beauty – dangerous?' If he came to an answer which satisfied him, that lay in the future. When at twenty-four he chose his hard vocation, his discipline for life, one may suspect that he already feared this danger and other dangerous elements in the self that he now denied. They could be dedicated, nevertheless; they could be refined. It might be argued that his choice, as well as his superior intellect and finer nature, saved him from a collapse analogous to the poetic and actual collapse of Swinburne (whom Hopkins detested as a poet); also that his vocation did in fact preserve, test, refine, and concentrate the power which eventually broke out in his exultant and his despondent poems.

v

Nature, 'excluding nature's most interesting productions, the works of man', according to Samuel Butler's remark, and in the usage of the time taken 'to mean mountains, rivers, clouds and undomesticated animals and plants', ringed the mid-Victorian sensibility in all its forms. In a new way elementary details from the sciences of nature did not repel either poets or painters. A poet (Tennyson's brother) might observe in his sonnets how 'passive jellies wait the turn of tide' or explain how a child (she had, of course, been gathering shells) took the homeward path which led

> Beneath yon dark-blue ridge, when, sad to tell,
> On her fair head the gloomy Lias fell.

This concern with nature could be indulgent, adding up simply or luxuriously to nothing, like Humpty Dumpty's recitation:

> In spring when woods are getting green
> I'll try to tell you what I mean –

or like Edward Lear's pie of pale purple amblonguses, to which a small pigeon, two slices of beef, four cauliflowers and any number of oysters were added before it was served up in a clean dish and then thrown out of the window as fast as possible; or else it could be justified, the justification for naturalist-before-Darwin or poet-before-Darwin being in one form or another a simple resort to the Christian god: everything was this god's handiwork. 'Do not study matter for its own sake, but as the countenance of God', Charles Kinglsey advised in the 1840s. 'Study the forms and colours of leaves and flowers, and the growth and habits of plants; not to classify them, but to admire them and to adore God. Study the sky! Study water! Study trees! Study the sounds and scents of nature!'

That might have been a programme entirely congenial to the young Hopkins twenty years later, had it not been for Kingsley's conclusion: that these beautiful things were to be studied 'in order to recombine the elements of beauty', were to be studied next 'as allegories and examples from whence moral reflections may be drawn', and last 'as types of certain tones of feeling'. Natural objects were thus, a little smugly, spiritual utilities. For Hopkins they were, if sources of possible danger, also divine concrete realities; and to such middle-protestant morality Hopkins the Catholic would much have preferred Philip Gosse the Plymouth Brother and fundamentalist, lamely and sincerely ejaculating over his marine animals: 'Yes, O Lord! the lovely tribes that tenant these dark pools are, like the heavens themselves, "the work of thy fingers", and do as truly as those glowing orbs above us "declare thy glory".'

Indeed, it was simply the case for nature as a declaration of his god's glory, an ultimately comprehensive nature centring upon man and the works of man (i.e. including language, poem, poetic structures), that Hopkins elaborated with subtlety and dignity; and it was this elaboration which allowed him to break at last into the exultancy of the poems of 1877. He had, one may believe, discovered what were the limits of self-abnegation, he had learned to recognize the irreducible solid minimum of self which could not be altered, whittled, or kept down. His particularizing science originated in his own being, in that self now so straitly and willingly disciplined; if by that self it was developed intellectually, it was also justifiable by religion and religious philosophy: it was indeed, as he came to see it, a part of his religion, which worked upon it and flushed it with its own increase and extra enthusiasm.

Hopkins was clear on that eventually; he was clear on the world 'charged with the grandeur of God', he was explicit, in season, that the world of nature is a leasehold let out by God, paying God for rent, he says, praise, reverence, service and God's own glory. 'Passionate science' is justified also as a description of his own activity, since Hopkins endeavours to be a reformed kind of poet, endeavours not to project *his* emotions into the objects of his enthusiastic attention, the world not being charged with any grandeur of his, of his own subjective devising. Endeavouring to let each object exist *per se* in his apprehension of it, in the most sheer language entirely and accurately correspondent to the sum of the qualities of the object, he would hardly have agreed with Newman, of an older generation, in setting science against poetry, in declaring that it was the 'aim of science to get a hold of things, to grasp them', while poetry's business was to delight only in the indefinite, having 'the vague, the uncertain, the irregular' among its attributes. Hopkins knew that it was poetry, then more than ever, which needed to hold and to grasp at least with the firmness, if not with all the other characteristics, of science. The school of Wordsworth, which expired, he thought, in Newman as a poet, was not his school, and was to be criticized as one of 'faithful but not rich observers of nature', not concrete observers. Crabbe, always underestimated by adherents of the indefinitude of poetry, was the poet Hopkins praised for 'a strong and modern realistic eye'.

VI

It is in the sermon which he based on the opening of the Spiritual Exercises of St Ignatius, that Hopkins has left the most precise explanation of the way in which creation, according to his belief, gives tongue to the glory of God. . . .

[Grigson cites Hopkins's sermon notes; see p. 29 above.]

But [non-human created things] do not know that they give

him glory, they do not know God, they are brute things thinking only of food or of nothing, giving by themselves, says Hopkins, 'poor praise, faint reverence, slight service', giving no more, a fine phrase, than 'dull glory'.

Yet amidst them all is man, created like the rest to praise, reverence, and serve this one God, to give him glory: but man is different – 'but man can know God, *can mean ic give him glory*. This then was why he was made, to give God glory and to mean to give it.' Hopkins sees glory given not only in prayer but in the common avocations of man:

Smiting an anvil, sawing a beam, driving horses, scouring, everything gives God some glory if being in his grace you do it as your duty. To go to communion worthily gives God great glory, but to take food in thankfulness and temperance gives him glory too. To lift up the hands in prayer gives God glory, but a man with a dungfork in his hand, a woman with a sloppail, give him glory too. He is so great that all things give him glory if you mean they should. So then, my brethren, live.

In other words, man alone of creatures on earth transforms dull glory into lively glory: if a man is a poet (Hopkins remarks in the sermon that poets, their minds and all, flower and fruit as well as tree, are creatures of God), in his poems he can transform the dull glory of the unintentional praise of God-created objects into the bright glory of the intended praise of man:

> And what is Earth's eye, tongue, or heart else, where
> Else, but in dear and dogged man?

For glory, objects and beholder have only to meet, Hopkins declared in that enthusiastic poem conceived as he walked home across the autumnal evening Vale of Clwyd on 1 September 1877:

> Summer ends now; now, barbarous in beauty, the stooks rise
> Around; up above, what wind-walks! what lovely behaviour
> Of silk-sack clouds! has wilder, wilful-wavier
> Meal-drift moulded ever and melted across skies?
>
> I walk, I lift up, I lift up heart, eyes,
> Down all that glory in the heavens to glean our Saviour;

And, éyes, heárt, what looks, what lips yet gave you a
Rapturous love's greeting of realer, of rounder replies?

And the azurous hung hills are his world-wielding shoulder
Majestic – as a stallion stalwart, very-violet-sweet! –
These things, these things were here and but the beholder
Wanting; which two when they once meet,
The heart rears wings bold and bolder
And hurls for him, O half hurls earth for him off under
    his feet.

Hurrahing, praising, glorying, and exclamation – these explain Hopkins as a poet. 'No single sentence', Humphry House
declared in a note to the sermon I have just quoted, 'better
explains the motive and direction of Hopkins' life than *Man was
created to praise*', and he maintained that the sentence should be
remembered always when the critic regrets anything or grieves
for anything in that full life of Hopkins which was more than
poetry – 'To remember it is not to share or advocate the belief;
but it is essential to an intelligent reading of his work.'

VII

Nature and glory in nature must be grasped by reaching to
nature's qualities and selfhoods. The god of Gerard Hopkins is
not inside nature – 'he is under the world's splendour and
wonder' – but one thing he does: through the nature he has
made he passes the voltage of the current of his love, his
grandeur. That current, in the words of one of the comments
of Hopkins on the Ignatian Exercises, is 'the Holy Ghost sent
to us through creatures'. So one penetrates to the full meaning
of his sonnet on 'God's Grandeur':

The world is charged with the grandeur of God.
    It will flame out, like shining from shook foil;
    It gathers to a greatness, like the ooze of oil
Crushed. Why do men then now not reck his rod?
Generations have trod, have trod, have trod;
    And all is seared with trade; bleared, smeared with toil;

And wears man's smudge and shares man's smell: the soil
Is bare now, nor can foot feel, being shod.

And for all this, nature is never spent;
  There lives the dearest freshness deep down things;
And though the last lights off the black West went
  Oh, morning, at the brown brink eastward, springs –
Because the Holy Ghost over the bent
  World broods with warm breast and with ah! bright wings.

And so his parallel statement that all things 'are charged with
love, are charged with God and if we know how to touch them
give off sparks and take fire, yield drops and flow, ring and tell
of him'. This current runs through Hopkins as creature, through
the stooks barbarous in beauty, through skies, clouds, stars; and
he hoped, if he was a true poet, that the great voltage of love
and grandeur would run through the best of his poems in their
hammer-forged equivalence of words, objects, and purpose, in
their close structure, in the roll, the rise, the carol, the creation
of 'The Starlight Night', for example:

Look, look: a May-mess like on orchard boughs!
  Look! March-bloom, like on mealed-with-yellow sallows!
These are indeed the barn; withindoors house
The shocks. This piece-bright paling shuts the spouse
  Christ home. Christ and his mother and all his hallows.

Deeply involved and involving all, is a concept it is necessary
to understand, so far as it can be coldly analysed – that 'inscape'
as he called it, which Hopkins had worked out in his twenties
and which he employed all through his life. Well examined by
Father W. A. M. Peters in his study of Hopkins, it includes
more than pattern and design: inscape includes the distinctiveness of objects, the 'outward reflection of the *inner* nature of a
thing', indeed all the 'set of its individuating characteristics'.
Hopkins used it first, so far as we know, in some notes on
Parmenides, on Being and Not-being, in the 1860s. Spanning
the years, he spoke in 1886 of 'the essential and only lasting
thing' which was lacking in certain poetry – 'what I call *inscape*
– that is species or individually-distinctive beauty'. So inscape

is akin to the 'self' Hopkins writes of, the totality of the animate
or inanimate individual; and both inscape and self were reinforced by the *haecceitas*, or 'this-ness' of the philosophy of his
admired Duns Scotus (see again the *Gerard Manley Hopkins* of
Father Peters). 'Self', 'selving', is strongest of all in human
nature, 'more highly pitched, selved, and distinctive than anything in the world'. Searching nature, says Hopkins, 'I taste
self but at one tankard, that of my own being'. But in all beings,
everywhere, self being and inscape can be recognized, must
indeed be recognized:

> As kingfishers catch fire, dragonflies draw flame;
>   As tumbled over rim in roundy wells
>   Stones ring; like each tucked string tells, each hung bell's
> Bow swung finds tongue to fling out broad its name;
> Each mortal thing does one thing and the same:
>   Deals out that being indoors each one dwells;
>   Selves – goes itself; *myself* it speaks and spells;
> Crying *What I do is me: for that I came* . . .

Thus in his passionate, god-praising science Hopkins is for
ever grasping at what is elusive, yet not vague; at what is
essence, yet solid, permeating quality, yet totality. Poetry itself
he describes as 'speech only employed to carry the inscape of
speech for the inscape's sake'. He grasps at the inscapes of Gothic
tracery, the horse, Edinburgh Castle rock, bluebells, a man, a
sonnet, a tree (in his journal, in 1874, he talks of a 'delicate
flying shafted ash' having 'single sonnet-like inscape'), a sunset,
the Milky Way, a view, a complicated swirl of water, a kestrel
hanging, as he describes it, at the hover. So inscapes, no less
than the things which have them, are of his god's glory.

VIII

Sunsets and water. Let us take these two, for a while. The
observed complexity of either one exemplifies the passionate
science of Hopkins, which is, after all, the science of inscaping.
He hangs over runs of water, breakings of water, spreading of

water, he stares at them, he describes them, he draws them as well in pencil with that kind of sureness and capture one sees in the notebooks of Leonardo. In 1872 he wrote in his journal of being unsatisfied with his observation of waves after they break, of how difficult it is 'to law out the shapes and the sequence of the running' – the running of milky surf up the beach. The natural complexities of individual sunsets he had been lawing out with a fantastic intensity from childhood, or the time of his early poems, as we have seen. Added to the sunsets in his verse, another fifteen at least are individuated by Hopkins in his journal. For the *materia* of all these sunsets his objects and substances include flowers – roses, yellow lilies, the pink to mauve flowers of the wild mallow, for example – plums and damsons, yellow and red candle wax, crimson ice, quilted crimson silk, oil, steel, gold, brass, bronze. As a climax to his sunset inscaping he was able to write letters to *Nature* at the time of the exceptional Krakatao sunsets in 1883 (after Krakatao in the Dutch Indies had stupendously erupted and ejected into the upper atmosphere dust which travelled round the world), in which he sets out the exact chromatic differences he was able to discern: he could do so because he held exactly in his knowledge, in that 'treasury of explored beauty', the inscapes of so many a sunset not interfered with by this volcanic dust from the other hemisphere.

He individuates the complex, he individuates the apparently simple – a species of tree, for instance, in its proper adjective: 'silk-beech, scrolled ash, packed sycamore, wild wychelm, hornbeam fretty . . .', in which only 'wild' proffers an unusual vagueness;[3] and it is clear that editors of Hopkins and commentators should really familiarize themselves rather more than they do with his inscapes, with the natural objects, in their activity, which may carry a weight of implication inside his poems – with metals, jewels, flowers, fruits, birds, and the rest. Again and again in the collected poems, in the books and the many essays about him, missing notes or understandings are required, sensual and scientific. A key plant may ask for a note – for instance, the 'fretty chervil' which leaves and laces the banks and brakes in one of the greatest of his sonnets, in contrast to Hopkins himself who was then the eunuch of time with no water at his roots:

> See, banks and brakes
> Now, leavèd how thick! lacèd they are again
> With fretty chervil, look, and fresh wind shakes
>
> Them; birds build – but not I build; no, but strain,
> Time's eunuch, and not breed one work that wakes.
> Mine, O thou lord of life, send my roots rain.

That 'fretty chervil' at least requires to be known for the plant it is, *Anthriscus sylvestris*; not any species, but that one which so whitely and lacily is part of the juice and joy of the dangerous vegetative month along every road and every lane of Hopkins's elmy England.

In the 'May Magnificat' Hopkins wrote of the thrush, 'star-eyed strawberry-breasted', above her 'Cluster of bugle eggs thin'. 'Bugle blue', goes the comment of the editor of Hopkins's poems, 'query, like blue beads'; which is dictionary scholarship. There does exist a kind of glass bead known as a 'bugle', though bugles are long tubular glass beads sewn on dresses as orna-ments, usually black, not blue. Bugle blue – bugle, or *Ajuga reptans*, is a common plant blossoming in May, the month of the poem, a plant which shines like the surface of eggs, which is juicy, lush, and in its flowers intensely blue, which grows con-spicuously in the damp hedgeside grass of meadows, an element of the 'greenworld':

> Flesh and fleece, fur and feather,
> Grass and greenworld all together;
>   Star-eyed strawberry-breasted
>   Throstle above her nested
>
> Cluster of bugle blue eggs thin
> Forms and warms the life within;
>   And bird and blossom swell
>   In sod or sheath or shell.

The plant meaning is the primary one; a hint of glass and thin-ness may be included as well.

Or consider again the superbly scintillating analogues for the stars, the fire-folk in 'The Starlight Night', including white doves, orchard blossom, sallow catkins, leaves of abele or white poplar – and whitebeam:

> Wind-beat whitebeam! airy abeles set on a flare!

Father Peters, generally one of the best critics of Hopkins, rashly thinks that *wind-beat whitebeam* has to do with white or silver beams of moonlight, though this night over Wales, which is giving Hopkins his ecstasy, is a starlight night in which the stars are sharp and fierce, not drowned or paled by a moon; and though the parallelism demands a tree. He does not believe that 'whitebeam' can be the tree *Sorbus aria*, which has that name, and which he and other commentators, one following another, only think of as a small tree which happens to have delicate white underleaves.

But what does this small tree do with the leaves? Hopkins knew: those who are expert on Hopkins but not upon inscapes, do not know.

With an exact appropriateness to the poem, to the starlight night, this whitebeam, in darker scrub or woodland, or among black yews, magnificently tosses its leaves back to front, the wind bears the whole tree magnificently white.

IX

These are small examples of neglecting the passionate science, and so the meaning of Hopkins. A big example of imperfect attention, by which Hopkins gives only half that he has to give, is in all the conflicting comments upon 'The Windhover', that poem of 1877 once more, which Hopkins looked upon as his best. . . . The discussions about this sonnet were opened in 1926 by the distinguished critic I. A. Richards, yet in no interpretation down to the most recent ones in England and America, does any commentator ever seem to have studied, as a watcher of the bird, the one exciting activity on which the fullness of the poem must hang. No commentator seems to have studied the

wing-beating, hovering, gliding, swooping and recovering of
the kestrel or windhover, the way the bird forces itself into
equilibrium against the wind, a study which cannot be con-
ducted inside a dictionary, a Cambridge college, or a religious
seminary.

There is no great trouble about the activity at least of the first
lines. The kestrel, favourite of the morning, drawn forward into
prominence by the dappled dawn, rides the air, a knight upon
its horse, it hovers into and on the wind; then strides to a new
position:

> and striding,
> High there, how he rung upon the rein of a wimpling wing.

He rings ecstatically on the rein of a wimpling wing. This ringing upon the rein – it may not be easy altogether, yet what ingenious technical explanations for it have been advanced! To
'ring upon the rein', as of horses reined to the trainer in the
riding school! – that suggestion was made first of all by I. A.
Richards. It doesn't do. It would be no credit to Hopkins, who
seldom stretches things so far. To 'ring' – it is a technical term
of falconry – to rise spirally in flight. Perhaps, but is that
required? The kestrel strides to its new position, it does not
spiral. After the stride, it must start hovering again, this hawk
which is rider and not steed, it must ring again upon the rein
of its wing, to keep place in and on the wind, its steed and its
environment. But it is not only the rider, the dauphin of daylight's kingdom, the favourite of the morning, it is a hung bell.
That it rings on the rein of its wing tells of the bird filling the
sky with its own ringing fame (a ringing rhyme runs through
the first eight lines), its own report, its own excellence, God's
fame, God's excellence; tells also of the tense ringing vibration
of the kestrel's typical movement. '*Myself* it speaks and spells',
as Hopkins affirmed of each mortal thing in the sonnet 'As
kingfishers catch fire'. And recall Hopkins declaring that all
things are charged with God: all things *give off sparks and take fire*
('the fire that breaks from thee then'), *yield drops and flow, ring and
tell of him.*

The hung bell is clinched by that Kingfisher or selving

sonnet, which Hopkins wrote some years later; he returned
there to the kestrel, its ringing and its swing on the bow bend:

As tumbled over rim in roundy wells
  Stones ring; like each tucked string tells, each hung bell's
Bow swung finds tongue to fling out broad its name.

There, too, internally, he uses the same ringing rhyme. But on
the rein? It is complex. The wimpling wing, however, is a rein
from the bird to the air it rides and controls, and the bird, the
rider, is also a bell ringing and jingling upon that moving rein.
'Wimpling' is rippling, quick-beating. Yet even this simple
word has had its esoteric interpretation: that Hopkins used it
(as if he had watched the bird with powerful field-glasses)
'because of the way the feathers appear in graceful folds when
seen from below'. Wimpling is no more than the activity, not
absolutely regular, but with a variation of speed and beat (the
bird misses a beat sometimes), expressed already in the quick-
acting words '. . . daylight's dauphin, dapple-dawn-drawn
Falcon', in which the missing of a wing-beat – so close and
material are the equivalencies between object and word, object
and verse movement – is indicated in the pause one has to make
after 'dawn': 'dapple-dawn-drawn Falcon'.

There is another crux of meaning later in the sonnet when
Hopkins continues

Brute beauty and valour and act, oh, air, pride, plume, here
  Buckle!

Much more ingenuity than is required has gone to unravelling, or smudging, the rest of the poem and its purpose – that
from the conjunctive AND in the tenth line Christ begins to
speak to the kestrel, or Hopkins begins to address his own heart;
that his 'heart in hiding' is in hiding from the kestrel's natural
world, lost in the dismality of his vocation. His heart for a while,
in fact, was in hiding *from* his vocation, from his proper being,
his God, as in a later fragment:

Once I turned from thee and hid,
Bound on what thou hadst forbid;

> Sow the wind I would; I sinned:
> I repent of what I did.

He was yielding for a while too much to the kestrel's dangerous mortal beauty:

> To what serves mortal beauty – dangerous; does set dancing
>   blood – the O-Seal-that-so feature, flung prouder form
> Then Purcell tune lets tread to? See: it does this: keeps
>   warm
> Men's wits to the things that are; what good means – where a
>   glance
> Master more may than gaze . . .
> What do then? how meet beauty? Merely meet it; own,
> Home at heart, heaven's sweet gift; then leave, let that
>   alone.
> Yes, wish that though, wish all, God's better beauty, grace.

Nevertheless, the kestrel was a portion of that dull glory given to God, it was charged with God, giving off sparks and taking fire, ringing and telling of God; it was, though dangerous, heaven's sweet gift.

As for the last three lines, the fire broke from the kestrel, the windhover, the standgale (to recall another of its excellent English names), in the course of, and by dint of, its natural avocation; as in the sheer plod of ploughing, the steel mould-board or breast of the plough becomes shiny from the turned earth down the long strips of land (sillions),[4] and as embers which have become blue-bleak reveal, when their dull surface drops away, the heat and colour inside them. He thinks, addressing Christ in 'ah my dear', of the sheer plod of his own nine years, as it would soon be, of long preparation; of his own natural avocation since he had chosen to enter the Jesuit Order; of the asceticism of those years. The sheer plod puts a shine upon the plough which is himself; his at times bitter asceticism and exhaustion of mind reduces him to bleak embers which nevertheless gall and gash themselves to gold-vermilion – which are, in fact, the ashes of his other poem 'Morning, Midday, and Evening Sacrifice'.

> The vault and scope and schooling
> And mastery in the mind,
> In silk-ash kept from cooling,
> And ripest under rind.

x

Of such a kind is the interweaving of subtleties, complexities, and force and fire which Hopkins can convey in the inscapes of his passionate science. His poetry can, of course, be read on different levels – for its delight in natural phenomena so ecstatically and so exactly caught in language-structures of superb energy, which so refreshes one's response:

> And a gray heaven does the hush'd earth house.

We can love him for that 'touching of things', which is not small; or we can read him as well for the thought which, in his words, was fathered by such fine delight, for the religious poetry of a man beyond poetry, who could have said, as in his translation of the hymn 'O Deus, ego amo te',

> O God, I love thee, I love thee –
> Not out of hope of heaven for me
> Nor fearing not to love and be
> In the everlasting burning.

Hopkins wrote for no public, had no care for publication, and as a Jesuit did not entertain the thought of poetic fame. Only to eleven people had he shown any of his mature poems, to four members of his own society, his parents and his two sisters, and the three poets Dixon, Bridges, and Patmore.

The Foundation Exercise of St Ignatius begins not only that man was created to praise, reverence and serve God and by that means to save his soul – which was sufficient for Hopkins – but that all things else on earth were created to help man towards that end: man should use them just so far as they afford him that help and should 'withdraw himself from them just so far as they hinder him'. Composition could interfere, composition was then abandoned: upon his premises there was a pursuit for Hopkins utterly more compelling, but that pursuit was none the less the condition of the greatness and power of the verse – the best of it – which he did allow himself to write.

He considered that poetry was unprofessional. Yet among those letters to Bridges, Dixon, and Patmore, which themselves added up to one of the most direct, strict, piercing, and convincing bodies of criticism in the English language, he establishes a test which does not, and never can, defeat his own poetry – that 'a kind of touchstone of the highest or most living art is seriousness; not gravity but the being in earnest with your subject – reality'. By that being in earnest he lives.[5]

> SOURCE: first printed as a pamphlet for the British Council and National Book League (1953); reprinted in *Poems and Poets* (1969).

NOTES

1. The story was first recorded by André Brémond ('Je l'ai pris pour un innocent, *a natural*'). See H. House (ed.), *The Note-books and Papers* (Oxford, 1937) p. 375. The edition of 1959, p. 408, adds another version from an old lay brother, who said that one of Hopkins's special delights was a path between the Seminary and the College of Stonyhurst. After a shower he would run and crouch down to stare at quartz glittering in the sun. 'Ay, a strange yoong man, crouching down that gate to stare at some wet sand. A fair natural 'e seemed to us, that Mr. 'opkins.'

2. 'The most lovely species was the exquisite *Eolis coronata*, with tentacles surrounded by membranous coronets, and with crowded clusters of papillae, of crimson and blue that reflect the most gemlike radiance' – P. H. Gosse, 1853.

3. Yet the wych-elm does display a flexible wildness of structure in contrast to the dark-pencilled masses of the common elm.

4. 'Ploughshare' is also intimated in 'sheer plod'. It must, I think, be the plough that acquires shine, though the mould-board also imparts shine to the furrow. 'Plough down sillion' could be a composite noun. However the context asks for shine self-acquired by an *active* instrument, bird, plough or priest. Hopkins's editor, and this typifies the refusal to see as Hopkins saw, glosses 'sillion' as 'furrow',

though sillions (or selions), the long separate strips of each furlong in the Open Field, were still frequently to be seen when Hopkins wrote. There is a record, by the way, of Hopkins, in Ireland, stopping the jaunting-car he was travelling in, and persuading a ploughman to let him have the feeling and experience of guiding the plough for a while as it cut through the soil.

5. I see that some of the annotations I suggested in this essay, which was first printed in 1953, have been adopted in the 4th edition of Hopkins's *Collected Poems* (Oxford, 1967), though the point has not been completely understood every time.

Dennis Ward

'THE WINDHOVER: TO CHRIST OUR LORD' (1955)

I caught this morning morning's minion, king-
    dom of daylight's dauphin, dapple-dawn-drawn Falcon, in
        his riding
    Of the rolling level underneath him steady air, and striding
High there, how he rung upon the rein of a wimpling wing
In his ecstasy! then off, off forth on swing,
    As a skate's heel sweeps smooth on a bow-bend: the hurl and
        gliding
    Rebuffed the big wind. My heart in hiding
Stirred for a bird – the achieve of, the mastery of the thing!

Brute beauty and valour and act, oh, air, pride, plume here
    Buckle AND the fire that breaks from thee then, a billion
Times told lovelier, more dangerous, O my chevalier!

    No wonder of it: shéer plód makes plough down sillion
Shine, and blue-bleak embers, ah my dear,
    Fall, gall themselves, and gash gold-vermilion.

This essay is an attempt to probe the question: What did 'The Windhover' mean to Hopkins? This is not the place to argue the value of such an approach; it must suffice that I state quite baldly my opinion that such a struggle for bearings as that illustrated in the body of this essay shows the best possible way into the poem – the essential first step in encompassing its experience.

I caught this morning morning's minion, king-
    dom of daylight's dauphin, dapple-dawn-drawn Falcon, in
        his riding

Of the rolling level underneath him steady air, and striding
High there, how he run upon the rein of a wimpling wing
In his ecstasy!

The poet catches sight of the Falcon flying high and solitary
in the early morning sky and responds with a burst of sensuous
delight. The movement of the verse follows first the upward
surge of the poet's spirit, then turns away to lift and swing with
the bird's flight as it 'rides' the wind, a monarch – 'kingdom of
daylight's dauphin'. The immediacy of the verb 'caught' conveys exactly that first swift shock of delight. From the initial
impact it is as though the poet – in spirit at least – is himself
snatched up to fly with the Falcon. The movement of this
opening is one of lift and pause and lift. The three *m*'s emphasize the running stress-words 'morning', 'morning's', 'minion';
but of first importance is the *grading* of the stresses. 'Morning's'
takes a more emphatic stress than 'morning' and forces a pause
between the two words. This pause allows the stress variation
full play and emphasizes the progression from the temporal
'morning' to the possessive impersonification[1] 'morning's'.
'Minion' takes the lightest stress of the whole of this first phase,
and, as a result, the natural grammatical pause between it and
'king–' is lengthened into a full-breath-pause, so that the exceptionally heavy stress on the latter – which ends the rising
movement and which takes some of its force from the echo of
the two preceding slack -*ing*'s – can be fully marked.

From there the movement follows the course of flight and
dips and swings and lifts with it. The chivalric terms 'dauphin'
and 'minion' seem appropriate to such a creature as the
'riding', 'striding' Falcon, who is certainly the morning's darling
and prince of daylight. Two interpretations are possible for the
image 'dapple-dawn-drawn Falcon'. Isolated, it may seem to
imply that the Falcon is drawn – outlined, etched – against the
dappled dawn; but this is too static, too lifeless. In its context,
it gives rather the impression of movement; and the most satisfactory explanation is that the Falcon is 'dawn-drawn' in the
sense of being attracted, of being drawn upwards, *into* the
'dapple-dawn' – as a royal 'minion' might well be attracted

into the royal presence. The romance terms 'minion', 'dauphin' and, later, 'chevalier' – combined with the description of the Falcon's *riding* of the rolling level underneath him steady air, and *striding* high there' – carry connotations of the mediaeval chivalry, knight-errantry and active pride. The very movement of the verse here seems to sway to the movement of a charger.[2] Here is the 'pride' and 'valour' and 'plume' of the bird; and its struggle against the elements becomes symbolic of the struggle of the Christian knight (Christ – to whom the sonnet is addressed) against the forces of evil.

In the adjectival compounds 'dapple-dawn-drawn' and 'rolling level underneath him steady', Hopkins has inscaped his objects. The Falcon is not simply a falcon – any falcon – seen at a certain time of day, performing a certain action in a particular setting. The Falcon is not separable from any of these circumstances; they are the outward expression of its essential features, part of its being, and are inseparable either from the Falcon or each other. It is the same with the inscaping of the 'air'; the significant thing about it is its complete identification with the Falcon's flight, which, as it were, renders it visible. The compound image provides an excellent example of how an oral reading will bring out the sense of a difficult passage. Sight-read it appears almost unintelligible; but when read aloud it resolves itself into a complex of three movements, which combine in expressing the control and supremacy of the 'dauphin' in his skyey kingdom, and we get: 'his riding of the rolling . . . level underneath him . . . steady air'. The air is rolling, but the Falcon's command is such that it appears level beneath him, and the final impression is of 'steady' (subdued – conquered) air. This emphasis on the Falcon's supremacy and control is further heightened later in the sonnet when his long, turning glide appears to have 'rebuffed the big wind'.

Now that the Falcon has been identified with the idea of the Christian knight, it is tempting to relate part of the next image to that concept and to interpret it on those terms. W. A. M. Peters, s.j., provides the extreme example: 'rung', he says, 'calls up the ringing bells with which the reins are adorned as befits a royal charger. But "rein" is a homophone of "reign" and this recalls once again that the hawk is a dauphin, is a prince.'[3]

W. H. Gardner gives a more sober and convincing reading: 'The technical term "rung upon the rein" compares the sweeping curves of the bird's flight to the circle described by a horse at the end of the trainer's long rein.'[4] This certainly does more justice to the sense of movement that is an important aspect of the Falcon's flight and its effect upon the poet. But even this is too earthbound and hardly does justice to a 'dawn-drawn' flight. R. V. Schoder, s.j., has offered the best explanation in his reminder that 'rung' is the correct hawking term for describing a spiral climb.[5] *The Oxford English Dictionary* quotes an example of this use of the term from the *Pall Mall Gazette* of August 20th, 1869: 'When flown at a rook, both birds at times "ring" into the sky, the rook striving its utmost to keep above its pursuer.' If this sense of 'rung' is combined with Professor Gardner's explanation of the 'running rein', the result is a vivid image of the Falcon's lifting flight: the control of the bird pulling against the curve of its climb would give exactly that impression of behing held on a 'running rein'. Yet a still further refinement is in order. As will be seen later (in the interpretation of the sestet) the important thing about the flight of the Falcon is that it is controlled in a double sense – is expressive of both determinate and indeterminate action. Its course is determined by the will of the bird in relation to the directing forces. Therefore it is worth while bearing in mind the idea of 'rein' contained in such phrases as 'giving the rein' or Shakespeare's: 'When she will take the rein, I let her run'[6] – which conveys the idea of *controlled freedom* or, less paradoxically, of governed impulse. According to Hopkins, man's actions are influenced by God; man, in a sense, is also on a 'running rein', though his free-will allows him the power to acknowledge or deny God's leading stresses.

Father Schoder says of the description 'wimpling wing': 'The falcon's wing is described as "wimpling" because of the way the feathers appear in graceful folds when seen from below (as Hopkins recalls from closer observation before), and also because the mechanics of banked flight require the pivotal wing to be contracted so that its shortened span forces the surface into bulging ripples.'[7]

This is very convincing, and it is exactly the sort of detail that Hopkins would have seized upon to inscape the Falcon's flight. Even so, I feel that the important thing is the movement that is suggested by the term 'wimpling' – especially when spoken aloud, as it should be.[8] 'Wimpling' suggests a rippling motion like the flickering of feathers in a wind, or like the shuddering movement of a wing held at tension, kite-like, against a stiff breeze – the sort of movement that a flapping wimple would make, rather like the ruffle of a flag, which Hopkins described in his Journal: 'and indeed a floating flag is like wind visible, and what weeds are in a current; it gives thew and fires it and bloods it in.'[9]

'In his ecstasy' again calls to mind the struggle of the Falcon in relation to the Christian knight. As the bird battles against the wind, he seems to rejoice in his strength as does the knight in his battle against evil; it is as though the protagonist can find his true strength only in the *trial* of strength and purpose, as though his might is drawn from the force of the opposition. Then the Falcon turns:

. . . then off, off forth on swing,
As a skate's heel sweeps smooth on a bow-bend: the hurl and
    gliding
Rebuffed by the big wind.

The similes of the 'skate's heel' persuades Father Schoder that 'bow' should be understood as representing the 'figure 8' – the skating figure – and that the curve of the Falcon's flight is expressed in terms of the curve made by the heel of the skate on the loop-bend. But the idea of a precisely skated figure hardly conveys the speed and strain of the turn into the wind. It is important that this sense of stress and strain should be fully realized, and it seems better caught in the image of an English long-bow held at tension.

Hitherto it has been the bird itself that has dominated the poet's thought – 'the achieve of, the mastery of the thing!' Now his thoughts turn inward to relate the experience to his own state of being, to his own struggle and aspiration. In a mere bird he has seen the image of Christian endeavour, 'caught' the essence of its spirit: the struggle and the achievement in face of all difficulties, the courage and pride in singleness of purpose that allows its possessor to triumph equally in open conflict or willing submission. Even as the Falcon can beat the wind beneath him or turn with it, submitting only to defeat it through its own impetus:

> . . . the hurl and gliding
> Rebuffed the big wind.

– so the true Christian knight, the ideal of the Jesuit priest, is He who brought his followers the offer not of peace but of strife and the trial of persecution – the Christ who could rise in wrath and cast the money-lenders from the temple and as willingly submit to the agony and humiliation of the Crucifixion. What Hopkins is saying in 'My heart in hiding stirred for a bird' is that the Falcon's example has re-animated his failing purpose. But he is saying much more than this. In exciting the poet's emulative desire, the bird has become the instrument of God (here it is worth remembering that a 'minion' is an instrument of the supreme monarch) and has brought the flash of recognition of God's stress. But this requires elaboration, which can best be done with a few extracts from Hopkins's other writings, especially from his *Comments on the Spiritual Exercises of St. Ignatius Loyola* – a work that has much to offer the commentator on 'The Windhover'.

First, a note on inspiration: 'The word inspiration need cause no difficulty. I mean by it a mood of great, abnormal in fact, mental acuteness, either energetic or receptive, according as the thoughts which arise in it seem generated by a stress and action of the brain, or to strike into it unasked.'[10] Now, for Hopkins, inspiration derives from God, is in fact God's 'assisting grace'; its function is 'elevating', and it '. . . lifts the receiver from one cleave of being to another and to a vital act in Christ: this is truly God's finger touching the very vein of personality, which nothing else can reach and man respond to by no play whatever, by bare acknowledgement only, the counter stress which

God alone can feel (*subito probas eum*), the aspiration in answer to his inspiration'.[11]

Directly after this passage Hopkins remarked, 'Of this I have written above and somewhere else long ago.' Mr. Humphry House, the editor of the *Notebooks and Papers of Gerard Manley Hopkins*, suggests, quite rightly, that the 'somewhere else' is the first part of 'The Wreck of the *Deutschland*'; but the elevating function of God's 'assisting grace' is a common theme in Hopkins's poetry; it is, in fact, the theme of 'The Windhover'. However, the phrase 'aspiration in answer to his inspiration' invites comment, and the fifth stanza of 'The Wreck of the *Deutschland*' provides a good starting point:

> I kiss my hand
>   To the stars, lovely-asunder
> Starlight, wafting him out of it; and
>   Glow, glory in thunder;
> Kiss my hand to the dappled-with-damson west:
> Since, tho' he is under the world's splendour and wonder,
>   His mystery must be instressed, stressed;
> For I greet him the days I meet him, and bless when I understand.

In short, this realization of God in natural phenomena must be made actual in the person by a contributive effort of acceptance; for: 'as a mere possibility, passive power, is not power proper and has no activity it cannot of itself come to stress, cannot instress itself.'[12]

Hopkins, then, in his reaction to the natural beauty of the Falcon, has felt God's stress, but so far his reaction has been passive, and to become active it must be 'instressed, stressed'. From this observation we may proceed to the sestet of the sonnet.

The sestet opens:

> Brute beauty and valour and act, oh, air, pride, plume, here
>   Buckle!

Here Hopkins calls on the qualities of the bird that have excited his admiration and inspired a 'heart in hiding' to come together in that heart and condition it for his life's purpose of struggle and sacrifice. It is not the refinements of the bird that are significant; it is the inspiration that is realized *through* them. The verb 'Buckle' has long been a debating point. If read as an indicative and not, as above, as an imperative, the meaning of the poem is changed completely and tends to become the weary surrender of the poet to the ascetic demands of the priest that many critics believe it to be. In such a reading, the sheer delight, the whole initiative and magnificent upward sweep, fails as the 'Brute beauty', 'valour' and 'act', the 'pride' and the 'plume' are made to crumble before the wearily submissive recollection of the priestly vocation. A variant of the imperative reading of 'Buckle' is that the bird represents only the 'valour' and 'pride' of 'brute beauty', which is purposeless, and that the poet-priest calls upon these qualities to submit – that is, his delight in these qualities – to the sterner demands of a spiritual life of plodding action: 'sheer plod makes plough down sillion shine'. This would again throw the emphasis upon the incompatibility of the poetic and priestly vocations. But neither of these readings is satisfactory. Hopkins rejects neither the natural beauties of the bird nor the sensuous delight that he finds in them; indeed, they are the source of his inspiration and strength. They must not be denied; they must be stressed – made more. Hopkins's 'here' in 'here Buckle' is not primarily temporal, less 'at this moment of recollection' than 'here in this place' – that is, *in my heart* – as later analysis will show.

The next problem is the reading of:

> . . . AND the fire that breaks from thee then, a billion
> Times told lovelier, more dangèrous, O my chevalier!

Why did Hopkins write 'AND' in capitals? Professor Gardner has the answer pat; it is, he says, a metrical subtlety: 'A very curious expedient was the writing of 'AND' in capitals. This could only be to point out that although the word counts in the scansion merely as a slack syllable, in the actual reading aloud it must be pronounced with speed and stress; by this means the poet hoodwinks the academic exciseman and slips in what is virtually a six-stress line under cover of a pentameter.'[13]

It is a pleasant thought, this hoodwinking of the 'academic exciseman'; but surely Hopkins's device has more to it than that. Again Father Schoder's observations point in the right direction and deserve quotation: 'The very way in which 'AND' is emphasized reveals its importance in the development of the thought. It is the 'and' of consequence, equivalent to 'and as a certain result'; for the preceding line is really the protasis, to which this is the apodasis – *if* this struggle is re-enacted in the poet's soul, *then in consequence* a glory, 'fire' will break forth from him too.'[14]

As has already been suggested, I believe that the important thing is not that the struggle – or for that matter any of the physical attributes of the bird – should be *re-enacted* in the heart or soul of the poet. Again it is the *significance* (the latent possibilities in relation to the poet) of the struggle – its implications when apprehended as God's 'assisting grace' and the exercising of that 'more particular providence' that incites the emulative desire of the 'receiver': 'When a man has given himself to God's service, when he has denied himself and followed, he has fitted himself to receive and does receive from God a special guidance, a more particular providence.'[15]

It is this realization of God's purpose that provides the motivation for the *active* life in Christ. The function of this emulative desire is explained in the *Comments*:

For prayer is the expression of a wish to God and, since God searches the heart, the conceiving even of the wish is prayer in God's eyes. For there must be something which shall truly be the creature's in the work of corresponding with grace . . . correspondence itself is on man's side not so much corresponding as the wish to correspond, and this least sigh of desire, this aspiration, is the life and spirit of man.[16]

So, too, in the poem 'To what serves mortal beauty', which expressly deals with this subject, we get:

What do then? how meet beauty? Merely meet it; own,
Home at heart, heaven's sweet gift; then leave, let that alone.
Yea, wish that though, wish all, God's better beauty, grace.

There we have it; it is the perception of that 'better beauty', God's grace, which lies behind the mortal beauty, that provides the incentive and is the end to be sought. And this again throws the emphasis on that key-word 'Buckle'; for now we realize that in the very act of engaging the 'receiver's' heart, the physical attributes, the 'mortal beauty', will give way, be elevated, to the spiritual. Our reading of this ambiguous 'Buckle' will, then, carry connotations both of 'engaging' and of 'giving way'.

From this we can continue the explanation of the sestet. The mortal beauty of the Falcon, the energy and valour and pride, will be a 'billion times told lovelier' when apprehended as the outward and visible sign of the creative force, God, which is 'under the world's splendour and wonder'. 'Then' (which is stressed and means 'when this has been accomplished') it not only will be immeasurably more beautiful; it will prove a source of spiritual strength, 'more dangerous' in that it will be actuated, will be stressed (made more) by 'corresponding' aspiration. The dangerous and active end to which this kind of inspiration draws the priest is the absolute submission to God's will, the effect of which is expressed in the Jesuit prayer: 'Dearest Lord, teach me to be generous; to serve Thee as Thou deservest, to give and not to count the cost, to fight and not to heed the wounds, to toil and not to seek for rest, to labour and not to ask for reward – save that of knowing that I am doing Thy will.'

It is not easy for those of us who do not share Hopkins's faith to appreciate the thrill of that 'dangerous'; it carries something of the primitive force of our earliest Christian poetry – 'The Dream of the Rood', for instance, where Christ is revealed as the ideal of heroic action, and his sacrifice is expressed in militant phraseology. . . . 'Then the young Hero, who was Christ Almighty, brave and unflinching, stripped Himself. He mounted on the high Cross, brave in the sight of many, when he was minded to redeem mankind.'[17]

Whom or what is Hopkins addressing with his 'thee' and his 'O my chevalier!'? According to our interpretation so far, it must be the re-animated heart; but this opinion, which is shared by Father Schoder but not by many other readers, is rather startling without further support; generally, it is considered easier and more logical to believe that he is addressing Christ, or perhaps the Falcon. Our help here may be a passage from the *Comments* which describes fully the ideal state of correspondence with God. As it is relevant to the whole idea of 'assisting grace' it will be worth while quoting the full passage:

For grace is any action, activity on God's part by which, in creating or after creating, he carries the creature to or towards the end of his being, which is self-sacrifice to God and its salvation. It is, I say, any such activity on God's part, so that so far as this action or activity is God's it is divine stress, holy spirit, and, as all is done through Christ, Christ's spirit; so far as it is action, correspondence, or the creature's it is *acto salutaris*; so far as it is looked at in *esse quieto* it is Christ and his member on one side, his member in Christ on the other. It is as if a man said That Christ is playing at me and me playing at Christ, only it is no play but truth, That is Christ *being me* and me being Christ.[18]

To which might be added another quotation, this time from his poetry:

> . . . for Christ plays in ten thousand places,
>   Lovely in limbs, and lovely in eyes not his
>   To the Father through the features of men's faces.[19]

With these extracts as support, I suggest that Hopkins is addressing Christ *and* his heart *and* the Falcon; for they are inseparable. In achieving that state of correspondence where the bird is recognized as the 'mortal' representation of the divine presence, he has achieved that perfect condition of 'Christ being me and me being Christ'. Now we can understand why the sonnet is addressed (and it is *addressed*, not merely dedicated) to Christ. It does not matter that the sub-heading 'To Christ Our Lord' was not in the original draft and was added years later; for the address is essential to its creation and is an integral part of the poem. 'Chevalier' is equally apt as the form of address for the high-riding Falcon, the hero Christ, or the newly dedicated knight and priest. 'Chevalier' echoes the chivalric terms 'dauphin' and 'minion', which it supersedes; for a 'dauphin' is less than a monarch and appears, with the first introduction of the bird, in conjunction with 'minion' – in other words, in the opening of the sonnet, the Falcon is at once the symbol of Christ, the intermediary of God, and of earthly beauty, as far as it represents God's influence or 'inspiration'. The comprehensive term of address, 'Chevalier', symbolizes the consummation of the whole process of 'correspondence' – of 'aspiration in answer to His inspiration'.

'Honour', Hopkins tells us in the sonnet 'In Honour of St. Alphonsus Rodriguez', 'is flashed off exploit', and so, too, in 'The Windhover' there is 'no wonder' – nothing surprising – that the highest Christian qualities should be struck out of conflict. It is the 'sheer plod', the sheer effort, involved in driving the ploughshare through the 'sillion' (selion) that makes it (Hopkins surely means the plough-share, not the 'sillion') shiny and bright; it flashes brighter for its use and friction. So also do 'blue-bleak embers' strike their brightest fire ('gold-vermilion' – blood colour) when they break from the self-consuming heat of the fire and gash and gall themselves against the outer world. It is usual to emphasize the laboured movement of the poem – what has often been described as the 'heavy, weary movement'.[20] But 'The Windhover' was not conceived in the self-damning mood of 'Carrion Comfort', and it is completely wrong to force it into compliance with the spirit of that and other 'agony' sonnets; nothing could be farther from the truth. Father Schoder may be right when he says that the close of 'The Windhover' brings out the contrast between the high ideals and the earthbound struggle of the priest; but he is surely mistaken when he suggests that the contrast is realized in a spirit of 'weary' submission. Rather has the contemplation of the higher flights of spiritual and worldly endeavour in the supreme example of Christ given *purpose* to the priest's humble struggle. 'Weary' is absolutely wrong; 'purposeful' better expresses the spirit and movement of this final phase:

> No wonder of it: sheer plod makes plough down sillion
> Shine, and blue-bleak embers, ah my dear,
>   Fall, gall themselves, and gash gold-vermilion.

'Sheer plod makes plough down sillion shine, and blue-bleak embers . . .' – the weight of the stresses and the alliterated explosives in 'plod . . . plough' and 'blue-bleak' give the impression of push and effort, while the slash and thrust of 'fall, gall themselves, and gash gold-vermilion' recaptures the battling spirit of the Falcon and the knight (dangerous indeed! – the essential spirit of the poem) and, which cannot be emphasized too strongly or repeated too often, is expressed not in the writhing agony of a 'terrible pathos' (Bridges unwittingly did Hopkins considerable disservice when he coined that phrase)[21] but in the spirit of militant zeal and sheer delight that animates the 'St. Alphonsus Rodriguez' sonnet:

> And those strokes once that gashed flesh or galled shield
> Should tongue that time now, trumpet now that field,
> And, on the fighter, forge his glorious day.

'The Windhover' is a declaration of Christian purpose and a triumphant confirmation of the poet's personal faith – the faith that was his very existence: 'I have not only made my vows publicly some two and twenty times but I make them to myself every day'[22] – we need not marvel that the sonnet was so dear to him.[23] In this sonnet we have the poetic expression of that intensely personal awareness of God's 'stress' that, in his tortured prose, he tried to analyse in his Comments on *The Spiritual Exercises of St. Ignatius Loyola* – the tremendous impulse of his religious faith acting upon that Self 'more distinctive than the taste of ale or alum, more distinctive than the smell of walnut-leaf or camphor':[24]

> Each mortal thing does one thing and the same:
> Deals out that being indoors dwells;
> Selves – goes itself; *myself* it speaks and spells;
> Crying *What I do is me*; for that I came.[25]

SOURCE: John Wain (ed.) *Interpretations* (1955).

NOTES

1. 'This most strange attitude towards self – whether joined to a rational or to an irrational nature – immediately proceeding from his habitual search for the inscape of things, drove Hopkins instinctively to their *impersonification*, a personification, that is, of the irrational selves on the level of sensitive perception, unconscious therefore, in so far as Hopkins neither reflected upon it nor intellectually accounted for it. I wish to stress the words "on the level of sensitive perception"; this restriction implies that the impersonification did not take place by an explicit act of comparison by and in which the intellectual presented the irrational object as a person. For this reason I have chosen the term "impersonification", and I preserve the term "personification" for that figure of speech which cannot exist without a conscious act of intellectual reasoning' (W. A. M. Peters, s.j., *Gerard Manley Hopkins*, London and Oxford, 1948).

2. Ibid. pp. 105–6.

3. Ibid. p. 105.

4. W. H. Gardner, *Gerard Manley Hopkins*, 1 (Harmondsworth, 1953; 2nd ed. 1966) p. 180.

5. R. V. Schoder, s.j., 'What does "The Windhover" mean?', in N. Weyand (ed.), *Immortal Diamond: Studies in G. M. Hopkins* (London, 1949) pp. 290–1.

6. *The Winter's Tale*, Act III, iii, 51.

7. Schoder, p. 291.

8. In a letter to Coventry Patmore, Hopkins wrote: 'Such verse as I do compose is oral, made away from paper, and I put it down with repugnance' (C. C. Abbott, ed., *Further letters of G.M.H.*, Oxford, 1938, p. 231). Again, in writing to Bridges about the poem 'The Leaden Echo and the Golden Echo', he defends his rhythmic subtleties with: 'The long lines are not rhythm run to seed: everything is weighed and timed in them. Wait till they have taken hold of your ear and you will find it so' (*Letters to Robert Bridges*, Oxford, 1935, pp. 154–5).

9. Humphry House (ed.), *Notebooks and Papers* (Oxford, 1937) p. 178.

10. Letter to A. Baillie, 16 September 1864.

11. *Notebooks and Papers*, p. 309.

12. Ibid.

13. Gardner, I, pp. 99–100.
14. Schoder, p. 298.
15. *Correspondence of G.M.H. and R. W. Dixon* (Oxford, 1935) p. 93.
16. *Notebooks and Papers*, p. 333.
17. 'The Dream of the Rood', lines 39–40.
18. *Notebooks and Papers*, p. 332.
19. 'As kingfishers catch fire, dragonflies draw flame'.
20. Schoder, p. 303.
21. The phrase was Canon Dixon's; see p. 33 above. [Editor's Note]
22. *Further Letters*, p. 75.
23. 'I shall shortly send you an amended copy of "The Windhover"; the amendment only touches a single line, I think, but as that is the best thing I ever wrote I should like you to have it in its best form' (*Letters to Robert Bridges*, p. 85).
24. *Notebooks and Papers*, p. 309.
25. *Poems*, p. 95. ['As Kingfishers catch fire'. Editor's Note]

Elisabeth Schneider

'THE WINDHOVER' (1960)

On 'The Windhover' I am disposed to be dogmatic. The poem conveys one direct meaning, and only one in which all the parts of the poem and all the images find a place. Belt buckles and buckles in armor are not part of it; they belong to some other poem, 'in another country'. Hopkins willingly employed puns when double meaning might be 'to one thing wrought' but not when two meanings fractured a poem. The instinct of critics to hover around the word *buckle* is nevertheless sound, for that word is the structural center, the pivot on which the sonnet turns.

Something buckles and something breaks through. Readers who buckle belts neglect the second half of this statement, though Hopkins capitalized the AND between the parts. It will not do to take *buckle* as an imperative either, as many writers do, for that leaves AND hanging loose and destroys the sentence. It is neither armor nor belt, nor Mr. Empson's bicycle wheel, that buckles or breaks; the pivotal image is of a higher order of magnitude. Deck or bulkheads of a ship buckle before fire breaks through; walls of a building buckle before they crash or burn. In 'The Windhover' the whole material world buckles, 'AND the fire' of the spiritual world – or Christ – 'breaks' through. *Buckle* and *break* control the sestet as it subsides from the climax of spiritual illumination to the everyday imagery of the conclusion.

'The Windhover' is one of several variations on a theme that occupied Hopkins in 1877. Other sonnets, particularly 'The Starlight Night' and 'Spring', display the same pattern of thought: a progression from the concrete beauty of nature described in the octave, to its spiritual meaning or analogue in the sestet. As is so often true in Hopkins, the plan is simple and straightforward; only the execution is complex.

'The Windhover' is addressed 'To Christ Our Lord', and

though Christ is not mentioned till the tenth line, He is prepared for in the first by epithets given to the falcon – morning's favorite (minion), 'kingdom of daylight's' crown prince – the Son, not the King or Father. *Dauphin* is more than an automatic bit of alliteration; it counts for the meaning and for unity. The falcon is an analogue, however, not a symbol of Christ. Though the power and beauty of its flight make it prince of the morning scene, it is not more than a bird, and it is described throughout the octave in the language of the material world. But the sight of it awakens the poet: 'My heart [which had been] in hiding stirred.' Beneath the word *hiding* I hear *hibernating*, but that may be an accidental personal association; at any rate, the poet's heart had been stagnant and perhaps reluctant to be moved.[1] Its awakening preludes the turn of the sonnet.

In the ninth line, the particularities of bird and morning are drained away, leaving abstractions and universals to represent the power and beauty in nature. This material world, so abstracted – 'brute beauty and valour and act, oh, air, pride, plume' – 'here [at this point, now] buckle[s],' and as it collapses before the poet's vision, the fire of Christ 'breaks' through, 'a billion times' more lovely and more dangerous. Only now does the poet address Christ directly: 'the fire that breaks from thee then . . . O my chevalier.' The image in Hopkins' mind probably derives from the crackling of timbers or plates in a fire at sea, a kind of disaster with which his father was professionally concerned and which from time to time furnished Hopkins himself, landsman though he was, with a surprising quantity of imagery. Such an image gives double significance to the epithet *dangerous*, applied immediately afterwards to Christ. From this point on, tension relaxes and the pitch drops to a quiet conclusion with the imagery remaining under the shadow of *buckle* and *break*. 'No wonder' this transformation occurs, Hopkins says, when the *breaking open* of the most drab things in life may reveal brightness within. Mere labor of plowing breaks open the earth and transforms dull clod into shining furrow ('the near hill glistening with very bright newly turned sods', he noted in his journal); and 'blue-bleak' coals of an apparently dead fire fall and break apart to show bright living fire within.

In the outline of its thought, then, 'The Windhover' is simple and strict. Its complexities lie, on the one hand, in the elaboration of the visual imagery interwoven with elaborately echoing patterns of sound, and, on the other, in the play between two counterpointed sets of opposites. The first is the opposition of the material and the spiritual which mark the two parts of the sonnet and are expressly brought together by the dauphin-Son parallel and more essentially by the primary theme of the poet's being stirred by one into more intense awareness of the other. The second pair of opposites appear in more shadowy form. The opposition of beauty and terror (or pain), present in so much of Hopkins' writing, runs through the poem without any reconciling of the two, though they are brought together in an uneasy harmony through the idea of power in the 'mastery' of the bird and the 'lovelier, more dangerous' fire of Christ. These opposites, however, are not evenly balanced in the poem: the terror or pain is no more than an undertone, reflected in one epithet of Christ, in the 'gall' and 'gash' of the close, possibly in the predatory character as well as the daring of the hawk and in the poet's 'hiding' heart. The unresolved suggestions of terror and pain give an edge to the overriding spirit of breathless admiration.

These complexities are enough. Richness of symbolic meaning cannot be had merely by reading into the poem a mechanical, dictionary-flavored ambiguity in *buckle*. For the interpretation of 'The Windhover' at least, an inveterate commitment to irony and paradox is apt to defeat itself by producing only disjointed structure and discordant associations that destroy, by neutralizing, the resonance of the poem. Quite a good deal of the resonance of 'The Windhover' comes from simplicity of theme, clarity of structure, and directness of movement. This is true even though the final effect is of an extremely complex poem.

SOURCE: *The Explicator*, vol. XVIII, no. 4 (1960).

NOTE

1. C. C. Abbott (ed.), *Letters of G. M. Hopkins to R. Bridges* (Oxford, 1935) p. 66.

Elizabeth Jennings

THE UNITY OF INCARNATION
(1960)

'There is no escape from incarnation' might well be an epitaph to all the work of Gerard Manley Hopkins.[1] So much has been written about his theories of 'inscape' and 'instress' and about the apparent conflict in him between poet and priest, that few critics have remembered that to write vital religious verse *at all* in the late nineteenth century was itself a problem. The lag-end of an age which was divided into insensitive materialism on the one hand and emotional pietism on the other was not a propitious time for the revival of religious literature, since it is harder to purify degraded symbols than to revive dead ones.

Hopkins, who is so often thought of as a twentieth-century poet (he was, in every sense of the word, a *modern* poet), is an example of the religious writer who first turns to the exploration of his own personality to test the validity of religious experience. And modern religious verse, unlike mediaeval religious verse, is a poetry of religious *experience* not of religion itself. This is also true of the plastic arts: the men who carved the statues on the walls of Chartres Cathedral were depicting the relationship between God and man in historical and scriptural terms. Dogma was sufficiently alive in their minds to be itself dramatic; it needed no individual colouring of personality or personal conflict to bring it to life. The creative power of the Chartres craftsmen sprang from their ability to play variations on traditional themes or, indeed, on the theme of tradition itself.

With Hopkins it is quite a different matter; the tradition of Catholicism which he inherited at his conversion was re-presented in his own poetry in entirely personal terms; yet it was completely orthodox in the theological sense. As I have said, he first turned inward, and perhaps for that reason alone is regarded as a master of modernity. But he did much more than this; he also turned outward and saw God's signature written on all creation, creation upheld by the love of God:

> Glory be to God for dappled things

and

> . . . Christ plays in ten thousand places,
> Lovely in limbs and lovely in eyes not his
> To the Father through the features of men's faces.

What is really new in Hopkins is not so much his ingenious and fastidious experiments with language and rhythm, as his double vision of the relations between God and man – God both substantially present in the centre of each man's soul, and God also pervading the whole universe. His poetry is therefore elemental rather than analogical; his unique vision reconnects the separated Christian symbols by putting them to work, as it were, in the context of all creation – of nature, astronomy, the seas, the tides, the earth, the air.

This extraordinary blending of acute self-consciousness with an intense awareness and observation of objects and likenesses in the physical world is achieved in and through an obsession with technique. For it cannot be stated too often that the most sublime reaches of a poet's work are only arrived at through discipline and through a never-ceasing effort to make language appear new. As Blake said, 'Technical excellence is the only vehicle of genius.'

Like all visionary writers, Hopkins had to learn himself before he could learn fully about God and the universe. The marvel of his poetry is that it describes all the stages in the struggle from obscurity to clarity; it does not simply celebrate the great moments of pure vision, as Vaughan's verse does, or the reconciling power of compassion which we find in Péguy. Nor does it arrive at truth through the medium of dreams and allegory as Edwin Muir's verse does. It is, in the strictest sense of the word, a poetry of *incarnation*, and therefore has a wholeness and a dynamic power which silence all questions about the problems of religious art.

The profundity of Hopkins's perception would have only a moderate value and conviction if his whole conception of poetry did not demand and include that contact with God which only the mystics know – a contact which reaches through and beyond the senses – and also that vision which must 'enjoy the world aright' *before* it can understand or be united with God. The sense of hierarchy is innate, in Hopkins's work, and it is the very struggle between different modes of being (plants, animals, man, God) which gives his poetry both its structure and its tension. But the vision is never impersonal; 'inscape' for Hopkins meant the unique individuality of every living thing, while 'instress' was the power, namely that of God, which keeps that individuality in being.

What is startling, and even shocking, in Hopkins's verse is not so much the audacity with language or the uninhibited play of imagery as the wholeness, the integration of the vision which these things embody. His images are never approximate counters or substitutes for some statement which for ever remains out of reach. They are the vision itself, both the subject and shape of the verse. It is rather ironic that a poet who has so often been praised or condemned for the idiosyncrasy of his style (as if style were an embellishment not an embodiment) should reveal, when his work is examined with concentration and without prejudice, that this style is entirely merged with what the poet has to say, and could say in no other way. The contemporary obsession with 'concrete imagery' becomes almost irrelevant when we find in, for example, the sonnet, 'No worst, there is none', an adherence not to concrete things for their own sake but for their supreme power of conveying and giving life to inner states of mind and conditions of the soul:

> My cries heave, herds-long; huddle in a main, a chief
> Woe, world sorrow; on an age-old anvil wince and sing –
> Then lull, then leave off. Fury had shrieked 'No ling-
> ering!' Let me be fell; force I must be brief!

O the mind, mind has mountains; cliffs of fall
Frightful, sheer, no-man-fathomed. Hold them cheap
May who ne'er hung there.

The equating here of unscaleable mountains with a condition of
despair and desolation tells us infinitely more about both the
mind *and* despair than any careful arrangement of abstractions
could. The mood is personal, the application entirely general;
the dark night of one particular man is disclosed and shared by
means of an image from the physical world. Even in his most
desperately personal conflicts, Hopkins first moves inwards and
then outwards. For him, this difficult objectivity is effected by
means of imagery; the mind is cleared, the senses satisfied.

Hopkins is perhaps the only 'modern' English poet who shows
no sign of that separation of thought and feeling which Eliot
called 'dissociation of sensibility' and which he traced back to
the seventeenth century. It may well be that it is the religious
nature of Hopkins's verse that permits this unity. Tormented
and battling as much of his work is, the battle always takes place
on solid ground and in a world of order. It is a world where dis-
ruption only occurs where there is a lack of innocence. It is not
surprising, therefore, that so many of Hopkins's poems are concerned with innocence and childhood. He shares this love of
and delight in innocence with Traherne, Péguy and Bernanos.
In 'Spring' he writes:

What is all this juice and all this joy?
A strain of the earth's sweet being in the beginning
In Eden garden. – Have, get, before it cloy,
Before it cloud, Christ, lord, and sour with sinning,
Innocent mind and Mayday in girl and boy,
Most, O maid's child, thy choice and worthy the winning.

And again, in 'The Bugler's First Communion', Hopkins praises
the freshness and simplicity of the young soldier:

Frowning and forefending angel-warder
Squander the hell-rook ranks sally to molest him;
March, kind comrade, abreast him;
Dress his days to a dexterous and starlight order.

Like Vaughan, Hopkins constantly pursues this 'dexterous
and starlight order' and his moments of clearest vision are
closely allied with his delight in the simplicity and innocence
of childhood:

> Margaret, are you grieving
> Over Goldengrove unleaving?
> Leaves, like the things of man, you
> With your fresh thoughts care for, can you?

This is a kind of foreshadowing, a pre-echo as it were, of the
children in Eliot's rose-garden – 'hidden excitedly, containing
laughter'. It is this passionate interest in the 'free and open
disposition' rather than the terrible sufferings of the later
sonnets which herald, for Hopkins, the awareness and reality of
union with God.

As I have suggested already, Hopkins's poetry is a poetry of
incarnation. His oneness with God is oneness with Christ, both
as God and man. His great devotion to Mary, the Mother of
God, is therefore an essential element in his verse:

> So God was god of old:
> A mother came to mould
> Those limbs like ours which are
> What must make our daystar
> Much dearer to mankind;
> Whose glory bare would blind
> Or less would win man's mind.
> Through her we may see him
> Made sweeter, not made dim,
> And her hand leaves his light
> Sifted to suit our sight.

('The Blessed Virgin compared to the Air we breathe')

'Made sweeter, not made dim' and 'sifted to suit our sight' are
important keys to Hopkins's own religious and mystical experience. The moments of pure illumination in his verse are almost
always concerned with Christ, God the Son, the incarnate God:

. . . . There he bides in bliss
Now, and seeing somewhere some man do all that man can do,
For love he leans forth, needs his neck must fall on, kiss,
And cry 'O Christ-done deed! So God-made-flesh does too:
Were I come o'er again' cries Christ 'it should be this.'

What Hopkins's most strenuous searches are trying to recover is, in effect, that state of innocence in which the human soul is a window for the concentrated light and reflexion of God. The sufferings which he describes in the so-called 'terrible' sonnets are dark nights in which the soul becomes obscured both by its individual infidelities to God and also by the fallen state of all mankind. Each vision of God is a recovery, a winning-back of some lost state. Like all deeply religious men, Hopkins never forgets the necessity and ennobling power of suffering. The Jesuit discipline and the practice of the *Ignatian Exercises* alone would have been sufficient to imprint this attitude towards suffering firmly on his mind.

Yet there is no masochism in Hopkins's agonies; he recognizes that suffering is part of the condition of man, a condition that has been made sweet and acceptable by Christ's passion and death. He recognizes too, as Bernanos does, that suffering is often undergone vicariously, that it is never wasted even at its darkest moments. His work is shot through with a joyous acceptance and with that patience or 'waiting on God' which is the mark of the true mystic:

We hear our hearts grate on themselves: it kills
To bruise them dearer. Yet the rebellious wills
Of us we do bid God bend to him even so.

In this sonnet there is nothing passive. God is sought with a personal, willing love and with a childlike confidence:

. . . He is patient. Patience fills
His crisp combs, and that comes those ways we know.

The poet knows too that he must be patient with himself and not demand from himself an inhuman courage and sacrifice:

> Soul, self; come, poor Jackself, I do advise
> You, jaded, let be; call off thoughts awhile
> Elsewhere; leave comfort root-room; let joy size
> At God knows when to God knows what . . .

One of the prerequisites of mystical experience is abandonment to God, an abandonment which is the only true source of peace. And, for the mystic, peace is not so much a state as a person, is, in fact, Christ Himself. Several of Hopkins's poems are explicit requests for this 'peace that surpasses all understanding':

> O surely, reaving Peace, my Lord should leave in lieu
> Some good! And so he does leave Patience exquisite,
> That plumes to peace hereafter. And when Peace here does house
> He comes with work to do, he does not come to coo,
>   He comes to brood and sit.
>   ('Peace')

>   And I have asked to be
>   Where no storms come,
> Where the green swell is in the havens dumb,
>   And out of the swing of the sea.
>   ('Heaven-Haven')

Poets and mystics who have experienced some close, personal but supra-rational awareness of God have always carried away from such moments of illumination an increased subtlety, a profoundly original understanding of human experience and of the apparent contradictions even in the physical universe. This kind of understanding is one of those gifts which Catholics refer to as 'the gifts of the Holy Ghost'. On a *natural* level all true poets have this understanding. When, however, such natural intuition is permeated by grace in a poet of more than ordinary talent, his whole work is flooded by perceptiveness and by a sensitiveness to truth in all its forms. In Hopkins's poem, 'The Wreck of the *Deutschland*', there is a remarkable example of this kind of power carried to the point where prayer and poetry meet. The poem's subject is the shipwreck of some Franciscan nuns in 1875, but that subject is only a jumping-off ground for a complete vision of creation held in the hands of God. The poem is a celebration of the glory of human and divine life, of both the physical and the spiritual world. It is also pervaded with a humble and intelligent charity; all things are seen in the light of God.

The first eleven stanzas of the poem are an astonishingly well-sustained lyrical expression of Hopkins's own knowledge and love of God; in the last lines of the first stanza, there is an unmistakeable description of a *mystical* experience:

> Thou mastering me
> God! giver of breath and bread;
> World's strand, away of the sea;
> Lord of living and dead;
> Thou hast bound bones and veins in me, fastened me flesh,
> And after it almost unmade, what with dread,
> Thy doing: and dost thou touch me afresh?
> Over again I feel thy finger and find thee.

This 'touch' of God, expressed in entirely concrete terms, is language familiar to readers of mystical literature throughout the centuries. The poem continues with an account of the 'terror' and 'stress' of the poet when confronted by God; this terror is the terror of awe not of craven fear. But the poet moves away from this sense of almost unbearable awe to the comfort and simplicity of the Holy Eucharist (the incarnation theme is beginning to emerge):

> I whirled out wings that spell
> And fled with a fling of the heart to the heart of the Host.

All is activity and the soul 'flings' itself into the mercy of Christ. Hopkins then acknowledges both his weakness and his strength. He is 'soft sift in an hour glass' and also 'steady as a water in a well'. The water can easily be stirred but is controlled and kept in balance by grace. What steadfastness he has, Hopkins asserts, springs from his priestly calling; he is one who can offer 'a pressure, a principle, Christ's gift'. Whatever he himself possesses is to be handed on to others.

The fifth stanza is the beginning of Hopkins's hymn to creation:

> I kiss my hand
> To the stars, lovely-asunder
> Starlight, wafting him out of it; and
> Glow, glory in thunder.

Like Eliot's last two *Quartets*, this part of the poem expresses a vision which embraces all creation. God is here seen as both immanent and transcendent, and Hopkins makes quite clear his belief that God can be found *in* natural things; his is the way of the affirmation of images:

> Since, tho' he is under the world's splendour and wonder,
>   His mystery must be instressed, stressed;
> For I greet him the days I meet him, and bless when I understand.

There is a pun here on the word 'stressed'. Hopkins is using it both in the sense of the individuality of every existing thing and also in the sense that God *desires* us to stress Him, to speak to Him and for Him. In other words, He *wants* our love and our willing surrender in order that He may fulfil His own plans for us.

'The Wreck of the *Deutschland*' goes on to state that this love is not received from and exchanged with some lofty being far removed from men but that it begins and 'dates from':

> his going in Galilee;
> Warm-laid grave of a womb-life grey;
>   Manger, maiden's knee;
> The dense and the driven Passion, and frightful sweat.

This love, which 'rides time like riding a river', entails suffering and submission, both ours and Christ's. It should, however, be noted that Hopkins is not here denying valid mystical experience to all those visionaries who lived before the coming of Christ; on the contrary, he states quite definitely:

> Though felt before, though in high flood yet –

From this exalted presentation of the Incarnation, Hopkins moves to a celebration of the Blessed Trinity:

Be adored among men,
God, three-numbered form.

. . . . .

Beyond saying sweet, past telling of tongue,
Thou art lightning and love, I found it, a winter and warm.

Even when speaking of a God who is pure spirit, Hopkins is able to introduce so simple and familiar a metaphor as that of one of the seasons. The proof of the success of such an image is the unquestioning delight with which we accept it. Once again, Hopkins illuminates and gives life to the abstract by presenting it in concrete terms. He may say that God and experience of God are 'past telling of tongue' but this does not prevent him from trying to tell these things and, what is more, from succeeding in doing so.

In all our reading of Hopkins, we should remember his deep sympathy with the thirteenth-century Franciscan philosopher, Duns Scotus. Duns Scotus was an important influence since his theology included the belief that God the Son would have become man even if Adam had not fallen from grace. This unusual attitude towards the Incarnation, not shared, for example, by Aquinas, had a powerful effect on Hopkins's poetry in that it enabled him to see the Incarnation as more than simply the means of man's redemption. For him, such a doctrine glorified the material world and was, perhaps, largely responsible for the lovely, carefree poems of praise such as 'Pied Beauty', 'God's Grandeur', 'The Starlight Night', 'The Windhover', and 'Hurrahing in Harvest'.

'The Wreck of the *Deutschland*' continues with a vigorous description of the voyage and wreck of the ship in which the Franciscan nuns were sailing. It is a powerful evocation of the strength of the elements, the elements which men struggle with and from the very struggle find peace. Hopkins's world is a dynamic world; all is moving, vital, urgent. The poem goes on to give a portrait of the leader of the group of nuns, and this portrait presents Hopkins with an opportunity to examine the meaning of the life of prayer:

> . . . Then further it finds
> The appealing of the Passion is tenderer in prayer apart.

And in the following lines he depicts the struggle to find words which will embody the experience of union with Christ. Here there is no sense of a vision recaptured in memory, but rather an attempt to portray it at its very moment of accomplishment and consummation:

> But how shall I . . . make me room there:
> Reach me a . . . Fancy, come faster –
> Strike you the sight of it? look at it loom there,
> Thing that she . . . there then! the Master,
> *Ipse*, the only one, Christ, King, Head.

After this, God is shown not simply as 'master of the tides' and 'of the year's fall' but also as 'ground of being and granite of it', immanent and transcendent, 'Past all,' says Hopkins, we can 'grasp God, throned behind Death.'

The God of 'The Wreck of the *Deutschland*' is a being who can be refused, wrestled with or surrendered to. There is nothing passive about man's approach to Him. He is terrible but also merciful and to be found, not simply through our sorrow for sin, but also through our insatiable desire for beauty:

> With a mercy that outrides
> The all of water, an ark
> For the listener; for the lingerer with a love glides
> Lower than death and the dark;
> A vein for the visiting of the past-prayer, pent in prison,
> The last-breath penitent spirits – the uttermost mark
> Our passion-plungèd giant risen,
> The Christ of the Father compassionate, fetched in the storm
> of his strides.

This is the Christ of Palm Sunday and of the Resurrection, not the gentle, effeminate creature, the travesty of divinity, which so many modern 'religious' statues and pictures portray. He is a person whom the poet knows through the confrontation of personalities.

In a sermon which he preached in November 1879, Hopkins
gave a detailed and impassioned portrait of Jesus Christ. After
speaking of Him as a warrior and a hero, he refers to His genius:
'I come to his mind. He was the greatest genius that ever lived.
You know what genius is, brethren – beauty and perfection in
the mind.' This idea is crucial to an examination of the relationship between art and religion, between poetry and mystical
experience. In Hopkins's view, human genius implied a likeness
to God similar to that of human sanctity. For him it *was* an
aspect of sanctity. . . .

This sermon shows clearly that Hopkins believed Christ to
be a supreme example of natural, *human* genius. The poet's
whole being was directed, with a kind of innocent passion, towards Jesus Christ, God and man. Such a devotion is a characteristic of the Jesuit priest, but in Hopkins it was a poetic as well
as a spiritual fervour. 'The Windhover', for example, is expressly dedicated 'To Christ our Lord', and in it Hopkins
likens Christ to a great soaring, plunging bird – 'kingdom of
daylight's dauphin, dapple-dawn-drawn Falcon' – and the
whole poem is full of movement and energy. Yet, within this
energy, the poet can make contact with God, can over again
'feel Thy finger and find Thee'. The image of Christ as a falcon
is the very source of the poet's ecstasy:

> . . . My heart in hiding
> Stirred for a bird, – the achieve of, the mastery of the
>   thing!

The bold play with language here, the use of 'achieve' as a
noun, the audacity which can conjure power even from a vague
word like 'thing' – all this is evidence of a blend in Hopkins of
artistic and ascetic discipline. He provides us, in fact, in his own
life with a perfect example of the similarities between spiritual
'ascesis' and poetic craftsmanship. For the poet's training cor-
responds in many ways with the training of the priest – the self-
mastery, the ability to discard what is inessential, the patient
waiting during the times when poems cannot be written, the terrible 'dark night of the senses' in which everything seems plunged
in meaninglessness and obscurity. In the life and character

of Hopkins we see the two disciplines interconnected. His achievement is to have endured and mastered both the priest's and the poet's sufferings, so that the two ways of life did not conflict with one another but complemented one another. It is a shallow judgement which blames Hopkins's priestly vocation for the unhappiness of much of his life. The tension in his poetry is caused by something much more profound than a conflict between passion and celibacy or between profane and sacred love. For the truth is that there is tension at the heart of all great poetry, but this tension is the source of life not of impotence or death. The poems which satisfy most are not those which simply give a sense of reconciliation and order, but those which show life and order as the fruits of conflict; and we need to *feel* this tension even in the most triumphant and reconciled poems. Poetry is not rationalization but revelation and what is healing in it, both for the poet and his readers, is the ability to depict conflict at its most vulnerable point; with Hopkins, this point is the wrestling of man with God – but also the surrender of man to God.

In the poem called 'Henry Purcell', Hopkins gives an account of the ecstasy which Purcell's music opened to him, an ecstasy in no essential way different in kind from Hopkins's experience of God at Mass or in his own prayers. The aesthetic experience of listening to Purcell's music is seen as a direct approach to knowledge of God. In his epigraph to the poem Hopkins explains clearly just why this particular music was so important to him: '. . . whereas other musicians have given utterance to the moods of man's mind, he has, beyond that, uttered in notes the very make and species of man as created both in him and in all men generally'. We are back once again with the theme of incarnation and also with the long-held belief of all Western Christian mystics that Christ, God made man, is at the heart of mystical experience. Purcell's music is for Hopkins, then, a window through which 'the very make and species of man' shine. Christian doctrine has always insisted on man's likeness to God so we are quite justified in interpreting Hopkins's epigraph as the belief that music too can contain and reflect the being of God. We are reminded also of the wonderful carving on one of the outer walls of Chartres which depicts God possessing the idea of man in his mind even before he created men.

In 'Henry Purcell', Hopkins declares that it is 'the forgèd feature' that delights him and he clearly means that, through Purcell's music, he can encounter the essence and soul of Purcell himself:

> Not mood in him nor meaning, proud fire or sacred fear,
> Or love or pity or all that sweet notes not his might nursle:
> It is the forgèd feature finds me; it is the rehearsal
> Of own, of abrupt self there so thrusts on, so throngs the ear.

It is in such words as these that Hopkins demonstrates his really original contribution to English poetry, and it is a contribution not so much of prosody or versification as of *subject-matter*. No other poet, religious or secular, has ever before used poetry as a means whereby men may encounter one another's inmost beings unprotected by masks or veils. In Shakespeare, Milton, Donne and Herbert, poetry often reaches a point where such encounters seem possible or even achieved (one thinks particularly of Leontes' discovery that his wife, Hermione, is alive at the close of *The Winter's Tale*); but what seems to me entirely new in Hopkins is the expression *within* his poems, not only of the possible meetings of personalities at a very deep level, but also of the emotions and ideas which accompany such meetings. Hopkins presents a kind of existentialism in action, so that what might have been simply a metaphysical abstraction is a warm, human experience. And in his descriptions of his own relationship with God, he writes with the same ardent, vigorous language.

It is surely significant that a number of Hopkins's poems are about particular people – the bugler, the soldier, Harry Ploughman, Purcell, Felix Randal. He was consumed by the true Christian charity which sees God in all things and all things in God. In the poem, 'Brothers', he gives a moving account of how affected he himself was by the love which a schoolboy showed towards his brother. The subject of the poem is the vicarious anxiety which the boy Henry suffers as he watches his brother John act in a play. John was 'brass-bold' and Henry need not have feared for him. That he did feel for and indeed wholly identify himself with his brother is what moves Hopkins almost to tears:

> Ah Nature, framed in fault,
> There's comfort then, there's salt;
> Nature, bad, base, and blind,
> Dearly thou canst be kind;
> There dearly then, dearly
> I'll cry thou canst be kind.

It is the grace of such a *natural* expression of love that moves Hopkins so deeply. There is nothing sentimental about the poem; Nature is seen as 'base' and 'bad'. What is remarkable, Hopkins is saying, is that out of baseness and evil such sweetness and selflessness can spring. 'Brothers' is, in fact, a very fine expression of Hopkins's attitude to nature and to all things in the natural world.

The same graciousness of natural love is celebrated in 'At the Wedding March'; this poem reminds us of the imagery of secular love which John of the Cross incorporated into his *Spiritual Canticle*. Hopkins writes:

> Each be other's comfort kind:
> Deep, deeper than divined,
> Divine charity, dear charity,
> Fast you ever, fast bind.

God is love and so *all* manifestations of love are reflexions and adumbrations of that love. In 'The Caged Skylark' Hopkins makes a triumphant affirmation of his belief that it is as *whole* men, body and soul with the soul 'the form of the body', that we can be most at one with Christ:

> Man's spirit will be fleshbound when found at best,
> But uncumbered; meadow-down is not distressed
> For a rainbow footing it, nor he for his bones risen.

This joyful vision of the created world, in which all things are seen to be good when they keep their appointed places in a universal hierarchy, is a vision which pervades all Hopkins's poems, even the darkest, most tormented ones. Like Eliot and like Edwin Muir, he sees man as an august creature who is free to choose good or evil. If he chooses evil, he is reponsible not only for imperilling his own soul but also for introducing a little more disorder into the whole universe – 'No man is an island . . . each is a part of the main.' Hopkins's own union with God is a union with absolute beauty, a union which he desires all men to share, but to share by freely choosing it:

. . . . deliver it, early now, long before death.
Give beauty back, beauty, beauty, beauty, back to God,
    beauty's self and beauty's giver.

SOURCE: *The Dublin Review*, vol. 234, no. 484 (1960);
    reprinted in *Every Changing Shape* (London, 1961).

NOTE

1. Cited from 'Religion and the Muses', an essay by David Jones in *Epoch and Artist: Selected Writings* (London, 1959); first published in *The Tablet* (November 1941). 'Epigraph' rather than 'epitaph', perhaps? [Editor's Note]

Donald McChesney

THE MEANING OF 'INSCAPE' (1968)

'All the world is full of inscape,' wrote Gerard Manley Hopkins in his journal at the age of 29, 'and chance left free to act falls into an order.'[1]

In a letter to Bridges, he explained that by the word Inscape he meant design or pattern, adding that 'design, pattern, or what I am in the habit of calling Inscape is what I above all aim at in poetry'.[2]

The first of the above statements – that the world is full of inscape – is about the world of nature as received by the mind. The second – about inscape being the chief aim of his poetry – is about language. It is doubtful if any universally true and final statements can be made about the relationship between human experience and human language, but one can trace the relationship in the case of individual poets. Inscape is a notion central to Hopkins' thinking and a key-idea when one is trying to figure out what his poetic aims were, and what he was trying to do with language. The basic question is therefore: what relationship is there between the inscapes Hopkins *saw* in nature and the inscapes he *created* in language?

INSCAPE IN NATURE

Hopkins' most significant experiences of inscape in nature seem to have occurred during the ascetic years of his Jesuit training, notably the years 1874–77 when he enjoyed the rural peace and contemplation of his studies at St. Beuno's in North Wales, and where he encountered the writings of Duns Scotus. It was as if asceticism sharpened his senses and drew aside an obscuring screen, revealing a world ablaze with energy, pattern and colour, each individual thing inexpressible in its unique selfhood, and all things falling into marvellous order.

The images he used to express these things are familiar: a world charged with the grandeur of God ('God's Grandeur'); the billion times told lovelier more dangerous fire of revelation born of the encounter with the falcon ('The Windhover'); the sense of enormous energies let loose in poems like 'Hurrahing in Harvest' and the 'Heraclitean Fire'; the glory given to God for the variety and 'dapple' of the world ('Pied Beauty'), where kingfishers catch fire, dragonflies draw flame, and each thing, just by being itself, seems to sing itself forth from the inner depths of its own identity ('As Kingfishers Catch Fire').

Hopkins, like many mystics, ascetics and visionaries, was given intermittent access to this world so described; a world in which forms shine by their own light, where colours glow from within and where all things fall into inexpressibly significant pattern. More recently – and be it noted only under specially controlled circumstances – access has been gained through drugs, notably LSD. Alan Watts, an authority on Zen Buddhism, was asked by a psychiatric research group to take 100 micrograms of this drug to see 'if it would reproduce anything resembling a mystical experience'. Watts was regarded as a suitable subject because he has a high degree of insight into his own states of mind, and can write about them with an almost preternatural clarity of prose style.

He took the drug, but did *not* have a mystical experience. What he did experience, and place on record, was a world seen as Hopkins must have sometimes seen it:

It seemed instead that my senses had been given a kaleidoscopic character . . . which made the world entrancingly complicated as if I were involved in a multidimensional arabesque. Colors became so vivid that flowers leaves and fabrics seemed to be illumined from inside. The random patterns of blades in a lawn seemed to be exquisitely organised without, however, any distortion of vision . . . What are ordinarily dismissed as irrelevant details of speech behaviour and form seemed to be in some indefinable way to be highly significant. Listening to music with closed eyes, I beheld the

most fascinating patterns of dancing jewellery, mosaic, tracery and
abstract images. . . . Ordinary remarks seemed to reverberate with
double and quadruple meanings. . . .[3]

The phrases used by Watts, unpack with uncanny accuracy
what Hopkins lumped together into the notion of inscape, and
what he strove to record in his poems and journals: a sharp
awareness of the kaleidoscopic character of sense impressions,
a flat world suddenly changed into a multidimensional arabesque, things glowing from inside themselves and random
patterns of things appearing as exquisitely organised. Watts'
imagery of dancing jewellery, mosaic and tracery is also highly
redolent of Hopkins – 'The Starlight Night', e.g. for dancing
jewellery, and poems like 'The Leaden Echo and the Golden
Echo' for dreamlike mosaic and tracery. Watts' last comment
on ordinary remarks *seeming* to reverberate with double and
quadruple meanings is especially interesting. It is just the kind
of language that Hopkins produced – language which seems,
and very often does, reverberate with additional meanings.

Hopkins saw nature thus from time to time, and when vision
failed to be granted him, he strove to attain it by conscious
effort. This is true at least of his earlier days, before his life was
blighted almost permanently by deep depression. 'Unless you
refresh the mind from time to time,' he wrote to Dixon, 'you
cannot always remember or believe how deep the inscape in
things is.' Refreshing his mind, to him, often meant intense and
solitary contemplation of a scene to make it yield its inscape. In
his journal, there is an interesting passage where he records a
close description of waves breaking on the shore, and an admis-
sion that he has failed to perceive the underlying inscape:
'About all the turns of the scaping from the *break and flood of the
wave* to its run out again I have not yet satisfied myself. The
shores are swimming and the eyes have before them a region of
milky surf but it is hard for them to *unpack the huddling and gnarls*
of the water and *law out the shapes* and sequence'[4] (Italics mine.)

The underlying faith is that the shapes and sequence *have* a
design or pattern if his vision were but clear enough – 'all the
world is full of inscape and chance falls into an order'. Inciden-
tally, apart from the characteristic eccentricity of 'huddling and

gnarls of the water' which is the linguistic equivalent of some of Hopkins' etchings of running water, the phrase 'break and flood of the wave' reappears as the 'buck and flood of the wave' in 'The Wreck of the *Deutschland*'. So often, Hopkins rough-hewed out the language for his experiences in his journal, and wrestled it gradually into shape in a poem, sometimes over a long period, a habit of his muse to which he referred in a poem to Bridges:

> Nine months she then, nay years, nine years she long
> Within he wears, bears, cares and combs the same.
>
> ('To R.B., 1889')

He was always delighted when he penetrated through to the true inscape of a scene, which thenceforth would be transformed for him. He recorded one such occasion in his journal, referring to a sunset. There is the usual painstaking, preliminary description which makes hard reading because of the minute, effortful accuracy of description: 'A fine sunset: the higher sky dead clear blue, bridged by a broad slant causeway rising from the right to the left of wisped or grass cloud, the wisps lying across; the sundown yellow moist with light but ending at the top in a foam of delicate white pearling and spotted with big tufts of cloud in colour russet between brown and purple but edged with brassy light.'[5]

He goes on to say however, that he has at last found the true inscape of the scene. Previously when looking at the sunset, he had covered the sun itself, blotting it out with his hand to avoid the dazzle. 'Today,' he wrote, 'I inscaped them together and made the sun the true eye and ace of the whole, as it is.' The result is a revelation, and the language leaps into a kind of visionary eccentricity as he tries to record the effect – one is reminded very strongly of Van Gogh: 'It [i.e. the sun] was all active and tossing out light and started as strongly forward from the field as a long stone or a boss in the knop of a chalice stem. It is indeed by stalling it so that it falls into scape with the sky.'

Inscape in nature then, to Hopkins, was sometimes a matter of visionary and ecstatic experience, and sometimes a matter of workaday effort. Either way, it was for him connected with God's presence in the world, revealed in energy, beauty and hidden pattern. It remains to be seen how he coped with these matters in the language of his poems.

INSCAPE IN LANGUAGE

The transition from the inscapes Hopkins *saw* in nature to the inscapes he *created* in language bring us to the usual gulf between two things: the ultimately inexpressible 'thisness' of experience and series of noises or marks-on-paper in which the 'thisness' is expressed, evoked and vicariously recreated in the symbolic meadium of language.

We have already noticed Hopkins' conscious wrestling with words to 'in-stall' a scene in his prose journals. The word is his own and seems to denote a kind of linguistic pickling process to preserve the flavour of the experience for future reference. This wrestling is raised to the nth pitch of intensity in his poetry where he is trying to inscape his sound-patterns as well as his logical meaning. In his poetry, he is not merely trying to reproduce in language his particular 'inscaped' vision of nature; he is *also* trying to produce inscapes or patterns of speech-sound which can be contemplated for their own sakes. To use an analogy, it is as if a craftsman in wood, not content with carving an object, also endeavoured to bring out and even to create the arabesques and patterns inherent in the very grain of the wood.

The following passage, for instance, basically describes the restless energies of cloud and sunlight on a windy day. The clouds swirl down the heavens, their shadows race across the sides of buildings, and the glancing sunlight flashes in shafts through the foliage of elm trees:

> Cloud-puffball, torn tufts, tossed pillows flaunt forth, then
>   chevy on an air –
> Built thoroughfare: heaven-roysterers, in gay-gangs they
>   throng; they glitter in marches.
> Down roughcast, down dazzling whitewash, wherever an
>   elm arches,
> Shivelights and shadowtackle in long lashes, lace lance and
>   pair.

The passage is, of course, from the 'Heraclitean Fire' sonnet. Its raison d'être however, does not lie in its descriptive merits, although it adequately describes and even enacts the 'million-fueled bonfire' of nature. Over and above its merits as communication, it is also an intricately patterned piece of language; language raised to an ecstatic pitch, the same kind of ecstasy as one might find on an intricately convoluted piece of carving. It is there for its own sake – or perhaps for the sheer glory of God. Some critics, especially earlier ones, have strained at a gnat to over-praise Hopkins for descriptive power or onomatopoeic skill. True he possesses both, but his use of language goes far beyond such mere utilitarian functions, and his poetic purposes stretch beyond these into the realm of pure 'play', pure pattern, pure energy of spirit.

To Hopkins, it is what he called the *shape* that matters – the pattern or inscape imposed by the artist on the raw material of his medium – paint, stone, wood or words. The correspondence of this 'shape' to anything outside itself is of secondary, even minimal, importance. 'Inscape is the soul of art', he said, and art to him had nothing to do with the reproduction of surface reality. He criticised a picture by Holman Hunt remarking 'It has no inscape of composition whatsoever.' He meant that Hunt, instead of shaping his colours and perspectives in obedience to inner vision, had simply produced a copy of external features. 'Inscape', continued Hopkins, 'could scarcely bear up against such realism' – a remark which anticipates the tenets not merely of the Impressionists, but of contemporary developments in art and sculpture.

However, there is a problem here. It is all very well to make shapes in wood, stone or paint, which exist for their own sakes and which do not correspond to, or copy, anything external to themselves. But language is a somewhat different medium, since it is basically a system of logical communication – an agreed system of noises or marks-on-paper by which we say things to people. Surely it is not just enough to make inscapes of speech-sound, however pleasingly intricate they may be, if they do not also make some sort of logical sense.

Hopkins' answer is that poetry, to him, lies somewhere be-

tween prose and music, but that it constantly aspires towards
the condition of music. Prose says things; it makes logical statements. Music also 'says' things, but not under a logical mode;
it is pure pattern of sound, and is contemplated by the mind as
such. Poetry lies in between, but, for Hopkins, constantly tends
towards the musical end. In his journal, he once defined poetry
as 'speech framed to be heard for its own sake and interest even
over and above the interest of meaning'.[6]

He did *not* exclude logical verbal meaning. He merely said
that it was secondary to the shape. The shape, in a poem, is the
total sound pattern as received by the listening ear and contemplated by the listening mind. 'Some matter or meaning is
essential to it,' he said, 'but only as an element necessary to
support and employ the shape, which is contemplated for its
own sake.' This remark is perhaps a key to the whole understanding of his poetry. All Hopkins' poems, even the most
verbally convoluted, have a core of logical meaning which can
be paraphrased. But more than most, Hopkins' poetry is totally
irreducible; you no more have the meaning of his poem when
you paraphrase it than you have the building when you strip it
to its girders. Syntactical 'maps' of his logical meaning are
useful for the newcomer to Hopkins, but only that he might
more quickly pass on to contemplate the shape of the poem –
i.e. the inscape or pattern of speech-sound.

Hopkins never deliberately cultivated obscurity. He merely
said on one occasion that one could not do all that he wanted to
do and *also* be immediately crystal clear. Nor did he deliberately cultivate mannerism or eccentricity, though he is guilty of
both at times – e.g. in some parts of 'The Loss of the *Eurydice*'.[7]
one feels very strongly that Hopkins himself, as well as his hero,
has lost his bearings, and in some of the rhymes in 'The
Bugler's First Communion'. He wrote to Bridges admitting
that his poetry was a bit queer at times, but that this was perhaps inescapable: 'Now it is the virtue of design, pattern or
inscape to be distinctive and it is the device of distinctiveness to
become queer. This vice I cannot have escaped.'[8] Add to this
his lifelong and unrequited need for an audience and much can
be forgiven him in this regard.

THE TECHNIQUES BY WHICH LANGUAGE IS INSCAPED

Given this intense desire to inscape his language into 'shapes', Hopkins ransacked all sources for devices of rhythm and sound. His lecture notes on rhetoric allude to Old English alliterative verse, Norse and Icelandic poetry, and classical metres notably the lyrical odes of Pindar and the chorus rhythms of the great plays.

What brought his technique to a fine degree of complexity was the Welsh art of *cynghanedd* (pronounced 'kung-hanneth'), which he studied and mastered in his years at St. Beuno's College, prior to his ordination in 1877. These are the years of such poems as 'The Wreck of the *Deutschland*', 'God's Grandeur', 'The Starlight Night', 'Pied Beauty', 'Hurrahing in Harvest' and 'The Caged Skylark'.

Cynghanedd is a Welsh bardic tradition of great antiquity, consisting of a highly sophisticated series of techniques for making intricate and beautiful patterns of speech-sound – i.e. for 'inscaping' speech-sound. All the devices are listed and codified, just as figures of rhetoric were once tabulated in 17th century English grammar books. Hopkins must have been delighted to find this ready-made art, systematising many patterns of alliteration and vowel sound. To some extent native Welsh poets seem to use *cynghanedd* naturally, even unconsciously. Dylan Thomas, for instance, does not use alliteration very markedly, but one can hear the rhyme and chime of the vowels in such lines as these from 'After the Funeral':

> After the funeral, mule praises, brays,
> Windshake of sailshaped ears, muffletoed tap
> Tap happily of one peg in the thick
> Grave's foot . . .

Hopkins imported these Welsh techniques into English and took them to a high pitch of conscious artistry; it was never, with him, a case of warbling native wood notes wild. Very roughly one can analyse his art under the headings of Vowelling and Alliteration.

VOWELLING

Hopkins frequently uses vowels for everyday onomatopoeic effects. There is the dreariness of 'seared with trade; bleared smeared with toil;/And wears man's smudge and shares man's smell', ('God's Grandeur'), or the lovely ding-donging of vowels in such lines as:

> like each tucked string tells, each hung bell's
> Bow swung finds tongue to fling out broad its name;
> Each mortal thing does one thing and the same.
>
> ('As kingfishers catch fire')

But Hopkins makes patterns of vowel sounds mainly for the joy of it. Patterns of internal rhyme for instance: 'Nothing is so beautiful as spring, When weeds, in wheels, shoot long and lovely and lush.' ('Spring')

He called this internal rhyming 'vowelling-on', and used it constantly. Some of his shapes of sound achieved by this device have an exquisite interwoven intricacy that must have cost him hours of work. This, for instance from 'The Wreck of the *Deutschland*', stanza 26. He is speaking of the sky, blue by day, glowing at sundown and radiant at night, symbolic of the glory of heaven.

> Blue-beating and hoary-glow height; or night still higher,
> With belled fire and the moth-soft Milky Way,
> What by your measure is the heaven of desire,
> The treasure never eyesight got, nor was ever guessed what
>   for the hearing?

Woven into these four lines are three sets of rhyming vowel sounds – height, night, higher, fire, desire,/moth, soft, got, was what,/measure, treasure. The total effect is a rich vocalic chiming, a lovely 'shape' of sound.

The opposite function to vowelling-on, is another aspect of the art of *cynghanedd* which Hopkins called vowelling-off. This consists of making a shape of sound not by assonance or internal rhyme as with vowelling on, but by employing contrasting vowel sounds or even running up or down a scale of vowels. Sometimes Hopkins used vowelling off for onomatopoeic effects. A line such as 'Left hand, off land, I hear the lark ascend', from 'The Sea and the Skylark', is to some extent onomatopoeic. The vowels, like the lark, seem to rise off the ground and go upwards. The final lines of 'The Windhover' about the blue-bleak embers that 'fall, gall themselves and gash, gold-vermilion', are about the glory that breaks forth from sacrifice; Christ's bloody and royal ('gold-vermilion') sacrifice or else the life-long self-abnegation ('blue-bleak embers') of those who follow him. But apart altogether from the rich associations of the words, the run of vowel sounds seem to *enact* a violent opening-out, a spilling-forth of hidden energy and beauty from a body of death.

Once again, however, Hopkins frequently uses vowelling off in the spirit of pure play, pure shape of contrasting sounds. The city of Oxford is described as 'Cuckoo-echoing, bell-swarmèd, lark-charmèd, rook-racked, river-rounded' ('Duns Scotus's Oxford') which, apart from making clear sense, is also pure exuberance of vowel play. Sometimes Hopkins contrived almost chromatic runs of vowels, using sharps and flats, so to speak. The sonnet 'Spelt from Sibyl's Leaves', for instance, is about the vivid colours and day merging, as the light fails, into grey confusion, and finally appearing as simple black silhouettes. To Hopkins it is a parable of the Day of Judgment, when all the 'skeined stained veined variety' of human conduct will be thrust into the simple and fearful polarities of right or wrong, white or black, heaven or hell. The vowel sounds in the poem, especially at the beginning, are chromatic: they are neither directly harmonious nor directly dissonant, but seem to proceed in half tones and quarter tones:

> Earnest, earthless, equal, attuneable, vaulty, voluminous . . .
> stupendous
> Evening strains to be time's vast, womb-of-all, home-of-all,
> hearse-of-all night.
> Her fond yellow hornlight wound to the west, her wild
> hollow hoarlight hung to the height
> Waste . . .

Hopkins once announced his intention of writing some music to

his poems, using half and quarter tones, and he certainly
manages to do it with his vowel sounds here. It does occur, in
passing, that the slightly disharmonious, atonal, chromatic
quality of the vowel runs here, may be profoundly onomatopoeic, in the sense of helping to convey the merging of daylight
colours into grey and finally into black. Nevertheless, Hopkins'
main thesis was that the sound-pattern or shape is there to be
contemplated for its own sake by the mind, over and above the
interest of meaning. This for instance:

> The blue wheat-acre is underneath
> And the braided ear breaks out of the sheath,
> The ear in milk, lush the sash,
> And crush-silk poppies aflash,
> The blood-gush blade-gash
> Flame-flash rudred
> Bud shelling or broadshed
> Tatter-tassel-tangled and dingle-a-dangled
> Dandy-hung dainty head.
>
> ('The Woodlark')

ALLITERATION

Apart from the art of vowelling, the Welsh tradition of *cynghanedd* also included a codified system of alliteration. It has
sometimes been suggested that Hopkins drew his alliterative
patterns from Old English verse. This is partly true, because he
loved Anglo-Saxon and Middle English, and in his lecture notes
on rhetoric he copied out a lovely alliterative lyric from the
Norse. But English alliterative verse of this period was really a
bit naive and club-footed:

> Wo-weary and wetshod went I forth after
> As a reckless renk that recketh not of sorrow
> And yede forth like a lorel all my life time
> Till I wex weary of this world and wilned eft to sleep.
>
> (*Piers Plowman*, Passus XXI)

When one compares this even with a simple Hopkins line: 'I
awoke in the Midsummer not to call night, in the white and the

walk of the morning' ('Moonrise'), one can see a world of difference. It is not merely that he shaped his vowels as well as alliterating his consonants. The alliteration itself is far more sophisticated than Old or Middle English which was content mainly with three alliterations per line. An example of the complexity of Hopkins', alliteration may be seen in a line from 'The Wreck of the *Deutschland*', which he wrote in the full flush of his enthusiasm for *cynghanedd*. He is writing of the nuns aboard the sinking ship, about to meet Christ in beauty and terror. He describes them as,

> sisterly sealed in wild waters
> To bathe in his fall-gold mercies, to breathe in his all-fire
> glances.

On analysis, as W. H. Gardner points out, the alliterative pattern of the first half of the line is almost exactly reproduced in the latter half. This is indeed a tour de force of alliterative technique, and Hopkins never again went to such lengths, realising doubtless that it is the *mixture* of vowel and consonant patterns that makes for inscape of language. It does show, however, the extreme care that he took in the 'lettering' (his term) of the syllables – the implied analogy is of a poet compared to a carver in wood or stone, taking infinite care with the shaping of the letters, one by one, of an inscription.

SPRUNG RHYTHM

The importance of the art of *cynghanedd* in assisting Hopkins to inscape his language has been discussed. Sprung Rhythm should be mentioned, but only to make clear that it is *not* a device for inscaping language, but a device for giving the poet freedom from the normal prosodic requirements of fixed quantity of syllables. Since the matter therefore is not particularly relevant here, the points one would make in passing are (a) that Sprung Rhythm gives flexibility and enables an approximation to normal speech to be made, (b) that it is not a systematic discipline, as Hopkins finally admitted, for although the line is 'sprung' upon a predetermined number of stresses, the poet can add extra stresses and call them outriders, (c) that a fairly clear idea of Sprung Rhythm can be found in nursery rhymes, or better still in the Gelineau Psalms, and (d) that prosodic freedom was not a new thing: Shakespeare, Donne and Milton had worked with astonishing freedom *within* traditional prosodic patterns. All Hopkins did in some (not all) of his poems was openly and 'professedly' to jettison these patterns. Quite frequently, however, he used traditional metres.

WHY INSCAPE?

Finally one might ask: why this enormous care for pattern, with the accompanying sense of strenuous and minute technical effort to inscape the language?

The reason Hopkins gave is that he thought English poetry sadly deficient in technique – abundant in inspiration but lackng in the elements of ordinary, teachable rhetoric:

The strictly poetical insight and inspiration of our poetry seems to me to be the very finest, finer perhaps than the Greek; but its rhetoric is inadequate – seldom first rate, mostly only sufficient, sometimes even below par. By rhetoric I mean all the common and teachable element in literature, what grammar is to speech, what throughbass is to music, what theatrical experience gives to playwrights.[9]

One would, of course, take leave to doubt the truth of this. The 18th century was perhaps over-smooth, the 19th century frequently turgid, but when one thinks of the 17th century with Shakespeare, Donne, Milton and company, one can hardly point to a deficiency in rhetoric. Nevertheless, this is the reason Hopkins gave for his lifelong concern.

The reason *we* give, in this psychological age, for Hopkins' concern with inscape in language is that we see a deep connection between his highly individual linguistic usage and the tensions and exhaustions of his highly charged personality. His technique, to quote Leavis, 'is much concerned with inner division, friction and psychological complexity in general'.[10] John Wain has written an article on Hopkins' language under the title 'An Idiom of Desperation',[11] and Thomas Merton has remarked that Hopkins' spiritual struggles fought their way out in problems of rhythm. He made his asceticism bearable by thrusting it over into the order of art where he could handle it more objectively.[12]

This is all true. The obverse side of Hopkins' ecstatic insights was a history of inner chaos, dereliction and depression, as he said himself approaching madness, though his judgment was never affected. Problems of order, control and balance pressed upon him almost unbearably in life and no wonder he thrust them over into the order of art into problems of inscape. A nervous vibrancy of language – alliterated and assonanced – was natural to him, as one can see from some of his journal passages. But he could not trust 'nature' either in life or art. A strong plainness of diction came only late in life when the Sonnets of Despair were 'wrung from him almost unbidden', under unbearable pressure of inner pain. But hidden under the apparent plainness, all the careful art and 'lettering' is still there – the alliteration and vowel play, to which are now added powerful elements of compression and inversion:

> I cast for comfort I can no more get
> By groping round my comfortless, than blind
> Eyes in their dark can day or thirst can find
> Thirst's all-in-all in all a world of wet.
> > ('My own heart let me more have pity on')

> Only what word
> Wisest my heart breeds dark heaven's baffling ban
> Bars or hell's spell thwarts. This to hoard unheard,
> Heard unheeded, leaves me a lonely began.
> > ('To seem the stranger')

This is the austere bone and sheer sinew of language, 'the chronicles of the Lord's suffering servant parched and bare', stripped of all inessentials. Yet the 'art' is still there, only now taken to a pitch of transcendence when it conceals itself.

It is perhaps providential that Hopkins did not find full publication till the 20th century. The 19th century did not understand him: Robert Bridges, who published his poems with loving care, was blind to some of Hopkins' main poetic concerns: Dixon, a lifelong friend, praised him highly, but more out of love than comprehension; and Coventry Patmore who was impressed, barely this side idolatry, by Hopkins' personality was baffled by his poetry. It is only perhaps because the 20th century understands more of the states of mind to which Hopkins (like Kierkegaard and Van Gogh) was exposed, that it is beginning to see the organic connection between these states and the tense taut language in which they found expression. Although Hopkins was in many respects a strict and convention-al Victorian he was, in the existential depths of his nature, ahead of his time, and he opened up these new dimensions of linguistic usage because he was driven to it by inner pressures.

SOURCE: *The Month*, new series, vol. 40 (July/August 1968)

NOTES

1. H. House and G. Storey (eds), *Journals and Papers* (Oxford, 1959) p. 230.
2. C. C. Abbott (ed.), *Letters to Bridges*, rev. ed. (Oxford, 1956) p. 66.
3. Alan Watts, *This is It* (London, 1961) pp. 131–2.
4. *Journals and Papers*, p. 164.
5. Ibid. p. 196.
6. Ibid. p. 289.
7. Oddities in the Eurydice poem include rhyming 'England' with 'mingle and', also 'portholes' with the 'messes of mortals' sliding over the heaving decks. Some passages, in comic banality, outstrip Wordsworth's best efforts in the *Lyrical Ballads* and approach the heights reached by that great owl of poesy, William MacGonegall. For instance, in Hopkins's poem, a survivor, Sydney Fletcher, swims around 'Till a lifebelt and God's will / Lend him a life from the sea swill'. Sydney is then picked up: 'Him after an hour of wintry waves / A schooner sights with another, and saves / And he boards her in, Oh, such joy / He has lost count what came next poor boy'.
8. *Journals and Papers*, p. 66.
9. C. C. Abbott (ed.), *Correspondence of G. M. Hopkins and R. W. Dixon*, rev. ed. (Oxford, 1955) p. 141.

10. F. R. Leavis, 'Essay on Hopkins', in *New Bearings in English Poetry* (London, 1950).

11. G. H. Hartman (ed.), *Hopkins: A Collection of Critical Essays* (New York, 1960).

12. T. Merton, *The Sign of Jonas* (London, 1953) p. 79.

Patricia A. Wolfe

HOPKINS'S SPIRITUAL CONFLICT IN THE 'TERRIBLE' SONNETS (1968)

[Editor's note: The original article begins by suggesting that the correct approach to understanding the 'Gethsemane of the mind' expressed in the 'terrible' sonnets is by a discussion of the paradoxical ideas that Hopkins entertained; 'for the contradictions arising from Hopkins's fundamental belief in natural individuality and in its duty to submit to the greater individuality of God provides a basis for interpreting his spiritual agony'. The critic then examines some of the theological (especially the Scotist) tenets held by Hopkins.]

The central conflict of the 'terrible' sonnets is a clash between impulses within the poet. He is caught between his desire to reach spiritual fulfilment and his reluctance to surrender human identity. Used to approaching the universal by way of the individual, the Scotist-oriented Hopkins often becomes dangerously enamored of earthly inscapes and forgets that these are only fragments of the supernatural inscape of God.[1] He must keep reminding himself that loss of one inscape means the attainment of another. 'It is not', the poet writes in his journal, 'that inscape does not govern the behaviour of things in slack and decay . . . but that horror prepossesses the mind.' In the 'terrible' sonnets, the poet tries to overcome this horror and to accept the supernatural destiny for which he has been created. Intensely sensitive, Hopkins understands the enormity of his problem. During a retreat in 1883, he writes: 'I have much and earnestly prayed that God will lift me above myself to a higher state of grace, in which I may have more union with him. . . . In meditating on the Crucifixion I saw how my asking to be raised to a higher degree of grace was asking also to be lifted on a higher cross.'[2] His prayer was answered; toward the end of his life, he was, in many ways, lifted on a higher cross.

Perhaps it was the loss of physical vitality which caused the depression and inner conflict of Hopkins' last years; perhaps the basis was primarily psychological.[3] At any rate, out of the gloom of those final years, the poet created six intensely introspective sonnets, outcries of a man to his tortured consciousness. Representing successive stages in the poet's spiritual crisis, the 'terrible' sonnets describe Hopkins' gradual recognition of the paradox of self. By degrees, he learns that a finite being must become infinitesimal before it can partake of the infinite. In the words of David A. Downes, therefore, 'It is not surprising . . . that Hopkins with his scrupulous turn of mind . . . gave expression to his feeling of terrible nothingness of self and the overwhelming all of God.'[4]

Hopkins once referred to himself as 'me, the culprit, the lost sheep, the redeemed' (*D.W.*, p. 187). In a very real sense, these appellations characterize the changing nature of his relationship to God as it is described in the 'terrible' sonnets. The poet is at first 'the culprit', fighting a power he refuses to acknowledge and acknowledging too late to avoid culpability the fact that his opponent is God. Having lost touch with the Divine, he sinks into desolation. As 'the lost sheep', he groped for the patch back to the fold; but he must contend with and overcome his own weakness before he can reestablish communication with the Divinity. The inner struggle continues until, with surprising suddenness, 'the lost sheep' becomes 'the redeemed'. The poet has once more established a relationship with his God. From this synopsis, it is apparent that several questions need to be answered before we can fully comprehend the meaning. Why, for instance, is the poet in conflict with his God? What is the nature of that conflict? And finally, how is it so suddenly resolved? By examining the sonnets individually and by putting them into context with relevant passages from Hopkins' other writings, we should be able to clarify their ambiguity.

In 'Carrion Comfort', the first stage of his spiritual crisis,

Hopkins battles with an enemy whose identity is progressively revealed. As the poem opens, however, Hopkins is fighting his own self-pity. Refusing to indulge in despair, the comfort of decaying flesh, the poet chooses to assert himself; but what can he do? He 'Can something, hope, wish day come, not choose not to be'. But, ironically, in not choosing not to be, he is pitting himself against the Almighty. Taking pride in the invincible human spirit, Hopkins is coming dangerously close to denying man's essential dependence on God; for it is not man's place to choose to be: man is made to serve, not to govern. A passage from one of the priest's spiritual exercises may help to clarify this point. In it, Hopkins explains what man *can* and *should* do on this earth. 'But man can know God, *can mean to give him glory*. This then was why he was made, to give God glory and to mean to give it; to praise God freely, willingly to reverence him, gladly to serve him.' (*D.W.*, p. 239.) By contrast, not choosing not to be is an ungodly answer: it is rooted in human pride rather than Christ-like humility; and because the poet suggests this as a possible way of asserting himself, he encounters a divine enemy.

Significantly, God the Son is the combatant described in images of rapacious mastery.[5] He is a 'lion-lamb' with 'devouring eyes' who menacingly scans the poet's 'bruised bones'. To discover why the poet is 'frantic to avoid' and eager to 'flee' Him, one must understand what Christ means to Hopkins. Again and again in his spiritual notebooks, the priest praises Christ's selflessness. In one such passage, he writes:

Consider our Lord's attachment to God's will at all times and this attachment ended in the very nailing of his body to the Cross. Try to attach yourself more to God's will and detach yourself from your own by prayer at beginning things.

The piercing of Christ's side. The sacred body and the sacred heart seemed waiting for an opportunity of discharging themselves and testifying their total devotion of themselves to the cause of man. (*D.W.*, p. 255.)

God the Son, then, is a constant reminder to Hopkins of divine self-sacrifice. Moreover, Christ, the perfect manifestation of God's spirit on earth, serves as a model for human behavior.

Hopkins develops this idea in a letter to his friend, Robert Bridges:

Christ Jesus . . . , finding, as in the first instant of his incarnation he did, his human nature informed by the godhead – he thought it nevertheless no snatching matter for him to be equal with God, but annihilated himself, taking the form of servant; . . . and instead of snatching at once at what all the time was his, or was himself, he emptied or exhausted himself so far as that was possible, of godhead and behaved only as God's slave, as his creature, as man, which also he was, and then being in the guise of man humbled himself to death, the death of the cross. It is this holding of himself back, and not snatching at the truest and highest good, the good that was his right, nay his possession from a past eternity in his other nature, his own being and self, which seems to me the root of all his holiness and the imitation of this the root of all moral good in other men.[6]

If Christ *spontaneously* chooses to ignore His divine claim to infinity in order to share the difficult and self-effacing fate of mankind, how blameworthy is the man who rejects *only reluctantly* his human identity in order to become an infinitesimal part of the infinite! In 'Carrion Comfort', therefore, Hopkins is battling an enemy who compels him to face his own inadequacy; and Christ, perfect in His selflessness, is trying to overpower the poet by force of divine example.

But the question remains: why does Christ want to vanquish the poet? In the sestet, Hopkins recognizes his enemy's truly unselfish motivation. The battle is waged, the poet reasons, so that 'my chaff might fly; my grain lie, sheer and clear'. If one acknowledges Christ as the poet's adversary, it becomes clear that the motive and result of the conflict is the divine gift of grace; for, as Hopkins puts it: 'grace is any action, activity on God's part by which . . . he carries the creature to or towards the end of his being, which is its self-sacrifice to God and its salvation. It is . . . divine stress, holy spirit, and . . . all is done through Christ, Christ's spirit.' (*D.W.*, p. 154.)

Hopkins has sensed the presence of divine stress throughout the conflict; for, paradoxically, 'in all that toil' there have been moments of happiness when he 'lapped strength, stole joy' from his enemy; and he has even felt the need to 'laugh', to 'cheer' someone. 'Cheer whom though?' Should he praise himself for daring to fight an overwhelmingly powerful force, or should he cheer the hero who in subjugating also elevates? The confusion is understandable because to Hopkins the process of giving and receiving grace is 'as if man said: That is Christ playing at me and me playing at Christ, only that it is no play at all but truth; That is Christ *being me* and me being Christ'. (*D.W.*, p. 154.)

Full of awe, the poet perceives the whole truth at the end of the sonnet; his paradoxical reaction to the conflict becomes completely natural when he recognizes, as his readers have suspected all along, that his dreaded adversary is also his beloved master. Exhausted by his ultimate discovery, Hopkins experiences a feeling of profound and appalling guilt when he utters, 'That night, that year/Of now done darkness I wretch lay wrestling with (My God!) my God.' The poet has undergone the first stage in his spiritual crisis. He has received a stress from Christ; 'it is a purifying and a mortifying grace, bringing the victim to the altar and sacrificing it'. (*D.W.*, p. 158.)

Sonnet sixty-five explores fear, but it is not emotional indulgence for its own sake; it describes the poet's need and search for strength. The flashes of power experienced in 'Carrion Comfort' are not enough to sustain his flagging courage; for just as Christ's grace 'did not avail [the Apostles] when he was no longer present to keep bestowing it' (*D.W.*, p. 158), so also it does not avail Hopkins when the hero's presence is no longer felt in the poet's soul. The emotional climate of the sonnet reminds one of the agony which Christ endured before his supreme sacrifice. In effect, the poet is suggesting to his readers, 'My soul is sad, even unto death. Wait here and watch' (Mark 14:34).

The language of the poem is compressed, giving the effect of emotional construction. At the beginning, the poet states cryptically: 'No worst, there is none'. To clarify this comment, one must look at a passage from Hopkins' spiritual notebooks in which he writes: 'All my undertakings miscarry: I am like a straining eunuch. I wish then for death yet if I died now I should die imperfect, no master of myself, and that is the worst failure of all.' (*D.W.*, p. 262.) Incited by divine example, the poet is confronted with an enormous spiritual ordeal. He realizes that he must become master of himself in life, for if he achieves self-lessness merely through death, he has not participated actively and willingly in Christ's sacrifice. He sees that he must pattern himself after his Savior, but wonders if he is strong enough to succeed. To the poet, then, there is no worse ordeal than seeing the right, trying to follow it, and being hindered by human weakness. It is the fear that he will not live up to Christ's example which leads him into a painfully emotional state of mind.

Hopkins laments that he is 'Pitched past pitch of grief'. By using the term 'pitch', he means to imply an exceptional degree of intensity as the following comment from his spiritual exercises suggests: 'I find myself both as man and as myself something most determined and distinctive, at pitch, more distinctive and higher pitched than anything else I see. . . .' (*D.W.*, p. 122.) When the poet states that 'Pitched past pitch of grief,/More pangs will, schooled at forepangs, wilder wring', we understand that he is tuned to a high degree of sensitivity, that he has known pain before, but that he has now been placed on a higher level of suffering than his previously-experienced grief. Christ's grace has pitched the poet into a new sphere of spiritual activity, for 'God . . . can shift the self that lies in one to a higher, that is/better, pitch of itself; that is/to a pitch or determination of itself on the side of good'. (*D.W.*, p. 148.) Hopkins' suffering, therefore, is desirable; it is an after-effect of Christ's stress. It is part of the poet's attempt to imitate his Savior. As Hopkins once wrote: 'The special grace to be asked for in the Passion is sorrow with Christ in his sorrow, a broken heart with Christ broken-hearted, tears and interior pain for the great pain that Christ has suffered for me.' (*D.W.*, p. 187.)

Just as in thinking of Christ's passion, man must 'contemplate the withdrawal and hiding of the godhead' (*D.W.*, p. 191), so also in enduring his own spiritual agony, man loses his sense of communication with God. Feeling this loss keenly, the poet cries out, 'Comforter, where, where is your comforting?'. In one of his sermons, Hopkins translates 'Paraclete' as 'Com-

orter'; and since 'both Christ and the Holy Ghost are Para-
cletes' (D.W., p. 69), his use of the word 'Comforter' creates
ambiguity in the sonnet. The poet is begging for more grace,
but he does not know to which person of the Trinity he should
address himself. Hopkins is clearly in a transitional stage: he
has received help from Christ, but he seems to need something
more; he wonders where, when, and from whom he can obtain
the extra grace he craves.

Continuing his plea for help, the poet prays, 'Mary, mother
of us, where is your relief?' Hopkins asks for the Virgin's inter-
cession, 'because it was her more than all other creatures that
Christ meant to win from nothingness and it was her that he
meant to raise the highest'. (D.W., p. 197.) Moreover, in
attempting to imitate Christ's selflessness, the poet quite naturally feels a kinship with Mary who 'died . . . of vehement love
and longing for God'. (D.W., p. 45.) Finally, because he is
approaching the paradoxical experience of surrendering his
mortal selfhood in order to become a part of the Divine, he is
attracted to one in whom 'met things that are thought to be and
even are opposite and incompatible, . . . courage and meekness,
height and lowliness, wisdom and silence, retirement and
renown'. (D.W., p. 29.)

Neither God nor Mary answers the poet's appeals, and no
relief presents itself to his tormented soul. For the time being,
no angel − metaphorical or otherwise − shall appear from
heaven to strengthen the poet in his agony (Luke 22:43).

Hopelessly, Hopkins proceeds to characterize his agony for
the reader: 'My cries heave, herds-long; huddle in a main, a
chief-/Woe, world-sorrow; on an age-old anvil wince and sing.'
Since the agony is both personal and universal, it must refer to
an experience which all men have in common. In *Metaphor in
Hopkins*, Robert Boyle equates this 'world-sorrow' with sin.[7] To
carry the idea one step further, perhaps the poet is bemoaning
a certain kind of sin. Certainly the grating 'wince and sing' of
the cries striking the anvil is reminiscent of another sound,
another discordant blend of the ugly and the beautiful, one
which Hopkins described in this way:

This song of Lucifer's was a dwelling on his own beauty, an instressing of his own inscape, and like a performance on the organ and instrument of his own being; it was a sounding, as they say, of his own trumpet and a hymn in his own praise. Moreover it became an incantation: others were drawn in; it became a concert of voices, a concerting of selfpraise, an enchantment, a magic, by which they were dizzied, dazzled, and bewitched. They would not listen to the note which summoned each to his own place . . . and distributed them here and there in the liturgy of the sacrifice; they gathered rather closer and closer home under Lucifer's lead and drowned it, raising a countermusic and countertemple and altar, a counterpoint of dissonance and not of harmony. (*D.W.*, pp. 200–1.)

Perhaps Hopkins' 'world-sorrow' echoes this dissonant, satanic music. If man surrenders freely to God, he becomes Christ-like in his perfection. If, however, man's pride in his inscape hinders him from willingly joining in his Savior's great sacrifice, he becomes one with Lucifer's discordant herd. This accounts for the poet's ignoble sorrow; his pride in his human nature has become an obstacle to his salvation. Having reached a climactic chord, Hopkins' emotional intensity subsides. His cries 'lull, then leave off', and the poet explains that the brevity of the emotion necessitates its fierceness.

In the sestet the poet reflects on the vast complexity of the human mind. 'O the mind, mind has mountains' expresses with simple majesty the twofold nature of man's consciousness. It enables him to reach for the sky, yet at the same time humbles him through an awareness of its own inadequacy. It hearkens back to its preexistent union with the mind of God, yet also clings to its present status as a fragmentary, but seemingly independent human being. It is the source of the greatest earthly happiness and the greatest earthly torment. The poet's own high-pitched consciousness has brought about his present desolation; for the 'keener the consciousness the greater the pain', and 'both these show that the higher the nature the greater the penalty'. (*D.W.*, p. 138.)

Hopkins knows the dangers of an overly sensitive 'mind'. There are, he explains, razor-edged cliffs which no mortal can ever fully understand or explore; but the human being who has never chosen to grapple with the paradoxes of his own consciousness cannot possibly understand their gravity or terror: 'Hold them cheap/May who ne'er hung there.' The poet cannot ridicule these people, however; for even a sensitive individual is unable to sustain himself for long under the pressure of such frightening insights. Contemptuously, the poet says, 'Nor does long our small/Durance deal with that steep or deep.' We cannot long face our inner conflict. The poem ends in dejection as Hopkins rushes to escape through sleep or death. He is asking, in effect, to have the sacrificial cup taken away from him; if he must imitate Christ and surrender his mortal selfhood, let it be as an ordinary man does through an acceptance of physical rather than psychological oblivion.

'To seem the stranger' is less fervent than the emotionally turbulent 'No worst, there is none'. It constitutes Hopkins' last attempt to assert his earthly identity. In the first quatrain, the poet indulges in '3 degrees of selfishness – love of our goods, which are wholly outside ourselves; love of our good name . . . , which is ourself indeed, but in others' minds; love of our own excellence, of our very selves, pride'. (*D.W.*, p. 180.) He laments his alienation from family and country; yet, if we are to believe a statement in his spiritual writings, he knows that these goods i.e. family and country, are merely superficial trappings of human nature, masking the essential self. As he points out in one of his exercises: 'even those things with which I in some sort identify myself, as my country or family . . . , all presuppose the stricter sense of self and me and mine and are from that derivative'. (*D.W.*, p. 123.) Yet, even knowing this, he goes on in the sonnet to lament his lack of reputation in England, 'whose honour O all' his 'heart woos'; but, he comments sadly, she 'would neither hear/Me, were I pleading, plead nor do I'.

The poet's inability to act distresses him, 'wear-/y of idle a being but by where wars are rife'. Lamenting his ineffectuality as priest, artist, and man, Hopkins seems to fear the loss of all his human potency; yet he knows that 'intellectual goods as learning, still more/talents and moral goods, as virtues, merits, graces, are . . . dangerous to be attached to and proud of'. (*D.W.*, p. 180.) Though he asserts that he can in Ireland 'Kind love both give and get', this is not enough; for his creativity has failed him. His depression leads him to question whether it is 'dark heaven's baffling ban' which 'bars' or 'hell's spell' which thwarts his originality. In a sense, it is both. Unable to face the sacrificial ordeal which he must undergo in imitation of Christ, the poet reacts in much the same manner as Satan did when he, too, was faced with the sacrifice. Compare Hopkins' reaction to his description of Satan's:

For being required to adore God and enter into a covenant of justice with him he did so indeed, but, as a chorister who learns by use in the church itself the strength and beauty of his voice, he became aware in his very note of adoration of the riches of his nature; then when from that first note he should have gone on with the sacrificial service, prolonging the first note instead and ravished by his own sweetness and dazzled, the prophet says, by his beauty, he was involved in spiritual sloth . . . and spiritual luxury and vainglory; to heighten this, he summoned a train of spirits to be his choir and, contemptuously breaking with the service of the eucharistic sacrifice, . . . he must have persuaded them, to the divine; and with this sin of pride aspiring to godhead their crime was consummated. (*D.W.*, pp. 179–80.)

In a sense, 'To seem the stranger' reveals a moment when Hopkins is tempted to join the satanic choristers. Concentrating on his own human inscape, he forgets that man's claim to divinity can be established only through Christ-like selflessness. In the last two lines of the sonnet, however, the poet recognizes his mistake. When Hopkins states, 'This to hoard unheard,/ Heard unheeded, leave me a lonely began', he is admitting the futility of his inscape without the stress of God's grace to make it productive. Nothing he attempts can ever come to fruition unless God, as well as the poet, wills it. Hopkins has advanced immeasurably toward the Divine Essence; pride in human potency is no longer possible for him.

Hopkins has passed through three stages in his spiritual crisis. He has recognized the nature of the conflict, experienced the cosmic fear resulting from this recognition, and admitted the futility of his own worldly efforts. He is now ready to undergo the tortuous suffering which, when finally completed, will have prepared him for his proper place in the divine scheme of things.

'I wake and feel the fell of dark' describes one episode in God's relentless quest for human self-sacrifice. The poet awakens to the surrounding darkness, a darkness which feels 'primitive, coarse, and . . . thick'[8] as it covers his sensitized soul. He recalls the hours of suffering which he had endured before his brief period of rest and understands that he must yet sustain more 'in . . . longer light's delay'. 'With witness', i.e., having experienced this torment,[9] he can describe this ordeal, but it is not simply the ordeal of a few hours; it is the ordeal of a lifetime. The poet realizes that his protests to God are at this point like 'dead letters sent/To dearest him who lives alas! away'. He must wait until the fulfillment of his sacrifice to achieve happiness with God, and even then it will be an entirely different kind from that which he expected as a self-concerned being.

Hopkins acknowledges the true nature of man when he comments: 'I am gall, I am heartburn. God's most deep decree/Bitter would have me taste: my taste was me;/Bones built in me, flesh filled, blood brimmed the curse.' The poet's extreme distaste for self becomes puzzling if one remembers other statements in which he marvels at 'that taste of myself, of *I* / and *me* above and in all things, which is more distinctive than the smell of walnutleaf or camphor, and is incommunicable by any means to another man'. (*D.W.*, p. 123.) Hopkins' thinking, however, is not inconsistent; when 'decree' is equated with 'curse', his ideas become logically united. 'God's most deep decree' is, in fact, that man should be cursed with bones, flesh, and blood. As Creator, God insists that the preexistent bare self assume a human nature, part of which is a body, the tangible symbol of man's finite existence. Because the poet is human, his perception is limited; he is unable to separate the infinite from the finite. He feels a singular godliness within him, singular because he was, is, and will be a unique portion of the Divine Consciousness. It is this sense of essential self which the poet so much admires, while he abhors the restrictions which his humanity places upon it. The body, for example, prevents man from understanding his infinitesimal place in the infinite; it is, in this sense, then, a curse.

When Hopkins states, 'Selfyeast of spirit a dull dough sours', he means that man's preoccupation with his earthly selfhood, his constant instressing of his human inscape, works on the dull dough of his material self and prepares it for the baking process, i.e. the struggle for unity with God. By asserting that human pride added to the material self forms sourdough, a kind of dough retained from one baking in order to start the next, Hopkins is suggesting that man's instressing of his own inscape is a developmental stage decreed by God. Man must be elevated by a sense of his own greatness before he can be humbled by a recognition of the greater selfhood of the Divinity. Boyle describes this stage as 'the self turning in on self instead of out toward God' (p. 155). To reverse this process, man needs the help of divine grace. Hopkins explains the creation-redemption procedure as follows:

The Trinity made man after the image of Their one nature but They redeem him . . . by bringing into play with infinite charity Their personality. Being personal They see as if with sympathy the play of personality in man below Them, for in his personality his freedom lies and this same personality playing in its freedom not only exerts and displays the riches and capacities of his one nature . . . but unhappily disunites it, rends it, and almost tears it to pieces. One of them therefore makes Himself one of that throng of persons, a man among men, by charity to bring them back to that union with themselves which they have lost by freedom and even to bring them to a union with God which nothing in their nature gave them. (*D.W.*, pp. 171–2.)

The struggle between selflessness and selfishness takes place in the souls of all men; and Hopkins admits the universality of his spiritual conflict when he writes, 'I see/The lost are like this, and their scourge to be/As I am mine, their sweating selves; but worse.' The redeemed indicate a 'correspondence with grace' and a 'seconding of God's designs'; it is as if they are 'taking part in their own creation, the creation of their best selves' (*D.W.*, p. 197). These fortunate ones are able to say and to mean: 'Take, O Lord, and receive all my liberty, my memory, my understanding, and all my will, whatsoever I have and possess. Thou has given it to me; to thee, O Lord, I return it: all is thine, dispose of it entirely according to thy will. Give me thy love and thy grace, for this is enough for me.' (*D.W.*, p. 193.) 'The wicked and the lost', however, 'are like halfcreations and have but a halfbeing' (*D.W.*, p. 197). They will remain for an eternity desolate and incomplete.

Hopkins once wrote: 'Let him who is in desolation strive to remain in patience, which is the virtue contrary to the troubles which harass him' (*D.W.*, p. 204). In sonnet sixty-eight the poet begins to arrive at a philosophy of endurance and recovery. He has somehow achieved the supreme insight into his conflict. He has discovered that his spiritual crisis is necessary, that without 'war', without 'wounds' he could never attain the ultimate virtue – patience. It is not something which man passively receives; he must actively 'pray' and 'bid' for it. But it is a 'rare' virtue; for in seeking patience, man seeks conflicts and with 'these away,/Nowhere' can he find what he was searching for. The price, then, for Hopkins is the spiritual crisis he has been experiencing.

Patience creates peace out of conflict. 'Natural heart's ivy', the poet calls it and explains, 'Patience masks/Our ruins of wrecked past purpose. There she basks/Purple eyes and seas of liquid leaves all day.' A passage from one of Hopkins' discourses clarifies this description. In it, he declares: 'No, we have not answered God's purposes, we have not reached the end of our being. Are we God's orchard or God's vineyard? we have yielded rotten fruit, sour grapes, or none' (*D.W.*, p. 240). It would seem, then, that the past purpose whose ruins patience masks is equivalent to the end for which man was created – union with God. The purpose is ruined by man's pride in himself, for he is not satisfied to be a part of the divine vineyard; rather, he wants to be the master of it. As a result, he becomes merely a vine yielding sour grapes. Patience is needed, therefore, if man is ever to fulfill the purpose of his existence. Basking in the sun and yielding divine fruit, it helps man to accept his conflict-ridden life.

Acceptance, however, does not imply Lethean forgetfulness.

In times of spiritual crisis, men's 'hearts' still 'grate on themselves'. When the poet states 'it kills/To bruise them dearer', he
is describing the loss of human inscape, the death, to which
his own spiritual crisis has led him. 'Yet', Hopkins tells us, 'the
rebellious wills/Of us we do bid God bend to him even so.' Man,
therefore, must take an active part in resolving his spiritual
conflict. As Hopkins wrote in his essay, 'On Personality, Grace
and Free Will': 'it is here that one creature, one man, differs so
much from another: in one God finds only the constrained
correspondence with his forestall . . . , in another he finds after
this an act of choice properly so called. And by this infinitesimal
act the creature does what in it lies to bridge the gulf fixed between its present actual and worser pitch of will and its future
better one.' (*D.W.*, p. 155.)

The sonnet ends on a peaceful note as the poet discovers the
Divine Essence in patience; for where acceptance lives, so also
does God. For the first time since his encounter with Christ in
'Carrion Comfort', Hopkins has established contact with the
Supreme Being. It is not surprising, because 'When a man has
given himself to God's service, when he has denied himself and
followed Christ, he has fitted himself to receive and does receive
from God a special guidance, a more particular providence'
(*Letters*, 11, 93). The poet has received another stress from God,
but of a different kind from the previous one. It is less dramatic,
but more sustaining. It is the kind of grace which was given at
Pentecost, an 'elevating grace . . . which fastened men in good.
This is especially the grace of the Holy Ghost and is the acceptance and assumption of the victim of the sacrifice' (*D.W.*, p.
158). Hopkins has learned that man must accept the limitations
of his finite existence. Man must not struggle *against* anything;
he must struggle *for* something – a reconciliation with the Spirit
from which he came. And in life man approaches this reconciliation through the complex virtue of patience.

'My own heart let me more have pity on' is a companion
piece to sonnet sixty-eight. It is a recognition that man, though
he can actively seek patience, cannot actively seek solace. This
must come unexpectedly after patience has taught man to
accept his place in the divine scheme of things. In essence, then,

the man who has achieved patience must strive for passivity i
he is ever to receive comfort.

Because sonnet sixty-nine begins 'My own heart let me more
have pity on; let/Me live to my sad self hereafter kind', one is
immediately impressed by the sincerity of the plea; for, to
Hopkins, 'the heart is of all members of the body the one which
most strongly and most of its own accord sympathises with and
expresses in itself what goes on within the soul. Tears are sometimes forced, smiles may be put on, but the beating of the heart
is the truth of nature' (D.W., p. 130). The poet has come to
understand that there is a place where self-torment ends and
living begins. He admits that he must allow for his own human
weakness, a weakess which becomes apparent when he likens
himself, a comfort-seeking 'Comfortless' soul, to daylight-seek-
ing blind eyes or a thirst searching for water – the one thing
unalterably opposed to its essence. In a sense, this insight into
human inadequacy is an answer to Hopkins' long-standing
prayer that God 'may give us a true knowledge and understanding whereby we may intimately feel that it is not in our own
power to acquire or retain great devotion, ardent loves, tears,
or any other spiritual consolation, but that all is a gift and
grace of God our Lord' (D.W., p. 205).

In the sestet the poet addresses a self shorn of its pride and
rebelliousness. 'Soul, self; come, poor Jackself', he counsels, 'I
do advise/You, jaded, let be; call off thoughts awhile/Else-
where. . . .' His long struggle has exhausted him, but it has also
prepared him for productive passivity. He will 'leave comfort
root-room; let joy size/At God knows when to God knows what.'
Comfort, then, is rooted inside of man; it is the consolation
which Hopkins once defined as 'any increase of hope, faith, and
charity, and any interior joy which calls and attracts one to
heavenly things and to the salvation of his own soul, rendering
it quiet and at peace with its Creator and Lord' (D.W., pp.
203–4). Since comfort comes from within, one can assume that
it, like patience, is a stress from the Holy Ghost who cheers
people 'not like Christ by his example from without but by his
presence, his power, his breath and fire and inspiration from
within' (D.W., p. 74).

In the concluding lines of the sonnet, Hopkins explains: joy's 'smile/'s not wrung, see you; unforeseen times rather – as skies/Betweenpie mountains – lights a lovely mile.' Thus, the soul which has agonizingly prepared itself will receive suddenly and surprisingly an ultimate stress from God, teaching it to value above all else the end for which it was created. Oddly enough, however, this ultimate consolation coexists with human misery; as Hopkins points out:

If you say that when all is said you feel your sorrows still; why yes, for comfort is not to undo what is done and yet it is comfort, yet it comforts. If we feel the comfort little, there, my brethren, is our fault and want of faith. . . . It *is* a comfort that in spite of all, God loves us; it *is* a comfort that the sufferings of this present world . . . are not worthy to be compared with the glory that is to be revealed in us; such thoughts *are* comfort, we have only to force ourselves to see it, to dwell on it, and at last to feel that it is so. (*D.W.*, pp. 47–8.)

The final image of the sonnet is admirably chosen to represent the resolution to Hopkins' spiritual crisis; for when the poet compares his chance feelings of joy to a dappled sky which unexpectedly appears between the mountains, he is once more demonstrating his preoccupation with natural inscapes. But, implicitly, he is acknowledging the unforeseeability, the incomprehensibility, of their patterns; implicitly, he is admitting that God alone can perceive an inscape in its entirety, God alone – because God *is* the ultimate infinite inscape of which man is merely an infinitesimal part.

Having watched the poet's spiritual torment, having studied his crisis and recovery, one can understand why Gardner states that the 'agony in the Garden constituted for Hopkins the prototype of all desolation' (II, 338). The poet could easily empathize with his Savior; for he, too, had been given a destiny by the Almighty; he had been chosen to see the paradox of self as clearly as a mortal can ever see it. It is not surprising, then, to find this entry in Hopkins' journal: 'One day in the Long Retreat . . . they were reading in the refectory Sister Emmerich's

. . . account of the Agony in the Garden and I suddenly began to cry and sob and could not stop.'[10]

SOURCE: *Victorian Poetry*, vol. VI (1968).

NOTES

1. Throughout his career Hopkins demonstrated a dangerous affinity for the selfhoods of the world. See, for example, 'Binsey Poplars', p. 78 and 'Felix Randal', p. 86 in W. H. Gardner and N. H. MacKenzie, *The Poems of . . . Hopkins*, 4th ed., rev. and enlarged (Oxford, 1967). All subsequent citations from the poems will be taken from this edition.

2. Christopher Devlin (ed.), *The Sermons and Devotional Writings of . . . Hopkins* (Oxford, 1959) pp. 253–4. Hereinafter referred to as *D.W.*

3. See W. A. M. Peters, S.J., *Gerard Manley Hopkins* (Oxford, 1948) pp. 48–9.

4. David A. Downes, *Gerard Manley Hopkins: A Study of his Ignatian Spirit* (New York, 1959).

5. There are a number of passages in his devotional writings in which Hopkins dwelt on this aspect of Christ; see, for example, *D.W.*, p. 268.

6. C. C. Abbott (ed.), *Letters of G. M. Hopkins to R. Bridges* (Oxford, 1935) p. 175.

7. Robert Boyle, *Metaphor in Hopkins* (Chapel Hill, 1960–1) p. 153.

8. Elisabeth W. Schneider (ed.), *Poems and Poetry* (New York, 1964) p. 471.

9. I do not subscribe to Gardner's view (W. H. Gardner, *Gerard Manley Hopkins*, New Haven, 1948–9, II, 338ff.) that the sonnet concerns Hopkins's desolation over the 'general loss of innocence and faith' in the world and that the poet's 'witness' to this loss is God. I interpret the word 'witness' by its first meaning, an attesting of a fact or statement, rather than by its second meaning, the person who is attesting to a fact or statement.

10. H. House and G. Storey (eds), *The Journals and Papers of Gerard Manley Hopkins* (Oxford, 1959) p. 195.

John Sutherland

'TOM'S GARLAND': HOPKINS'S POLITICAL POEM (1972)

'Tom's Garland: Upon the Unemployed' is Hopkins' single poem on public affairs. It reminds us of what is easy to forget and sometimes held to be irrelevant[1] – that he inhabited the England of Morris and Shaw. Not that he shares many political opinions with these contemporaries, but for once the poet seems, incontestably, to be in the same age as the priest. Recorded by the poet as being written in 1887 (September), 'Tom's Garland' reflects on the two great and suggestively opposite events of that year, the riots which shook England and Ireland, and Queen Victoria's Jubilee in June. From this historical irony it moves out to a largely metaphysical discussion of cosmos and chaos. Itself an uncompromisingly loyal poem, it diagnoses the current troubles as a failure of loyalty or, in the older-fashioned political terminology which Hopkins preferred, allegiance. Carlyle, who was similarly backward-looking in such matters, would have called it servantship. In the ideal of the corporate state which is glorified the sovereign is 'the lordly head', Tom and his fellows 'the mighty foot', both sharing a 'common honour'[2] and more importantly a common stability, only so long as subordination is kept. Thus, by resolute anachronism, Hopkins simply annuls the 'problem' of the unemployed: food, work, and a proper sense of station are what is needed, not social reorganization. The 'fools of Radical Levellers' who give the working classes ideas above themselves (i.e., a destiny of gold crowns rather than hobnails) are simply 'pests'.

One of these pests was William Morris. Morris as editor of *The Commonweal* was a direct instigator of the climax of this year

of convulsion and jubilation, 'Bloody Sunday', and the Trafal-
gar Square riots by the unemployed in November. As well as
our normal alertness to semantic duplicity in Hopkins' poetry
we should, I feel, bring an awareness of the immediate social
context. So when Tom declares 'Commonweal/Little I reck ho!'
Hopkins, I am sure, is merging the senses of (1) Commonwealth
little I wreck; (2) *The Commonweal* (i.e. inflammatory journalism)
little I reck (i.e., in the sense of heed or care about); (3) Political
theory doesn't concern me. The urgency of the poem, too, can
only be appreciated by also appreciating the hysteria which
seems to have possessed the country that autumn at the prospect
of the red flag unfurling in the heart of London – an emergency
which engaged even Hopkins' apolitical muse.[3]

The unemployed, however, were only half of England's
problem. 1887 was a year of unprecedented upheaval in Ireland
with Home-Rule and eviction riots. And Hopkins, moving as
he was between the two countries, must have known that the
jubilated crown was also the symbol of imperial dominion.
Loyalty to Victoria's 'lordly head' meant not only subservience
in the theocratic state but also in the Colonial Empire. When
therefore Tom, who is presumably in one of his guises an Irish-
man navvying in England, bellows 'What! Country is honour
enough in all us', he disowns Home-Rule. Despite the apparent
naïveté of the thinking of 'Tom's Garland', its John Bullish
patriotism and medievalism, it is, in the actual historical situation, cleverly comprehensive. By its very lack of specification it
manages to cover the simultaneous crises of emergent socialist
movements in England (the I.L.P., for example, was formed in
this year; Hopkins may not have known this but he certainly
sensed it) and Parnellism in Ireland, and to blot them out with
a timely hurrah for the crown. It is in this respect a misleadingly
confident poem. The poet's letters show him to have been
privately more fearful of the future and the wrecking capacity
of the lower classes than at any time since the Paris Commune
of 1871. To Bridges in February he writes:

You will see, it is the beginning of the end: Home Rule or separation
is near. Let them come: anything is better than the attempt to rule
a people who own no principle of civil obedience at all, not only

to the existing government but to none at all. I should be glad to see Ireland happy, even though it involved the fall of England, if that could come about without shame and guilt. But Ireland will not be happy: a people without a principle of allegiance cannot be; moreover this movement has throughout been promoted by crime.[4]

The 'principle of allegiance' which the poem celebrates was, Hopkins realized in one part of his mind, forever lost. So for all its forced virility of tone and certitude of opinion 'Tom's Garland' was written in a defeated spirit. And this, I suggest, accounts for that feature which all commentators have noted, the almost wanton complexity of the expression, a complexity which implies that the poet was indifferent, or felt it was of no importance whether he was understood or not, even by his restricted readership. Hence the paradox that the unique poem of public affairs is uttered in a uniquely private language. 'Tom's Garland' is, arguably, the most unattractively difficult poem in the Hopkins canon, so thickly enfolded in its own technique as to be almost strangled by it. Certainly the poet seems to have seen in it a boundary beyond which he would lose himself. To a bewildered Bridges he confides: 'It is plain I can go no further on this road: if you . . . cannot understand me who will?'

In expression the poem is ultra-Hopkinsian, a prime example of the 'mannerism', the deliberate 'oddity and obscurity' against which Bridges felt he had to warn the Edwardian reader. But although the syntactic gaps are even wider than usual, and the lexical units even more compressed, the poem is not absolutely obscure; at least not so if one pays full attention to the given sub-title, 'upon the Unemployed'. It is, however, undeniably odd. The hearty mimicry of the navvy's roaring voice and the poem's subtle, reactionary argument do not mix well. In the uncomfortable falsetto which results there is a more than passing resemblance to the self-conscious contrivances of Meredith's prose – in this extract from *The Ordeal of Richard Feverel*, for example: 'There lay Tom; hobnail Tom! a bacon-munching, reckless, beer-swilling animal! and yet a man; a dear brave human heart notwithstanding; capable of devotion and unselfishness. The boy's better spirit was touched, and it kindled his imagination to realize the abject figure of poor clodpole

Tom, and surround it with a halo of mournful light.'[5]

The resemblance between this and 'Tom's Garland' may not be entirely accidental. Meredith's Tom Bakewell is under arrest for rick-burning, the standard symptom of industrial unrest. But more probably Hopkins is drawing on an extraliterary tradition of social discussion in which 'Tom' is the paternalistic eponym for working class man, or as the *O.E.D.* puts it, 'a generic name for any male representative of the common people'. As with Uncle Tom it is a consoling image becuse it suggests that there is an instinctive docility in him, if only one is kind to the animal. In the political huckster Johnson, in *Felix Holt*, George Eliot gives us an example which places another of the spurious simplifications which the argument by reference to Tom is liable to: 'I should like to ask them, "What colliers?". There are colliers up at Newcastle, and there are colliers down in Wales. Will it do any good to honest Tom, who is hungry in Sproxton, to hear that Jack at Newcastle has his bellyful of beef and pudding?'[6] Felix recognizes the divisive tendency of this and answers, unexpectedly, 'yes'.

Hopkins was not the first to celebrate this generalized Tom in verse. Almost a century before, Hannah More had written 'The Riot, or, Half a Loaf is better than no Bread, In a dialogue between Jack Anvil and Tom Hod. Written in '95, a Year of Scarcity and Alarm.' This doggerel propaganda begins:

> *Tom:*
> Come Neighbours, no longer be patient and quiet,
> Come let us kick up a bit of a riot;
> I'm hungry, my lads, but I've little to eat,
> So we'll pull down the mills, and we'll seize all the meat.[7]

Tom, however, is talked out of his anarchic courses by Jack, who urges that king and parliament should be trusted to arrange a remedy and clinches his remarks with the (unironic) consolation: 'The gentlefolks too will afford us supplies;/They'll subscribe – and they'll give up their puddings and pies.' Finally persuaded, Tom throws down his pitchfork and returns to work. As a poem 'The Riot' has nothing more than curiosity value, but for all his refinement of expression Hopkins, in his year of scarcity and alarm, is saying much the same as Hannah More – that the social hierarchy and its Toms are divinely created and, more practically, that hard work and a full belly are benign sedatives for a discontented working class.

So far I have mentioned some of the contemporary background of 'Tom's Garland', outlined a little of Tom's literary genealogy, and touched on the overwrought nature of the poem's language. Any of these could provide the basis for extended discussion. But I want instead to concentrate my remarks on the poem's remarkably sustained and homogeneous 'underthought', as W. H. Gardner would call it. As he wrote 'Tom's Garland' Shakespeare's *Coriolanus* seems to have been constantly in the poet's mind, and its presence is interfused with the finished work. Whether it is there as influence, allusion, or analogue is hard to say and probably pointless to investigate. But it is, indisputably, there. The relationship has yet to be shown but some advance reasons may be given for the evocation. *Coriolanus* is a play angry in tone and conservative in attitude; it shows the destructive nature of an insubordinate plebeian class and returns time and again to the reference point of the body-politic.

On a casual reading the link between *Coriolanus* and 'Tom's Garland' is suggested by one word – 'mammock'. The word occurs but once in all Shakespeare's plays and once in all Hopkins' extant poetry. Both poets employ it as a verb while its most common usage is as a noun; it is thus, the *O.E.D.* tells us, that 'mammock' is first recorded in Skelton's *Colin Clout* with the meaning 'scrap of food'. Shakespeare is apparently the first to have used it as a verb denoting a violent tearing into pieces.

The context of this rare verb in poem and play attaches it to an implied violation of maternal tenderness. Young Marcius, his 'father's son', is described to his mother (the only gentle character is a very rugged play) and to his grandmother smashing the gilded butterfly: 'and when he caught it, he let it go again; and after it again; and over and over he comes, and up again; catched it again; or whether his fall enraged him or how 'twas, he did so set his teeth and tear it; O, I warrant, how he mammocked it!'[8] (I, iii, 61–5).

This crude destructive response to situations requiring delicacy is one of the key motifs of the play. There is a similar blind violence in the poem's version of the word, and a similar emotive heightening aroused by associating it with motherhood: 'or mother-ground/That mammocks, mighty foot'. An intensification of effect is gained here not so much by narrative circumstance as by alliteration, rhythm, and animation of language ('mighty foot' is both subject and object of 'mammock'; 'mammock' itself evokes the gigantism of 'mammoth').

The appearance of 'mammock' and its parallel usage establishes a coincidental identification which one can support by further comparison of the texts. 'Garland' is a peculiar term with which to approach the labor problems of the nineteenth century. Superficially it seems to be a rather fanciful combination of a spontaneous visual impression: 'Tom – garlanded with squat and surly steel' (i.e. with his pick over his shoulder thus forming a metal collar) and the more reflective metaphysical idea of a badge of station – 'gold go garlanded/With, perilous, O, no' – and of a mark of socially awarded merit. This is quite different from the way in which garlands are brought in as vaguely classical and picturesque furniture in much Romantic poetry. It is possible that Hopkins was thinking of Arnold's 'Friendship's Garland', which dealt with social problems, or Ruskin's *Crown of Wild Olive*, which the worker could win by the sweat of his brow.[9] There is, however, a strong concurrence between the nature of Tom's garland and those we find in *Coriolanus*. Coriolanus' garlands are all won in his rightful occupation, war; as Tom earns his with the pick Coriolanus earns his by the sword:

> Caius Marcius wears this war's garland (I, ix, 60)

> He comes the third time home with the oaken garland
> (II, i, 122)

> He lurch'd all swords of the garland (II, ii, 101)

'Garland' signifying preeminence and duty well done occurs four times in *Coriolanus*. In no other play of Shakespeare, the *Concordance* tells us, is the term found more than twice, and then often with variant meanings. More interesting than this statistical evidence, though, is the invariable association of the idea of the garland with the unfortunate hero (there is a similar juxtaposition of reward and exile in the poem); *The Soldier's Garland* would be an ironically effective subtitle to the play.

In his gloss of the sonnet for Bridges, Hopkins explains 'iron' garland as 'the nails they wear' (i.e. in the soles of their boots) and from the poem itself we can infer the addition of the 'surly steel' pick. 'Steel' and 'iron' in *Coriolanus* have a very different but in some ways an analogous meaning; they are the metonymic emblems of war. 'This peace is nothing but to rust iron' (IV, v, 225), complains a disgusted Volsce. For steel picks we can read 'steel pikes' (v, vi, 151). To the military Roman state, war is what work is to industrial England, an honorable employment of the nation's manpower. War and work respectively are the antidotes to the inertia and internal dissension paralyzing a society where there is 'No way sped,/Nor mind nor mainstrength' and 'steel grown soft as is the parasite's silk' (I, ix, 45).

It is perhaps apposite to refer here to the attraction the military life seems to have held for Hopkins, an attraction we can infer from the subjects and imagery of many of the poems, and also his frequent blending of military terminology in his poetic diction:

> Of a fresh and following folded rank
>   Not spared, not one ('Binsey Poplars')

> Sometimes a lantern moves along the night,
> That interests our eyes. And who goes there?
>   ('The Lantern out of Doors')

> Though as a beechbole firm, finds his, as at a roll-call, rank
> And features, in flesh, what deed he each must do –
>   His sinew-service where do ('Harry Ploughman')

And in 'Tom's Garland' 'bold steel' has an overtone of the more familiar 'cold steel'.

Coriolanus opens not merely with restless 'musty' peace but with bread riots; the first citizen voices the general grievance: 'Let us revenge this with our pikes, ere we become rakes: for the gods know I speak this in hunger for bread, not in thirst for

revenge' (I, i, 21–4). This too finds an echo in 'Tom's Garland':
'Commonweal/Little I reck ho! lacklevel in, if all had bread.'
Both works maintain that hunger causes dissidence, and, more
importantly, that lack of employment (war/work) causes hunger.

Rebellion motivated by privation finds its cause, and its
refutation, in the ideal of the Commonweal. This is a concept
structural to both *Coriolanus* and 'Tom's Garland'. Its allegori-
cal model, the body-politic, is by no means original. In his
letter to Bridges explaining the poem Hopkins writes: 'As St.
Paul and Plato and Hobbes and everybody says, the commonwealth or well ordered human society is like one man; a body
with many members and each its function.' The body-politic is
also, according to Caroline Spurgeon, the 'central image'[10] of
Coriolanus: 'It obtrudes,' she says, 'throughout the play; anyone
on a first reading will notice and remember it' (p. 349). It is
outlined explicitly very early in the action by Menenius' 'pretty
tale' of the time 'when all the body's members rebell'd against
the belly' (I, i, 94). Society, according to this anthropomorphic
fable, has its 'kingly-crowned head' (I, i, 114) and at its base the
foremost of the mob 'you, the great toe of this assembly' (I, i,
154). In 'Tom's Garland' we have the 'lordly head' (the sovereign as Hopkins tells us in his note) and 'the foot is the day-
labourer'. In both works the hierarchy is justified by parity of
function, and in both the demand for equality of privilege is
radically antisocial.

Partnering this view of the serving member of society as
humble but necessary limb is that of him as predatory animal
when he ceases to be corporate and turns rebel. Coriolanus is
exiled from Rome as a gangrenous foot (III, i, 303); he returns
as the 'osprey' who will take the city 'by sovereignty of nature'
(IV, vii, 35). Similarly the ranks of the people are transformed
by disaffection into a 'cry of curs' (III, iii, 120). The last couplet
of the sonnet could well be an example of Coriolanus' own
numerous invectives against the 'beast with many heads' (IV,
i, 2): 'This by Despair, bred Hangdog dull; by Rage,/Manwolf,
worse; and their packs infest the age.' Hopkins' mention of
'infest' also recalls one of the major thematic strains of imagery
in *Coriolanus*, that of disease, contagion, and epidemic:

> you herd of – Boils and Plagues
> Plaster you over, that you may be abhorr'd
> Further than seen and one infect another
> Against the wind a mile! (I, iv, 31–4)

In his letter on the poem Hopkins refers contemptuously to 'Loafers, Tramps, Cornerboys, Roughs, Socialists and other pests of society'. The organizers of the equivalent pests in *Coriolanus* are the crafty tribunes of the people, Brutus and Sicinius. The Commonweal is always in their mouths: they talk of 'the body o' the weal' (II, iii, 179) and proclaim Coriolanus 'A foe to the public weal' (III, i, 173) and assert: 'The commonwealth doth stand and so would do/Were he more angry, at it' (IV, vi, 14–15). As Menenius employs the argument of the Commonweal to pacify the mob, using a parable made up of their own political notions, so with the same ideas the tribunes (like the 'fools of Radical Levellers' Hopkins accuses) stir up insurrection. In the poem too there is a certain ambivalence of meaning: 'Commonweal', the order of society, is contrasted with 'world's weal', the order of nature. As *Coriolanus* shows, the concept is sufficiently adaptable to be used polemically by either of the conflicting parties. Against this too flexible theory Hopkins and Shakespeare introduce the too simple emotional appeal to nationalism: 'What! Country is honour enough in all us', cries Tom. In the play the patricians are as constantly invoking 'country' as the tribunes do the commonweal:

If any think that brave death outweighs bad life/And that his country's dearer than himself (I, vi, 72, Coriolanus)

induced/As you have been; that's for my country (I, ix, 17, Coriolanus)

The blood that he hath lost . . . he dropped it for his country (III, i, 296–8, Menenius)

> I do love
> My country's good with a respect more tender,
> More holy and profound, than mine own life (III, iii,
> 111–13, Cominius)

So far the analogies observed have been direct or parallel. To whatever degree derivative, Hopkins' poem contains imagery, diction, progress of thought, and attitudes similar to those contained in the larger work. The next stage of the comparison becomes more speculative, however. It will be suggested that, consciously or unconsciously, Hopkins transferred certain of the characteristics of Coriolanus to his own less individual Tom. Thus the image of power in 'Tom's Garland' is not the patrician warrior but the manual worker. Both these 'garlanded' heroes embody an irresistible and primitive massiveness, both are portrayed with heroic exaggeration:

when he walks, he moves like an engine, and the ground shrinks before his treading (v, iv, 18–20).

> piles pick
> By him and rips out rockfire homeforth.

In the sonnet it is Tom who is 'undenizened', in the play Coriolanus who is 'hooted' out of Rome into banishment. Exile turns 'Tom Heart-at-ease' to 'Hangdog' and 'Manwolf'. Coriolanus disgarlanded goes 'alone/Like to a lonely dragon' (IV, i, 30).

The clause in the poem, 'mother-ground/That mammocks, mighty foot', in addition to its primary affinity through 'mammock', has another in its echo of Volumnia arguing her son out of sacking Rome:

> thou shalt no sooner
> March to assault thy country than to tread –
> Trust to 't, thou shalt not – on thy mother's womb
> That brought thee to this world (v, iii, 121–4)

At their best Tom and Coriolanus evince a noble disinterestedness:

> What! Country is honour enough in all us.

> Our spoils he kicked at,

. . . .

> rewards
> His deeds with doing them, and is content
> To spend the time to end it (II, ii, 124-9)

In their proper element both are invulnerable:

> Tom seldom sick,
> Seldomer heartsore; that treads through, prick-
>   proof, thick
> Thousands of thorns, thoughts.

Coriolanus similarly belittles his multitudinous wounds as 'Scratches with briers,/Scars to move laughter only' (III, iii, 52-3). Both Tom and Coriolanus are sublimely unthinking and unpolitical creatures whose lives should ideally be those of natural reflective activity, 'making no hardship of hardness, taking all easy' (Hopkins to Bridges).

One could conceivably justify this transfer of attributes from patrician to plebeian as attendant on the change from oligarchic to semidemocratic in the social schemes of the two worlds. But it would probably be casuistic to rationalize it other than as a process of very unsystematic association of ideas. On a purely fortuitous level, however, the resemblances are many. Both works are untypical of their authors and have been somewhat neglected, perhaps on account of a joint complexity of expression and austerity of mood. Nowhere is Hopkins less the nature poet (or indeed the priest); nowhere is Shakespeare less lyrical. 'Tom's Garland' conspicuously lacks 'the roll, the rise, the carol, the creation' of the poet's other works. It is almost unique, for example, in having no color references (except for the neutral 'fallow' which has a complex of meanings – the earth which Tom and Dick tread, the suggestion of rest after work or 'lying fallow'). The language of both play and sonnet is elliptic, violent, and tending to hyperbole.

It is unlikely that having come this far the reader will echo Hopkins' 'O, once explained, how clear it all is!' Apart from the word 'mammock' and the idea of the body politic, *Coriolanus* permeates the poem as a miasma which defies complete distillation. One's conclusion about 'Tom's Garland' is probably the same as one's first impression – that it is very odd: a social-problem poem by a poet of whom John Wain has said that his only connection with the nineteenth century was that for forty-five years he drew breath in it, a poem whose closeness to contemporary events is contradicted by an exceptionally remote language and allusive infrastructure.

SOURCE: *Victorian Poetry*, vol. x, no. 2 (1972).

NOTES

1. See, for example, John Wain, 'Gerard Manley Hopkins: An Idiom of Desperation', in *Essays on Literature and Ideas* (London, 1963).
2. This is Hopkins's explanatory letter to Bridges of Feb. 10, 1888. Bridges, W. H. Gardner, and Gardner and Mackenzie quote it in their notes to the poem where it is most conveniently to be found. Cf. Gardner and Mackenzie (eds), *The Poems of . . . Hopkins*, 4th ed. (Oxford, 1967) pp. 291–2. References to this letter, as to the sonnet (p. 103), are from this edition.
3. I am aware of Hopkins's confession that he was a Communist at the time of the Paris Commune. One assumes that his views had become more conservative in the following sixteen years, or that he was able to view a revolution across the English Channel with more complacency than one across the Irish Sea.
4. Feb. 16, 1887; see C. C. Abbott (ed.), *Letters . . . to Robert Bridges* (Oxford, 1935) p. 252.
5. *The Works of George Meredith* (London, 1896) I, p. 61.
6. George Eliot, *Felix Holt* (London, 1896 reprint) p. 125.
7. *The Works of Hannah More* (London, 1853) VI, p. 62.
8. Line references are to the 'Arden' edition; they may vary slightly from other standard texts.
9. More recently the image of the garland is rich in allusion. Hopkins's reference to thorns in the prose reinforces an association with Christ's crown of thorns and crown of glory. Donne similarly confuses these with the classical laurel crown in 'La Corona'. It is also possible that Hopkins was thinking of Pliny's famous description of still garlanded generals returning to the plough in Rome's Golden Age.
10. Caroline Spurgeon, *Shakespeare's Imagery* (Cambridge, 1935) p. 347.

BIBLIOGRAPHY

I   TEXTS AND SELECTIONS

W. H. Gardner and N. H. MacKenzie (eds), *The Poems of G. M. Hopkins*, 4th ed. (Oxford, 1967). Professor MacKenzie is preparing a Variorum Edition of the *Poems*.

C. Devlin (ed.), *The Sermons and Devotional Writings of G. M. Hopkins* (Oxford, 1959).

H. House and G. Storey (eds), *The Journals and Papers of G. M. Hopkins* (Oxford, 1959). These two volumes constitute the 2nd ed., revised and enlarged, of the *Notebooks and Papers*, edited by Humphry House and published in 1937 (Oxford).

C. C. Abbott (ed.), *Letters of G. M. Hopkins to R. Bridges, Correspondence of G. M. Hopkins and R. W. Dixon*, 2 vols (Oxford, 1935; revised 1955); and *Further Letters of G. M. Hopkins* (Oxford, 1938; 2nd ed. 1956).

Among the Selections may be mentioned:

W. H. Gardner (ed.), *G. M. Hopkins: A Selection of Poems and Prose* (Harmondsworth, 1953; 2nd ed. 1966).

J. Pick (ed.), *A Hopkins Reader* (Oxford, 1953; 2nd ed. London, 1966).

G. Storey (ed.), *Hopkins: Selections* (Oxford, 1967).

2   SELECT BIBLIOGRAPHY

Books referred to in the Introduction have not been included in this list, which is chronological in arrangement.

Alan Heuser, *The Shaping of G. M. Hopkins* (Oxford, 1958). An interesting attempt to relate all Hopkins's artistic activities, music and drawing as well as poetry.

T. K. Bender, *G. M. Hopkins: the Classical Background and Critical Reception of his Work* (Baltimore, 1966). Exceptionally valuable; makes use of unpublished notes.

N. H. MacKenzie, *Hopkins* (Edinburgh, 1968). A useful introduction, in the 'Writers and Critics' series.

Patricia Ball, *The Science of Aspects: Coleridge, Ruskin & Hopkins* (London, 1971). The note-books of the three writers, and the use they made of them, supply the point of departure for a very interesting study.

W. S. Johnson, *G. M. Hopkins: the Poet as Victorian* (Cornell, 1968). Brief but very valuable study, concentrating on poems rather than biography.

Elisabeth W. Schneider, *The Dragon in the Gate* (Berkeley, Calif., 1968). A series of studies of individual poems and of the poetry in general. Very well-informed and perceptive.

A. G. Sulloway, *G. M. Hopkins and the Victorian Temper* (London, 1972). Stimulating in its way; a useful chapter on Hopkins and Ruskin.

R. K. R. Thornton, *G. M. Hopkins: the Poems* (London, 1973). A brief introduction, in the 'Studies in English Literature' series. Very well done.

3   ESSAYS AND ARTICLES

The Kenyon Critics, *G. M. Hopkins* (1945; London, 1949). Contributions by A. Warren, H. M. McLuhan, J. Miles, R. Lowell, A. Mizener, H. Whitehall.

N. Weyand (ed.), *Immortal Diamond: Studies in G. M. Hopkins* (London, 1949). Contributions by M. C. Carroll, A. McGillivray, J. L. Bown, W. J. Ong, C. A. Burrows, R. V. Schoder, M. V. McNamee, W. T. Noon, Y. Watson, R. Boyle.

G. H. Hartman (ed.), *Hopkins: A Collection of Critical Essays*, Twentieth-Century Views Series (New Jersey, 1966).

F. N. Lees, article on Hopkins in *Pelican Guide to English Literature*, vol. VI (London, 1958).

J. E. Stevens, 'Hopkins as a Musician', in *Journals and Papers of G. M. Hopkins*, ed. H. House and G. Storey (Oxford, 1959).

W. Walsh, 'G. M. Hopkins and a Sense of the Particular', in *The Use of Imagination* (London, 1959).

J. Hillis Miller, chapter on Hopkins in *The Disappearance of God: Five Nineteenth Century Writers* (Cambridge, Mass., 1963).

M. Ochshorn, 'Hopkins the Critic', *Yale Review*, vol. LIV (1965).

D. Donoghue, chapter on Hopkins in *The Ordinary Universe: Soundings in Modern Literature* (London, 1968).

B. Hardy, 'Forms and Feelings in the Sonnets of G. M. Hopkins' (Hopkins Society, London, 1970).

F. R. Leavis, 'G. M. Hopkins: Reflections after Fifty Years' (Hopkins Society, London, 1971).

K. J. Raine, 'Hopkins: Nature and Human Nature' (Hopkins Society, London, 1972).

R. Preyer, 'The Fine Delight that Fathers Thought', in *Victorian Poetry*, Stratford-upon-Avon Studies, 15 (London, 1972).

W. Nowottny, 'Hopkins's Language of Prayer and Praise' (Hopkins Society, London, 1973).

W. W. Robson, 'Hopkins and Literary Criticism' (Hopkins Society, London, 1974).

4 COMMENTARIES

D. McChesney, *A Hopkins Commentary* (London, 1968). An explanatory commentary on the main poems, meant for 'the average student'. Besides glossing all the major poems, there are notes on Inscape, Instress, Duns Scotus's leading ideas, and so on.

Peter Milward, s.j., *A Commentary on G. M. Hopkins' 'Wreck of the Deutschland'* (Tokyo, 1968); and *A Commentary on the Sonnets of G. M. Hopkins* (Tokyo, 1969; London, 1970). Very detailed, almost word by word expositions. Though intended primarily for Japanese university students, others could benefit from these well-informed guides.

P. L. Mariani, *A Commentary on the Complete Poems of G. M. Hopkins* (Cornell, 1969). Another useful guide.

R. V. Schoder, 'An Interpretive Glossary of Difficult Words in the Poems', in *Immortal Diamond: Studies in G. M. Hopkins*, ed. N. Weyand (London, 1949).

5 BIBLIOGRAPHIES

J. Pick, 'G. M. Hopkins', in *The Victorian Poets: a Guide to Research*, ed. F. E. Faverty (Cambridge, Mass., 1956).

G. Storey, 'G. M. Hopkins', in *New Cambridge Bibliography of English Literature* (Cambridge and New York, 1969); and 'G. M. Hopkins', in *English Poetry: Select Bibliographical Guides*, ed. A. E. Dyson (Oxford, 1971). The latter gives a most useful account of the development of Hopkins studies.

NOTES ON CONTRIBUTORS

ROBERT BRIDGES (1844–1930). A contemporary and close friend of Hopkins at Oxford. Practised medicine, but devoted much time and talent to poetry. Corresponded with G.M.H. for many years, and became his literary executor. Poet Laureate 1913–30.

CHRISTOPHER DEVLIN, S.J. (1907–60). Editor of Hopkins's *Sermons and Devotional Writings* (Oxford, 1959). Like Hopkins, studied theology at St Beuno's College, and was much interested in Scotist philosophy.

R. W. DIXON (1833–1900). Anglican clergyman, historian and minor poet. At one time taught G.M.H. at Highgate, and corresponded with him for many years.

T. S. ELIOT (1888–1965). Poet and critic.

WILLIAM EMPSON. Poet and critic, now Emeritus Professor of English, Sheffield University. His *Seven Types of Ambiguity* (1930) remains the most influential of his critical works.

GEOFFREY GRIGSON. Critic, poet, and editor of *New Verse* 1933–9.

HARMAN GRISEWOOD. Retired in 1964 after a distinguished career in the B.B.C.

HUMPHRY HOUSE (1908–55). Scholar and critic. First editor of Hopkins's *Notebooks and Papers* (1937).

ELIZABETH JENNINGS. Poet and critic. Her essay on Hopkins is included in a collection of studies on the relation between mystical experience and the making of poems, *Every Changing Shape* (1961).

BERNARD KELLY. His study of G.M.H. was privately printed, under Jesuit auspices, at St Dominic's Press, Ditchling, Sussex, in 1935.

C. N. LUXMOORE (1844–1936). A school-friend of G.M.H., and a student of painting under Arthur Hopkins, Gerard's brother.

DONALD MCCHESNEY. Principal Lecturer in English, De la Salle College of Education, Middleton, Manchester.

J. MIDDLETON MURRY (1889–1957). Literary critic and influential journalist. Editor of *The Athenaeum* (1919–21) and *The Adelphi* (1923–48). At one time married to Katharine Mansfield.

COVENTRY PATMORE (1823–96). Poet and, after 1864, ardent convert to Roman Catholicism. Corresponded with G.M.H.

PLURES. Collective *nom de plume* of some Jesuits who contributed to a feature on G.M.H. in *The Dublin Review* (September 1920), together with Frederic Page, s.j.

I. A. RICHARDS. Critic of language and literature, latterly a poet. An influential teacher in Cambridge during the twenties; held professorship at Harvard 1943–63. He was associated with C. K. Ogden in the invention of Basic English.

EDWARD SAPIR (1884–1939). Linguist and anthropologist, interested also in general culture and its relation to personality. Worked in the United States and Canada.

ELISABETH SCHNEIDER. Author of a valuable study of Hopkins, *The Dragon in the Gate* (see Bibliography). Emeritus Professor of English at Temple University, California.

Sir ROBERT STEWART (1852–94). A well-known organist, teacher and conductor in Dublin, whom G.M.H. consulted about his own musical compositions.

JOHN SUTHERLAND. Lecturer in the Department of English, University College, London.

VINCENT TURNER, s.j. Contributed an article to *The Dublin Review* in celebration of the centenary of Hopkins's birth. Now at Campion Hall, Oxford.

CHARLES WILLIAMS (1886–1945). Poet, man of letters and writer of allegories. Edited the second edition of Hopkins's *Poems* (1930).

INDEX

Abbott, C. C.   16, 23 n., 24 n.,
    30, 31, 34, 36, 38, 39, 138 n.,
    139 n., 181 n., 185 n., 216 n.,
    234 n., 246 n.
Allingham, W.   144
Aquinas, St Thomas   113, 195
Arnold, Matthew   240
'As kingfishers catch fire'   132,
    158, 162, 163, 178, 182 n., 187,
    203, 210
'Ashboughs'   116, 123
'At the Wedding March'   200
Auden, W. H.   17

Baillie, A.   31, 130, 136, 181 n.,
Barnes, William   69, 145
Baudelaire, C.   108
Beeching, H. C.   13, 40
Bender, T. K.   23 n.
Bergson, H.   99, 116
Bernanos, G.   189, 191
'Binsey Poplars'   61, 148, 234 n.,
    241
Bischoff, A.   20
'Blessed Virgin, The'   36, 65, 84,
    121, 190
Bourget, P.   95, 100 n.
Boyle, R.   19, 23 n., 224, 229,
    234 n.
Brémond, H.   17, 98, 115, 166 n.
Bridges, Robert   11, 12, 13, 14,
    16, 18, 19, 20, 22, 30, 31, 34,
    37, 38, 49, 50, 55, 56, 60, 64,
    69, 70, 83, 92, 95, 96, 101, 102,
    106, 112, 129, 131, 133, 139 n.,
    145, 149, 151, 165, 166, 180,

181 n., 185 n., 202, 205, 208,
    215, 221, 234 n., 236, 237, 241,
    242, 245, 246 n.; 'Preface and
    Notes'   41-8
Brooke, Stopford   59
Browning, Robert   36, 55, 56,
    59, 143, 144
'Brothers'   56, 85, 199, 200
'Bugler's First Communion, The'
    46, 57, 85, 189, 208
Butler, Samuel   152
Byron, Lord   102

'Caged Skylark, The'   102, 133,
    200, 209
'Candle Indoors, The'   42, 57,
    58, 82
Carlyle, Thomas   235
'Carrion Comfort'   59, 75, 106 n.,
    148, 179, 219-22, 231
Cecil, Lord David   138 n.
Cézanne, P.   143
Champneys, B.   38
Claudel, P.   98, 125
Coleridge, Mary   55
Coleridge, S. T. C.   19
Cormac, Father   35
Crabbe, George   154
Crashaw, Richard   91 n., 128
Croce, B.   17
Cowper, William   57
Cummings, E. E.   16

Dante   127
Davie, D.   20, 21, 24 n.
Darwin, Charles   153

Descartes, R. 99

Devlin, C. 16, 19, 24 n., 29, 234 n; 'Hopkins and Duns Scotus' 113–16

Dixon, R. W. 11, 12, 16, 22, 70, 96, 112, 138, 139 n., 165, 166, 182 n., 204, 216, 216 n.; Correspondence 32–5

Donne, John 91 n., 127, 128, 148, 199, 214, 246 n.

Downes, D. A. 19, 23 n., 219, 234 n.

Dryden, John 106

'Duns Scotus' Oxford' 33, 148

Eliot, George 238, 246 n.

Eliot, T. S. 93, 139 n., 189, 190, 194, 201; 'A Note on Hopkins' 107–8

Empson, W. 13, 15, 183; 'Ambiguities in Hopkins' 87–91

'Epithalamion' 50, 86 n., 94

'Felix Randal' 46, 58, 85, 234 n.

Flaubert, G. 133

Francis of Assisi, St 116, 121

Froude, H. 136

Gardner, W. H. 17, 23 n., 128, 171, 175, 181 n., 182 n., 213, 233, 234 n., 239, 246 n.

Gilby, T. 123, 125 n.

'God's Grandeur' 65, 133, 156–7, 195, 203, 209, 210

Gosse, Sir Edmund 92

Gosse, P. H. 149, 153, 166 n.

de Gourmont, R. 100 n., 133

Graves, Robert 13, 15, 99, 100 n.

Greenwood, F. 37

Grigson, G. 17; 'A Passionate Science' 143–67

Grisewood, H., 'The Impact of Hopkins' 92–100

'Habit of Perfection, The' 42, 101, 131

Hake, T. G. 93

'Handsome Heart, The' 56, 85, 86 n.

Hardy, Thomas 49, 55, 83, 143

'Harry Ploughman' 58, 94, 102, 241

Hartman, G. H. 17, 24 n., 217 n.

Haydon, B. R. 150

'Heaven-Haven' 101, 192

'Henry Purcell' 21, 122, 148, 198, 199

Herbert, George 19, 89, 91 n., 128, 148, 199

Hobbes, Thomas 242

Hopkins, Arthur 39

House, Humphry 16, 19, 20, 31, 138 n., 139 n., 156, 166 n., 174, 181 n., 217 n., 234 n.; 'A Note on G.M.H.'s Religious Life' 109–12; 'In praise of G.M.H.' 140

House, M. 24 n.

Hulme, T. E. 99

Hunt, Holman 207

Hunt, Leigh 102

'Hurrahing in Harvest' 102, 103, 116, 124, 155–6, 195, 203, 209

'I am in Ireland now' 64

'I wake and feel the fell' 52, 106 n., 148, 228–30

Ignatius Loyola, St 19, 109, 111, 131, 154, 165, 173, 180

'In honour of St. Alphonsus Rodriguez' 95, 179, 180

'Inversnaid' 42, 102

James, Henry 143

Jennings, E., 'The Unity of Incarnation' 186–201

John of the Cross, St 104, 110, 111, 200

Jowett, B.   62
Joyce, James   94, 95, 108

Keating, J.   13, 40
Keats, John   50, 96, 102, 110, 149, 150
Keble, John   130
Kelly, B., 'The Wreck of the *Deutschland*'   117–25
Kierkegaard, S.   216
Kilmer, A. J.   15, 65
Kingsley, Charles   153

Lahey, G. F.   16, 23 n., 40, 95, 104, 122
Lang, A.   44
'Lantern out of Doors, The'   83, 241
Lawrence, D. H.   65
'Leaden Echo and Golden Echo, The'   42, 52, 66, 67, 102, 116, 204
Lear, Edward   152
Leavis, F. R.   17, 18, 23 n., 214, 217 n.
Leonardo da Vinci   159
Liddon, H. P.   130
'Loss of the *Eurydice*, The'   32, 44, 46, 57, 61, 72, 208, 216 n.
Luxmoore, C. N.   38

McChesney, D., 'The Meaning of Inscape'   202–17
MacDonald, G.   59
MacGonegall, W.   216 n.
MacKenzie, N. H.   23 n., 234 n., 246 n.
MacLeod, Father,   23 n.
McLuhan, H. M.   18
Maritain, J.   98
Marlowe, Christopher   83
'May Magnificat, The'   50, 52, 95, 160
Meredith, George   55, 108, 237, 238, 246 n.

Merton, T.   214, 217 n.
Miles, A. H.   13, 23 n., 40, 42
Milton, John   21, 33, 34, 44, 50, 84, 129, 199, 214
Mizener, A.   18
Monro, H.   93
'Moonrise'   116, 213
More, Hannah   238, 239, 246 n.
'Morning, Midday and Evening Sacrifice'   164, 165
Morris, William   235
Muir, Edwin   187, 201
Murry, J. Middleton   48–55
'My own heart. . .'   16, 69, 76, 106 n., 135, 192, 215, 231–3

'Nature a Heraclitean Fire'   203, 206–7
Newman, J. H.   131, 147, 148, 154
'No worst, there is none'   76, 106 n., 137, 148, 188, 222–6

'O Deus ego amo te'   165
Ogden, C. K.   15, 23 n.
Ong, W.   18

Page, F.   55–60
Parmenides,   157
Pascal, B.   60
Pater, Walter   97, 98
'Patience'   106 n., 111, 119, 230–1
Patmore, Coventry   12, 16, 21, 31, 57, 58, 59, 96, 143, 145, 165, 166, 181 n., 216; Correspondence 35–8
Paul, St   242
'Peace'   53, 71, 75, 111, 148, 192
Péguy, C.   187, 189
Pick, J.   20, 24 n.
'Pied Beauty'   102, 103, 123, 133, 146, 187, 195, 203, 209
Pindar   209
Plato   242
Pliny   246 n.

'Plures' 60–4
Poe, E. A. 66
Pope, Alexander 83
Purcell, Henry 140
Pusey, E. B. 130

Read, Herbert 95, 100 n.;
    'Creativity and Spiritual
    Tension' 101–6
Richards, I. A. 13, 15, 23 n.,
    69–77, 88, 89, 91, 161, 162
Rickaby, J. 109, 112 n.
Riding, Laura 13, 15
Rimbaud, A. 95
Ritz, J. G. 20, 24 n.
Ronsard, P. de 93
Rossetti, D. G. 64
Ruskin, John 63, 143

Sambrook, J. 35
Sandburg, C. 67
Sapir, E. 14, 15, 65–9
Schneider, E., 'The Windhover'
    183–5, 234 n.
Schoder, R. V. 18, 171, 172,
    176, 178, 179, 181 n., 182 n.
Scotus, Duns 19, 60, 62, 113–15,
    122, 131, 135, 158, 195, 202
'Sea and the Skylark, The' 97,
    102
Shakespeare 81, 199, 214;
    Coriolanus 239–45
Shaw, G. B. 235
Shelley, P. B. 50, 61, 96, 102
Sitwell, Sir Osbert 93, 100 n.
Skelton, John 239
'Soldier, The' 15, 191
'Spelt from Sibyl's Leaves' 17,
    73–4, 103, 116
'Spring' 42, 102, 183, 189, 210
'Spring and Fall' 15, 42, 85,
    87–9, 103, 190
'Starlight Night, The' 33, 42, 68,
    85, 102, 133, 157, 161, 183, 195,
    204, 209

Stewart, Sir Robert 22, 38, 151
Storey, G. 16, 31, 216 n., 234 n.
Sutherland, J., 'Tom's Garland'
    235–46
Swinburne, A. C. 50, 66, 81, 82,
    97, 152

Taine, H. 34
Tennyson, Lord 143, 144, 145,
    151
Teresa, St 104, 110
Thomas, A. 20, 24 n.
Thomas, Dylan 209
Thompson, Francis 84
'Thou art indeed just' 19, 84,
    104, 106 n., 160
'To R. B.' 42, 54, 99, 205
'To seem the stranger' 75, 106 n.,
    215, 226–9
'To what serves mortal beauty'
    58, 164, 176
'Tom's Garland' 22, 98, 235–46
Traherne, Thomas 189
Turner, V., 'Many a poem'
    126–39
Turner, W. J. 126, 138 n.

Van Gogh, V. 205, 216
Vaughan, Henry 128, 187, 190
Verlaine, P. 49
Victoria, Queen 235, 236
Villon, F. 108
'Vision of the Mermaids, A' 42,
    149–50

Wain, J. 180, 214, 246, 246 n.
Ward, D., 'The Windhover'
    168–82
Warner, Rex 17
Watts, A. 203, 204, 216 n.
Weyand, N. 18, 181 n.
Whitman, Walt 58
Williams, Charles 16, 48;
    'Introduction' 81–6, 95

'Windhover, The' 15, 18, 33, 53,
    72–3, 85, 89–90, 92, 98, 102,
    103, 116, 133, 161–2, 163, 164,
    168–82, 183–5, 195, 197–203, 211
Winters, Yvor 20, 21, 24 n.
Wolfe, P. M., 'The Terrible
    Sonnets' 218–35
'Woodlark, The' 66, 67, 97, 116,
    212

Wordsworth, William 96, 97, 102
    127, 154, 217
'Wreck of the *Deutschland*, The'
    13, 14, 15, 17, 33, 36, 47–8, 56,
    57, 61, 82, 94, 97, 101, 112, 114,
    117–25, 137, 147, 174, 192–6,
    205, 209, 210, 213
Wust, P. 98

p 163
    -164

p 203
= the scourion times told
loveliest more dangerous
fire of revelation
p   241